THE PHILOSOPHY OF HUMAN LEARNING

This study addresses current concerns with the nature of human learning from a distinctive philosophical perspective. Using insights derived from the work of Wittgenstein, it mounts a vigorous attack on influential contemporary accounts of learning, both in the 'romantic' Rousseauian tradition and in the 'scientific' cognitivist tradition. These two schools, the author argues, are more closely related than is commonly realised.

The book examines the early modern and enlightenment origins of contemporary learning theory before developing an original, socially-based perspective, which challenges the excessive individualism of most work in this area. Professor Winch covers a wide range of topics. These include: training, contemporary representationalist accounts of the mind and their implications for our understanding of learning, developmental theory, language learning, concept formation, memory, attention, later learning, and, in several chapters, learning in moral, religious and aesthetic contexts. The author shows that learning pervades all aspects of our lives and that in order for us to understand it in all its variety and complexity, we must go beyond the narrow perspectives of most empirical psychological study.

The Philosophy of Human Learning will be of interest to all who have a professional interest in learning, including psychologists as well as philosophers, of education.

Christopher Winch is currently Professor of Philosophy of Education at Nene College, Northampton, UK. He has taught in primary schools and in higher education. Among his publications are *Language, Ability and Educational Achievement* (1990), *Reading, Writing and Reading* (with Gavin Fairbairn) (1991, 1996), and *Quality and Education* (1996).

ROUTLEDGE INTERNATIONAL STUDIES IN THE PHILOSOPHY OF EDUCATION

THE PHILOSOPHY OF
HUMAN LEARNING

Christopher Winch

London and New York

First published 1998
by Routledge
11 New Fetter Lane, London EC4P 4EE

Simultaneously published in the USA and Canada
by Routledge
29 West 35th Street, New York, NY 10001

Phototypeset in Garamond by Intype London Ltd
Printed and bound in Great Britain by
T.J. International Ltd, Padstow, Cornwall

British Library Cataloguing in Publication Data
A catalogue record for this book is available from the British Library

Library of Congress Cataloguing in Publication Data
Winch, Christopher.
The philosophy of human learning/Christopher Winch.
p. cm.
Includes bibliographical references and index.
1. Learning. 2. Learning—Philosophy. I. Title.
LB1060.W56 1998
153.1′5—dc21 97–28095

ISBN 0–415–16190–8

This book is dedicated to the memory of Peter Winch

CONTENTS

CONTENTS

PREFACE

My motive in writing this book is easily stated. Despite the enormous contemporary interest in human learning and the amount of research that is done on it, we are in danger of knowing even less than we knew at the beginning of this century. This is not because we have failed to accumulate information about the subject, but because we have too much, a lot of it misleading, and we have been obsessed with theory-building at the expense of attention to particular cases. The rapid growth of the study of learning as a branch of psychology has been largely responsible both for the increase in information and the decline in clarity on the topic. We have failed to take account of what we already know, of what is embedded in what is sometimes called 'folk psychology' and consequently we are saddled with large-scale theories that contradict or conflict with older and deeper understandings of human learning.

This book represents a puny but nevertheless worthwhile attempt to question the pretensions of the scientific study of learning as an exercise in grand theory-building. It suggests instead an approach that is based on reminders of what we already know, a judicious scientific investigation where this is appropriate, and a self-denying ordinance on the construction of grand theory in this area. By following these suggestions we may gain greater clarity at the expense of vaulting scientific ambition; but that will be no bad thing.

The male pronoun is used generally to denote both males and females unless otherwise stated.

ACKNOWLEDGEMENTS

I have benefited greatly from conversations with John Gingell, David Carr, John and Patricia White and Paul Standish in increasing my understanding of the topics dealt with in this book. Written comments from John Wilson, Jim Walker, Nicholas Burbules and anonymous referees for Routledge, for the *Oxford Review of Education*, *Educational Theory* and *Educational Philosophy and Theory* have also been very helpful. In addition, I would like to record my thanks to participants at seminars at the University of London Institute of Education, the Philosophy of Education Society of Great Britain in Oxford, and the West Midlands Branch of the Philosophy of Education Society of Great Britain. I have also greatly benefited from the writings of Ludwig Wittgenstein, Norman Malcolm, G.P. Baker and P.M.S. Hacker and Nicholas Dent, to name a few.

I would like to thank the editors of *Educational Theory* (No. 4, 1996), *Educational Philosophy and Theory* (1997), *Westminster Studies in Education* (1987, published by Carfax), the *Oxford Review of Education* (No. 4, 1995, published by Carfax), for permission to reproduce material previously published in their journals. This material appears in Chapters 3, 5, 6 and 12 respectively.

All errors are my own responsibility.

1

INTRODUCTION

Reconsidering Learning

Why the subject is important

This book is a philosophical treatment of the concept of learning as it applies to child-rearing and education. Such a book is necessary because of the distorted way in which learning has been treated by many psychologists and those educationists who have been influenced by them. Learning is an important part of human life and the major concern of our education and training systems, not to mention the institution of child-rearing in any society. In addition, life is a matter not just of having more experiences but of preparing for and reflecting on experience. These activities can be called 'learning' just as much as the acquisition of knowledge, skill and understanding in childhood and early adulthood. Learning is, then, at the heart of human experience and, as such, a proper matter for a philosophical treatment, particularly where a rescue operation is necessary.

First, a word of clarification. I use the term 'learning' generically to cover not only those situations where people apply themselves deliberately and carefully to acquiring knowledge, skill and understanding, but also to those situations where they acquire these things either without apparent effort or through the normal processes of growth. The terms 'acquisition' and 'development' respectively are usually applied to these cases and I shall follow such usage but cover the full range of my concerns under the term 'learning', constantly bearing in mind both the similarities and the differences between the cases. The idea of learning through a quasi-biological form of development will, however, be critically discussed in Chapter 7. In addition, I shall be concerned with learning in both the task (trying to learn) sense and the achievement (having succeeded in learning) sense, and the discussion and context should make clear the distinction if it is necessary to do so.

My particular concerns in writing this book are as follows.

1 I wish to rescue learning from the exclusive concern of the social

sciences (psychology and linguistics in particular) and to defend the importance of a distinctive philosophical perspective on the subject.

2 I shall be challenging representationalism, behaviourism, developmentalism and Rousseauian romanticism as influential accounts of learning. I hope that it will be evident from the development of my argument that these approaches are far more closely related to one another than is commonly supposed and that all four have common roots which themselves stand in need of a vigorous critique.

3 I wish to treat aspects of learning that are neglected by most writers, as well as those more commonly considered. The former category includes the concept of attention and religious and aesthetic aspects of learning. In the latter category, memory, language and moral learning have all received extensive treatment which has largely passed into conventional wisdom. These conventional accounts will be given a thorough critique and an alternative point of view will be put forward.

4 I wish to emphasise the *social*, *affective* and *practical* nature of learning. These are three features that have received relatively little attention, but they are, I believe, of fundamental importance in gaining any understanding at all of how or why human beings learn anything.

Towards the end of *Philosophical Investigations*, Wittgenstein remarks that:

> The confusion and barrenness of psychology is not to be explained by calling it a 'young science'; its state is not comparable with that of physics for instance, in its beginnings.... For in psychology there are experimental methods and *conceptual confusion*....
>
> The existence of the experimental method makes us think we have the means of solving the problems which trouble us; though problem and method pass one another by.[1]

These remarks remain as true as they were nearly fifty years ago and can also be applied, to a large degree, to educational and linguistic thinking (both of which are heavily influenced by psychology).

When I say that the concept of learning needs examination, I do not wish to be understood as saying that we need an alternative theory. This is not necessary, desirable or even possible. In the course of the book, I shall show that much current thinking about learning (including what is called 'acquisition' and 'development') is confused and barren and should be discarded without regret. But the possibility of giving a *scientific* or even a *systematic* account of human learning is also mistaken.

One of the reasons why it has seemed possible to provide such accounts is that psychologists interested in learning have consistently failed to pay enough attention to certain aspects of human life, particularly those concerned with religion and the arts and, more generally, those aspects that have an irreducibly social, practical and affective dimension. Indeed, one of the main themes will be that the social, practical and affective dimensions of human life are central and need to be implicated in virtually every aspect of accounts of learning in different practices and situations. When one does so, the importance of *context* in understanding learning becomes apparent and this undermines the tendency to see our understanding of learning in terms of a grand theory.

These cautionary notes should not be taken to imply complete pessimism about our understanding of learning. The cautions are more about the dangers of theory-building than they are about the possibility of understanding. What we need, it will be argued, are not more theories but more *description* and more *understanding* of what is already before us. In certain important respects, the theories stand in the way of our understanding. What has been said should not be taken to mean that it is not possible to gain new knowledge and insight into the way in which people learn; it is, however, more likely that such knowledge will be piecemeal and related to particular activities than that it will form or be derived from grand theory.

It is inevitable that much of what I have to say will be concerned with children, often very young children, and the years in which most education takes place. This is inevitable, given that so much learning takes place in the earliest years of our lives. Certainly, the world of education has been deeply influenced by some of the theories that are described in subsequent chapters. To the extent that I am critical of practices based on those theories, there are implications for the way in which education is organised. But there will be no attempt to prescribe exactly what should go on in the nursery or the classroom, although the possible implications should, in most cases, be clear enough. There has, however, been too much dogmatic prescription of pedagogical practice in recent years for anyone to venture into this area without a great deal of humility and respect for the particular circumstances in which learning takes place. Instead, I shall be content if the implications of the criticisms of learning theories that are made here are debated within the teaching profession as a means of reviewing and reconsidering current practice. But learning does not take place solely in childhood and so the scope of the book will be broader than what is directly relevant to education.

That area of philosophy known as epistemology has been concerned with questions of how knowledge is acquired and the distinction between knowledge and belief. Epistemology is not concerned with empirical questions about how we learn, but with providing a framework in which such questions can be answered. Questions about how we learn are closely related to these epistemological preoccupations and rest on them to a large extent. The scientific enterprise of learning theory rests on a variety of related epistemological positions and cannot be understood except in terms of them. Much of the book will be concerned with those positions and why they are wrong. To the extent that learning theory rests on faulty epistemology it is, to a large degree, compromised. Therefore much of my concern will be epistemological, looking at the presuppositions behind learning theories and showing how empirical results derived from those theories are largely irrelevant to the questions in hand.

Most, if not all, modern learning theory derives from a tradition of thinking about human knowledge and human nature that stems from the work of Descartes on the one hand and Locke on the other. Despite the fact that these two philosophers are commonly thought to belong to different camps (rationalist and empiricist respectively), and despite the fact that there are significant differences in approach between the two of them, chiefly to do with the existence or otherwise of innate mental principles or ideas, there are enough similarities for it to be possible to talk of a common epistemological position from which modern learning theories draw their inspiration. It is also fair to say that there has been a growing *rapprochement* between empiricism and rationalism in contemporary philosophy which builds on the common ground that exists between them.[2] The starting point of both epistemologies is the existence of individuals, whose conscious awareness forms the basis of all knowledge. This individuality is conceived of more in mental than in corporeal terms. The common epistemological position that, historically, both empiricism and rationalism share is, then, a form of methodological individualism based on a conception of human beings as mental primarily and corporeal secondarily. This is one of the assumptions that will come under attack in subsequent chapters and the consequences of that attack ramify through the accounts offered of various aspects of human learning. Briefly, this assumption results in accounts of learning that neglect the practical, social and affective.

The picture is, however, complicated in various ways that make an onslaught on mentalism and individualism inadequate in itself. The first of these is the tendency of one strand in empiricism to eschew its mentalist assumptions and to concentrate on the corporeal nature of humanity and its continuity with the animal world. In doing so, it adopts a view, inspired by Descartes and continued by Kant, that, in so far as humans are part of the natural world and, hence, subject to causality, they can be treated as automata for the purposes of scientific understanding.[3] This empiricist-derived approach, known as *behaviourism*, has been and continues to be influential in psychology and education. Behaviourists seek to explain learning in terms of modifications to bodily movements by external stimuli. Ironically, the behaviourist programme requires the observer or scientist who investigates learning to be in the position of the empiricist's individual, who takes in raw sense data concerning the behaviour of the creature observed (whether it be animal or human is not to the point) and forms generalisations on the basis of it.[4]

The second complication lies in the way in which some strands within Cartesianism have become subordinated to a physicalist view of the world, in modern linguistic and learning theory. This tendency has been boosted by the growing importance of computer technology and the seeming promise that this gives for providing a model for the operation of the human mind. Modern *cognitivism*, as the most influential contemporary variants of Cartesianism are now called, tends to be a physicalist version, where the mind and the brain are identified and the symbolic abilities of the human mind are explicable in terms of neural structures and processes.[5] The third complication lies in *developmentalism*: an approach to human growth and learning derived from Rousseau, but continued through the work of Piaget and others, which emphasises the *qualititative* differences in learning capacity which relate to the different stages of childhood and young adulthood. It is arguable though, that developmentalism is more of an elaboration than a wholesale revision of mentalistic individualism.

The fourth and final complication is the *liberationism* that again derives from the work of Rousseau. Rousseau stresses the need to free humans from the overt subordination of one human will to another if education is really to be achieved. This implies, as I shall argue, a freedom from authority. Much modern learning theory therefore has a distinctly utopian, liberationist and anti-authoritarian bias which has had a profound influence on Western patterns of child-rearing and education. In fact, a failure to appreciate the normative nature of human life, particularly including childhood, lies behind all these approaches to learning; it is therefore not surprising to find explicit connections between, for example, cognitivism (with its emphasis on methodological individualism) and Rousseauian progressivism (with its emphasis on individual freedom) in the work of some influential modern writers.[6]

Insights from the work of Wittgenstein

The long tradition of thinking about the human mind and the nature of learning that I have described as mentalistic individualism has reigned, practically unchallenged during this century, up to and including the present time. The only challenge of really major importance to have emerged has come from the work of Ludwig Wittgenstein. While his challenge to the epistemology of mentalistic individualism has received some attention, the profound implications of his work for the various projects of explaining human learning have been much less considered. These implications can be summarised briefly, but the detail of the book will spell them out.

First, Wittgenstein cast doubt on the view that knowledge should be assimilated to *certainty*. This view, expressed in the Cartesian *cogito* argument and in the direct awareness of ideas and impressions in the empiricists, is replaced with reference to beliefs and attitudes that underpin all our behaviour and which can be expressed as agreement in reactions and in judgement. There are certain beliefs to which we hold fast and which form the basis of all other judgements; it makes no sense to doubt them as there is no framework within which they can be doubted. Certainty about some general matters of fact is a prerequisite of our ability both to gain knowledge about and to cast doubt on other matters of fact.[7] Therefore, although we learn to be certain about many things from our earliest days (for example, that everyday objects do not disappear and reappear all the time), when we learn, we do not thereby become certain about what we know. In fact, it is possible for us to come to *doubt* what we know and for our doubts to exist within a framework of bedrock beliefs about which we are certain. It follows that knowledge exists within a system of practices and beliefs that are not themselves properly describable as knowledge but which are the prerequisites of knowledge. Wittgenstein makes certainty normative, prescribing a framework for knowledge, while, at the same time, acknowledging that the boundaries between certainty and knowledge are sometimes vague and may fluctuate over time. These ideas are of importance to the understanding of later learning (see Chapter 12).

Second, Wittgenstein drew attention to human natural history. He did not mean by this that we should regard ourselves as automata as the Cartesians regarded animals. Rather he wanted to question the view that we are composed of two parts – one mental, the other corporeal – and to stress that a general separation of the two is unintelligible. There are a number of implications that follow from this shift in emphasis:

- The connection between cognitive, conative and affective aspects of human nature is very close; although they can be conveniently separated for certain purposes, it is a mistake to think that they are in a sense distinct faculties of mind. In particular, our feelings and emotions (which themselves have a cognitive aspect) as they are manifested to others are important in understanding our behaviour in ordinary life; they do more than provide clues to what we think and feel, they are, to a large extent, constitutive of it.
- We understand thought, feeling and action as attributes of *people* rather than of minds. Learning from the reactive behaviour of others is fundamental to our becoming human and is bound up with our ability to recognise and respond to gestures and facial expressions that are themselves part of the agreement in reaction that forms the background to knowledge.
- The affective side of human nature is very important for understanding motivation, interest and desire, including the desire to learn. Behaviour-

ists have, it is true, paid attention to motivation as important to learning, as have developmentalists, but they have both dealt with it in a hopelessly crude and inappropriate way.

- A further consequence of emphasising our animal nature is Wittgenstein's stress on the importance of *training* for learning. Most cognitivists regard training with horror and behaviourists tend to conflate it with *conditioning*, but for Wittgenstein it was of fundamental importance. It is through training that we develop the responses that allow us to take part in human life: to use and understand language; to perform simple and then more complex everyday and practical tasks; and to become morally, religiously and artistically aware. Human training is a normative activity whose possibility rests on agreement in reactions. It is through training that we first learn to follow rules, and it is through being able to follow rules that we can go on to learn more through instruction, explanation and discovery.[8]

- I shall argue that it is a further, although unstated, consequence of this approach that learning to *act* and to *acquire abilities* is both intimately bound up with learning that certain things are the case and is also important in its own right.[9] This again is an area of learning that has suffered relative neglect, apart from very crude treatments on the part of behaviourists.

Third, Wittgenstein drew attention to the social nature of human life. He did this primarily through arguing that there could be no such thing as private rule-following.[10] The truth of Wittgenstein's claim has been contested by many philosophers, but so has its interpretation. I shall deal with both of these in subsequent chapters but will confine myself to a couple of observations here. Wittgenstein's claim does not rest on scepticism about individual memories as some commentators have thought, nor does it apply only to rules that are necessarily unshareable, like those that govern a private sensation language. The claim is more radical than that; it is that one cannot get a grip on the notion of right or wrong, correctness or incorrectness, without there being a *social institution* of rule-following. No normative activity could exist *ab initio* in the life of a solitary. Since the possibility of memory claims rests on the possibility of being wrong as well as right, it makes no sense to appeal to memory claims except in a social context where such claims can be meaningfully assessed.[11]

The social nature of rule-following implies that human learning is more than just an individualistic activity.[12] Most psychologists, linguists and educators who concern themselves with learning pay little attention to this social dimension and, even where they do, it is given an extremely superficial treatment in terms of, for example, the importance of co-operation. Taken seriously, understanding the social nature of learning goes far deeper than this, at a variety of levels ranging from the interpersonal to the political. Exploring this implication is one of the major themes of this book.

Learning and institutions

If human learning has an irreducibly social basis, then what is there to be said about the importance of *society* in shaping learning? In what follows I shall concentrate particularly on the kinds of society in which we live, namely advanced, post-industrial societies. But I shall move to a consideration of them from a wider anthropological perspective. All human societies, whatever their diversity, have to take account of certain limiting factors which are to be found, in one way or another, in their conceptual schemes.[13] These concepts, relating to the biological factors of birth, reproduction and death, are taken account of in different ways in different cultures. In different ways, they inform all aspects of human existence: domestic, economic, moral, religious and artistic. It is an important implication of these limiting factors that they give each society the task of producing the next generation and thus of reproducing themselves.

How this is done will vary enormously, but any society will have some form of child-rearing practices, some form of cultural and institutional initiation and some form of vocational preparation. It is not difficult to see that these categories are, to some extent, artificial. It is quite conceivable, for example, that all these aspects can be found within the same activity or group of activities. One could imagine a tribe where child-rearing involves the learning of myths, the making of artefacts and of paintings and sculptures, as well as moral formation. As a child grows older he learns to identify plants and animals, to hunt and to make tools and to learn more about the beliefs and practices of the tribe. Since these beliefs and practices inform the vocational activities of hunting and making, it would be wrong to say that they were learned separately; they are all bound together as part of the life of the people. As the child grows to adolescence, he learns more about the institutions and rites of his people and becomes fully initiated as a grown man (or woman) ready in turn to take on the role of trainer and educator. This is not a fanciful scenario, but describes the conditions of societies that we call hunter-gathering, which exist in different and diverse parts of the world. The example illustrates that not only is learning part of everyday life, but its different aspects are extremely difficult to keep separate from one another.

Our society is not like this. It is institutionally complex and specialised. It was this feature that allowed Marx in the nineteenth century to talk of an economic base and a residual superstructure. Whatever the myths generated by that particular image, it is nevertheless true that modern people are inclined to compartmentalise their lives to a great degree. This is not just because we run a very finely organised division of labour (although that is an important part of it), it is also because we are far more ready to think of society as composed of different categories than we were in the past, even though, paradoxically, we are more inclined to think of people as fundamentally the same, irrespective of race, culture, age or sex. It now comes naturally to us to think of the economy, religion, art and domestic life as separate spheres of life through which we move in the course of the day or the week.

This means that there are aspects of life about which most of us are relatively ignorant. It also means that the upbringing of the young has become a specialised task, entrusted to workers who bear the main responsibility for it and who work in institutions such as nurseries, schools and colleges with, to some extent, their own rules and priorities. While there exist lines of accountability and an ability and willingness to negotiate about the implementation of what are sometimes different and opposing sets of values, conflicts between different institutions can be handled. But one of the prices of such institutional separation is that, inevitably, relatively autonomous institutions develop their own values and cultures (beliefs and ways of doing things), that both reflect broad movements in society and dominant intra-institutional preoccupations.[14] In the specific case of learning and the educational institutions with which it has come to be connected, this amounts to a dominance of two forces, sometimes in conflict but sometimes working in harmony. One is that of *scientism* and the other is that of *anti-authoritarian romanticism*. Both these tendencies are very influential in the societies taken as a whole, but they tend to be particularly influential within education systems. They are also greatly influenced by the common root of mentalistic individualism outlined earlier.

That they can sometimes work symbiotically may perhaps seem surprising, but should not be. To a large extent, science has developed through emancipation both from traditional authority and traditional institutional connections. Rousseauian ideas of society, morality and religion have developed from largely the same source; the Creed of the Savoyard Vicar is an attempt to retain some form of religious belief in the face of a growing scientific worldview in the mid-eighteenth century.[15] There are common themes of emancipation and the rejection of authority both in the rise of science and of democratic political theory. There is a darker side to both as well, an arrogance and a need for control that verges on the totalitarian; this is more difficult to resist, perhaps, because it comes couched in the rhetoric of freedom and emancipation.[16]

These two tendencies have shaped modern ways in which we teach, learn and the ways in which we think about these activities. The way we think about teaching and learning has led quite naturally, through the influence of scientism, to the attempt to build theories about learning that profess to cover the whole gamut of human activity, while in reality neglecting some aspects in favour of others. I shall try to recover the diversity at the expense of grand theory-building; to reinstate the importance of learning in other relatively neglected areas of life; and to suggest that in pursuing the vision of the Enlightenment, we have incurred significant losses in our understanding of some aspects of human life, particularly as they relate to our views on learning. Lest this be thought as a fogeyish diatribe against modernity, let me say at once that my purpose is not a reactionary one of trying to return to a 'pretopia' of integrated and holistic social institutions, but to redress a balance in our thinking which has needed correction for some time. I hope also to show how, through scepticism about the importance of unbridled individualism in successful learning, one can nevertheless make sense of the enormous diversity of individuality and individual ability that results from learning that takes place in many different ways through the impact of political, cultural, social and familial factors on the individual and his or her particular circumstances.

Outline of the book

Chapter 2 will look more closely at the Cartesian and empiricist roots of learning theory, seeking to emphasise their points of similarity as much as their differences. Chapter 3 will look critically at the work of Rousseau, particularly those considerations of education to be found in *Émile*, critically examining both Rousseau's awareness that humans have a natural history that shapes the way in which they think, and his anti-authoritarianism and refusal to appreciate the normative nature of human life, particularly in relation to education and child-rearing.

Chapter 4 looks more closely at this normative nature and examines what it implies in terms of social interaction, reactivity and the affective side of our nature. The importance of the private language argument for our understanding of learning is also assessed. Chapter 5 examines the importance of *training* to rule-following, and to learning more generally. This chapter also considers the limitations of modern behaviourism as a scientific learning theory. Chapter 6 looks critically at the currently dominant scientistic account of learning: cognitivism in its representationalist form, and suggests that it is incoherent because it is based on applying the concept of representation to a context (the 'mind/brain') where it makes no sense. Chapter 7 is a critical account of the most influential form of developmentalism and suggests that, in so far as it is correct, it is largely platitudinous. In so far as it is not valuable, it has contributed to consistent underestimates of learning ability. Chapter 8 looks critically at current scientific accounts of how we learn to speak and suggests that they attempt to explain a mystery that does not need to be explained. Chapter 9 concerns concept formation and defends the view that concepts are capacities exercised in judgement and shows how they can be developed in the normative context described in earlier chapters. Chapter 10 re-evaluates the role of memory in learning while Chapter 11 looks at the somewhat neglected role of the concept of *paying attention* and the place that it has in learning. Chapter 12 examines later learning and casts doubt on the notion that it is, above all, important to 'learn to learn' considered as some kind of super-thinking skill.

Chapters 13, 14 and 15 are all concerned with aspects of learning that have been relatively neglected (moral learning is a partial exception to this, but has mainly been influenced by developmentalism), but which are closely connected with one another. These chapters also draw on themes developed in earlier chapters. Chapter 16 concludes and summarises the issues.

2

THE CARTESIAN AND EMPIRICIST HERITAGE OF LEARNING THEORIES

Introduction

Both Descartes and the empiricists have profoundly affected modern thinking about learning. Modern cognitivism owes an enormous debt to Descartes, while associationist accounts of learning issue from the theorising of Berkeley and Hume. Both behaviourism and much modern thinking about memory remain steeped in the thinking of both Descartes and the empiricists.

Both Descartes and the empiricists start from the solitary individual as the source of knowledge. Descartes' individualism is qualified by his reliance on God to provide veridical perception but *that* knowledge is itself underwritten by the solitary examination of ideas. The individual starting point for learning is also shared by the empiricists; they do not however hold, like Descartes, that some ideas are planted in the mind before birth. This view has had a very strong influence on some modern theories of learning. It is, however, important not to confuse the historical views of Descartes with the doctrines associated with 'Cartesian dualism' which, in some important respects, resemble empiricism more than views that Descartes himself held.[1]

It is to the empiricists rather than to Descartes that we owe the idea that experience consists in acquaintance with necessarily private objects of which the individual mind is aware. This awareness is incorrigible and inaccessible to anyone other than the perceiving mind. The particulars of which the mind is aware, on this account, consist of sense impressions in the first instance, and secondarily, thoughts, volitions, memories and imaginings. The mind is aware of these objects through a faculty of inner sense (modelled on visual perception). In this respect, popular accounts of the views of Descartes make them coincide with those of the empiricists in grouping all mental phenomena together as objects of perception of the conscious mind. According to this view, where Descartes differs from the empiricists is in thinking that some at least of these mental phenomena

12

are *innate* rather than acquired through experience. In fact, Descartes is not committed to the view that conscious experience is of objects and hence that our experience of these objects is *private, incorrigible* and *subjective*. Since the logical account of judgement to which Descartes subscribed did not recognise relational propositions, he could not regard judgement as expressing a relationship between a judger and certain kinds of objects.[2] It is fair to say, however, that under the influence of post-Aristotelian logical categories, it is largely taken for granted that Descartes thought in these terms as well.[3]

Descartes thought he had proved that his essence was that of a thinking being (*res cogitans*). By 'thinking' he meant 'making judgements' so that, although animals can perceive, have sensations, remember and imagine, they cannot judge or will. The essence of a human is thinking and, unlike animals, their behaviour is not wholly subject to mechanical laws of explanation. Human learning would, then, seem to be of two kinds: first modifications of bodily movements that can be accounted for mechanically, in the way that the bodily movements of animals can. Second, through learning to make judgements and issue volitions (both of these are examples of voluntary action).[4]

Descartes is well known as an exponent of the thesis that certain ideas exist within the mind at birth and do not come to us from experience. This thesis has an obvious impact on any Cartesian account of learning since, at the very least, any account of human knowledge that involves the existence of innate ideas will influence an account of how knowledge is gained from experience. It was a new departure in philosophy to use the term 'idea' to refer to the contents of the human mind and Descartes appears to have used the term to mean jointly certain concepts that we now prefer to keep distinct. For example, in *Meditation I*, he appears to mean by 'ideas' what we would now mean by the term 'proposition', while in *Meditation III*, he refers to the ideas or thoughts of such things as 'Earth, sky, stars and the rest of what I got from the senses'.[5] However, there does seem to be something pictorial about ideas and this is not a contingent feature of them.

> Some of these experiences are as it were pictures of objects and these alone are properly called ideas; e.g. when I think of (*cogito*) a man, a chimera, the sky, an angel or God. These ideas cannot in themselves be considered false, only judgements.[6]

Although alike in all having a pictorial or quasi-pictorial character, they are not alike in their origins. Hearing a noise, seeing the sun, or feeling the fire seem to proceed from external objects, while sirens, hippogriffs, etc. are Descartes' own invention. However, such ideas as 'thing', 'truth', and 'consciousness' seem to come from Descartes' own nature and thus are innate. It is not claimed that these are pictorial.

These comments raise as many questions as they answer, for on the one hand, the term 'concept' appears appropriate to some of the items, both pictorial and non-pictorial, while others appear to be not just experientially based but experiential in character, while others again appear to be products of the imagination.[7] Furthermore there can be different kinds of ideas of the same object. Descartes gives as an example the idea of the sun, which I gain experientially on the one hand and through innate notions *via* astronomical reasoning on the other.[8] The latter idea more closely resembles the sun than the former. Descartes' reluctance to define ideas suggests that he uses the term 'idea' as a special kind of portmanteau concept, with generic pictures and experiences at the core, and non-generic pictures, propositions and judgements at the periphery.

Across these distinctions cuts a further set of distinctions concerning the origins of ideas. Ideas can be innate, adventitious (experiential) or factitious (imaginary) in their origins.[9] At the same time, one should not assume that adventitious ideas are resemblances of what they are ideas of. It is quite likely that they are pictorial but non-resembling (*vide* the idea of the sun above), but are so constructed as to enable us to flourish in the world in which we live.[10] Descartes, who thought that the essence of material substances was extension, seems to attribute something like what Locke was later to call 'secondary qualities' to material substances, although he thought that those that arise in our minds as the result of contact with the material world are somewhat different and perhaps confused ideas of properties of material substances.[11] However, if the ideas of which we are conscious are not caused by qualities of material substances, then there is a sense in which they are not adventitious but properties of the mind. If this is the case, then they are properties (at least for humans) of a *res cogitans* and are properties that the mind must have had from its origin.

There is, then, a major difficulty about interpreting Descartes' doctrine of ideas. The term 'idea' can mean anything from a present experience, to a mental image, to the result of the exercise of an ability, to an ability, to a capacity.[12] It is not clear, for example, that a baby's innate idea of God is in some sense in the baby's mind although not attended to, or whether it is an ability to acquire the idea of God (a capacity).[13] Kenny argues that Descartes seems unwilling to distinguish between two cases of potentiality: (1) where the potentiality exists to acquire a concept; (2) where the concept has been acquired but is not currently being exercised. In order to account for most kinds of human learning, it might be argued, it is necessary to have the first kind of potentiality. The doctrine of innate ideas, by relying on the blurring of this distinction, threatens to make much learning a kind of recollection on the Platonic model, i.e. a potentiality to recall what has been acquired before birth.[14] Thus, if a baby has an innate idea of God, rather than a capacity to learn about God, then what we would normally call 'learning about God' would involve recollection of the already existing idea of God.[15] Kenny remarks: 'There seems no real room in his system for the concept of learning.'[16]

On the one hand, if I already have an idea innately, then I cannot have learned it. On the other hand, if I have acquired an idea and do not currently hold it in my mind, it is unclear in what sense I do 'have' it and therefore in what sense I have really learned it.[17] One way of dealing with this problem is to take Chomsky's path, and to account for innate ideas as a kind of structure in the mind which is both a capacity and, in some sense, a representation of the range of ability which the holder of the capacity exercises. Thus, an innate language is both an ability to communicate (if only for the mind with itself), but also a general structural representation of all natural languages, which allows them to be learned given appropriate inputs. In this sense, it is a kind of capacity.

As we have noted, ideas that result from experience (adventitious ideas) are also in a sense innate. Since the causes of experience do not in any way resemble the ideas that they excite, these ideas must have existed in us beforehand and are in a sense excited or brought forward by the impact of material objects on our senses.[18] Kenny's gloss on this is as follows: the idea *qua* ability (he uses the term capacity) is innate. The idea *qua* episode is adventitious; when the ability is exercised during a judgement about something outside the mind, it is adventitious. However, no idea is like the sensory stimulus that brings it to mind. According to Descartes, ideas are not pictures of the objects that exist outside the mind, although they are, in a sense, pictorial. This is clear enough in the case of ideas *qua* abilities, but not *qua* episodes. He is clear that ideas (*qua* episodes) are not images in the brain, but they may be images in the mind's eye when it is directed to a part of the brain.[19]

In fact, his ideas have some of the properties of material pictures, some of mental images, and some of concepts. Like material and mental pictures, they are representations that exhibit things. Like mental pictures and unlike cerebral pictures, they are not made of any matter. Unlike either, they can represent immaterial things (e.g. God) without doing so by representing something material (e.g. a bearded sage). Like material pictures, but unlike mental images, they exist even when not before the mind, and when before the mind they can contain details that the mind has not noticed.[20]

It can be argued that the notion that the exercised concept is a representation, in some sense, leads to a vicious regress. If my judgement that here is a man implies that the man corresponds to a mental representation of a man, then the representation would itself have to be correctly recognised in order for the judgement to be correct. In order for this judgement to be made, a further representation of the relationship between the representation of a man and the man himself would have to be available which would be subject to the same requirement to ensure that it too was correctly recognised. This kind of problem is characteristic of attempts to describe the mind as a solitary homunculus. Because the homunculus is solitary, there is no clear way in which it can distinguish between correct and incorrect representations (see Chapters 4 and 7 for further discussions of this issue). The only clear sense in which it is possible to talk of ideas as innate is when 'idea' is taken to mean not 'concept', but the capacity to acquire concepts. Even then, when one attempts to characterise this capacity as a form of representation, confusion is likely to follow. However, no one, empiricists included, is likely to deny that humans have an innate rather than an acquired capacity to form concepts, in some sense of 'innate'. The thesis, although uncontroversial, is not very interesting as a distinctive philosophical account of the origin of ideas, because all that it asserts is that we are so constituted as to be capable of forming concepts.[21]

Descartes' attempt to construe ideas as a kind of representation analogous to a picture leads to further problems. Cases where what is thought about is something that has no extra-mental existence are run together with cases where that something is outside the mind. Thus, to think of a unicorn may, for Descartes, be to have an idea of a unicorn in one's mind; there is no presumption that a unicorn is in one's mind or that one is thinking of a real unicorn. On the other hand, if thinking of the sun involves having an idea of the sun, then there is a sense in which the sun is present to the mind, since the sun, unlike the unicorn, is not an imaginary entity. Descartes moves between saying that thinking of the sun involves a purely extrinsic property of the sun, that it has an objective existence in my understanding (I am not thinking of an imaginary sun), and saying that in so far as it has an objective existence in the understanding, it is as an idea. It would seem to follow from this that when I think of the sun, then I think of an idea of the sun, since this is the way in which the sun can have an objective existence in me, which is necessary for me to be thinking of a real sun. However, this conclusion seems to be false, because the two kinds of thought (sun and idea of the sun) can be distinguished. The difficulty arises in taking the idea of the sun as a kind of representation of the sun, and then having this idea as being the only way in which I can think of it. This difficulty applies both to adventitious and factitious sun-concepts since both are representational.

When the idea of X is seen, on the other hand, as a thinking about X (with or without an image), then it is best seen as an aspect of the exercise of the concept X in various activities. That is to say, the concept X is employed in, for example, an act of judgement. Where the concept applies to non-existents like unicorns, the judgements in which it occurs are true and false in somewhat different ways from those cases where something external corresponds to the concepts. Acts of judgement are to be described in many different ways, including assertions, actions and what Geach has

16

called 'mental acts', which can be construed on the analogy of real acts of assertion, questioning, etc.[22] Concepts in this sense are abilities that can be employed in acts of various kinds, including acts of judgement and mental acts (see Chapter 9). Performing a mental act may be part of what is involved in thinking about X, but should not be what is to be identified as the thinking about X. *Thinking of* or *thinking about* X is a wider and more diffuse notion than that of making a judgement (mental act or not) about X. One may think about X in various ways without necessarily making judgements or carrying out mental acts concerned with X (see Chapter 11). The associationist account of learning developed by Berkeley and Hume attempted to show how a mental image might represent a concept and will be discussed further in Chapter 9.

Locke and the doctrine of innate ideas

Locke's ideas seem to have the same heterogeneity as Descartes'. He denies, however, that any of them originates in anything other than experience. On the one hand he seems to have meant *concepts*, as understood in the previous section, but what he, like Descartes, ambiguously calls ideas. These include concepts like *existence* and *unity*.[23] He also seems to mean analytic propositions such as:

It is impossible for the same thing to be and not to be.[24]

Episodes that involve mental attributes called up by excitations of the sensory organs are also ideas. They include some of the properties of material things not directly present in the objects themselves but created by excitations of our sensory system; they do not subsist in the objects themselves but are called up (rather than abstracted) from the objects. The mechanism for the calling up of these ideas is a mental faculty about which we appear to know nothing. Locke holds that ideas in this sense are created by objects outside the mind. The only sorts of ideas that he appears to reject are those that are not acquired as a result of the impact of the world on our senses. He prefers an account of the origins of these that ties them to the experience of the world. In some respects the views of Locke and Descartes are quite similar:

1 They both assume that ideas in some sense *represent* that for which they stand in the world.
2 They both postulate unknown functions of the mind which allow ideas to be generated by objects outside the mind, to disappear from consciousness and to be called up again.

The empiricists postulate other functions, such as that of the *imagination*, which allow ideas to be associated and combined with one another. Locke's strategy is to show that if all ideas can be demonstrated to arise from experience, then there is no reason to suppose that they should be innate. His first argument is directed against the view that there is universal consent for the principles of identity and non-contradiction. In the first place, idiots and children have no conception of them; if they were innate, they would unavoidably perceive them, but they do not and so they cannot be innate. Against this argument, a Chomskyan category of tacit knowledge which is available to the subject but not available to conscious thought might help the Cartesian account, but Locke seems to reject it. For a content to be available to the mind it must satisfy one of two conditions. First, that the mind is actually conscious of the content; second, that it was once conscious of that content but is no longer so. In this latter case, the content appears to leave a kind of trace in the memory. Innate ideas, supposedly available at birth, satisfy neither of these two conditions; they are not currently attended to, neither have they ever been attended to by the individual in question.

> To say a notion is imprinted on the mind, and yet at the same time to say that the mind is ignorant of it, and never yet took notice of it, is to make this impression nothing.[25]

Yet Locke, like Descartes, must admit that notions can in some sense be imprinted on the mind and the mind not take notice of them, in order to account for memory or, indeed, any retention of what is learned. If learning occurs through the generation of ideas by experience and these ideas only exist so long as they are present in awareness, then it is difficult to see how we could learn anything. Descartes argued that images stored in the brain could be perceived by the subject and these images are what is called memory.[26] It is arguable that, in this way, he is not subject to the criticism levelled against him by Kenny that he cannot account for learning. If an image (and it need not be a likeness) of something is imprinted on the brain, then the mind may, at any time, inspect it. There is thus a difference between someone who has not acquired an idea but is able to do so, someone who has acquired one and is not currently using it, and someone who is currently making use of an acquired idea. Locke maintains that

> there is an ability in the mind, when it will, to revive them again.[27]

Yet, as Don Locke points out, this cannot be a satisfactory solution, for the reason that one is unable to attach any sense to the proposition that the same idea as before is called up in an act of memory. This is one of the main points of the 'private language argument' of Wittgenstein, that it cannot make sense to speak of 'the same' or 'not the same' in cases like this, as there is no independent principle of individuation available. Locke, who treats ideas as particulars capable of occurring as terms in relational judgements and as the logical subjects of judgements, is vulnerable to this criticism in a way that Descartes, who only allows a modal existence to ideas, is not.[28] Descartes is not, however, invulnerable to the criticism that the brain impression that constitutes the basis of memory does not have available to it clear criteria of identity and is thus dubious as means of checking memory. In the case of Descartes, it is the *solitary* rather than the *private* nature of the source of memory that is troublesome (see Chapter 4).

In order to avoid the first objection that Locke makes to Descartes, it is sometimes said that people assent to logical truths through the use of reason and this is what renders them innate. But in this case, Locke replies, reason must have led them to discover truths already imprinted in the mind which that person was not aware of before. This, Locke holds, leads to a contradiction: if the ideas were already imprinted, then a man knows them already; if they are not, then he does not know them. But since he does know them, it is self-contradictory to suppose that he did not, in some sense, know them before he used his reason to discover them, since this would violate Locke's two necessary conditions for knowing something, namely that it either is or has been previously before the mind.[29]

It is also a confusion, Locke holds, to think that merely because one cannot but assent to certain propositions, they must be innate.

> This cannot be denied: that men grow first acquainted with many of these self-evident truths upon their first being proposed; but it is clear that whosoever does so finds in himself that he then begins to know a proposition that he knew not before, and which henceforth he never questions, not because it was innate, but because the consideration of the things contained in those words would not suffer him to think otherwise, how or whensoever he is brought to reflect on them.[30]

Locke goes on to deal with the suggestion that these ideas are implicitly in the mind, even if they are not brought to consciousness. He dismisses this view as meaning nothing more than that the mind has a capacity to understand such propositions.

It is natural for us to talk about learning as if we recognise that we have both a capacity to learn and a capacity to bring to mind what has been learned. As Ryle pointed out, the concepts of knowledge and belief are *dispositional* rather than *episodic*.[31] This does not mean that all knowledge is practical 'know-how', but that knowing is not to be identified solely with *episodes of bringing something to mind* as both empiricists and Cartesians have thought. While it would seem that empiricists have little to add on this matter, the position is more complex for Cartesians. We have already noted in Descartes a trace theory of memory, whereby knowledge is stored through a physical representation in the brain. One can develop this thought further and argue that it is the trace that provides an implicit sort of knowledge which exists even when the subject is not aware of it.

This kind of physical representationalism has been extensively developed in modern cognitivism, much of which is self-consciously an extension of Descartes' philosophy.[32] The difficulties that arise with it come from the notion that a physical trace in the brain could represent anything at all (See Chapters 6 and 10).

Conclusion

In their epistemological writings, Descartes, Locke and Hume describe learning as a solitary activity. For Descartes, it involves attention to innate ideas or to representations of brain-traces. For the empiricists it involves retention and recall of ideas whose existence as objects is necessarily *private*. The empiricists are vulnerable to the criticisms made of the possibility of intelligible discourse about necessarily private objects made by Wittgenstein in *Philosophical Investigations*, paragraphs 258–265.[33] These criticisms do not apply to the claim that learning is essentially a solitary activity because paragraphs 258–265 are not directed against that claim. Modern cognitivism is committed to the latter but not to the former view and so is invulnerable to the strictures of the private language argument. Whether or not there can be *ab initio* solitary learning is much disputed. What is beyond doubt is that the *foundationalist* view of human knowledge, held by Descartes and the empiricists, takes the knowledge of a solitary individual as the basis on which all knowledge is built up.

This preconception is built into most contemporary theories of learning. When it is combined with a version of the anti-society normative account of learning offered by Rousseau (and critically discussed in the next chapter), a distorted view of how humans learn emerges. Not only is the learning in its most fundamental forms a solitary process but the *best* learning is solitary. Inevitably, the confluence of such views poses a considerable challenge to any understanding of learning that sees it as fundamentally a social activity whose success may be dependent on other individuals through, for example, training and instruction. In Chapter 4 the view that the most important features of human learning could be *ab initio* solitary will be challenged.

3

THE ROMANTIC VIEW OF LEARNING

Rousseau's *Émile*

Introduction

This chapter examines Rousseau's theory of learning and assesses its strengths and weaknesses. The theory is an integral part of the account of education developed in *Émile*.[1] Not only is *Émile* a work of sustained literary brilliance but it is rigorously worked out from its own premises.[2] It also prefigures some of the insights in epistemology and the philosophy of mind that are attributed to Wittgenstein. Any attempt to deal with the theory of learning that it sets out needs to engage closely with the fundamental ideas of the book and how they hang together, before criticism can be effective.

Rousseau's positive contribution to philosophical and psychological thinking about learning can be described as follows. Human beings are not disembodied intelligences but embodied creatures who are part of the natural world. The thrust of Rousseau's educational programme and, by implication, of his epistemology, is to take individuals as whole, organic beings, part of the natural order of things and to develop them in more than narrowly intellectual ways.[3] This remains the case despite the empiricist character of his description of the genesis of ideas and of their use.[4]

Rousseau does not take the view that human beings are essentially solitary individuals; however, the idea of human society that he develops as the proper medium for mutual association and self-expression does not allow him to give a satisfactory account of either human learning or of the nature of social relations. His unwillingness to see that a normative order is constitutive of *all* social relations of the human type runs through his writing and keeps him from appreciating the importance and indeed, the necessity of normative intervention in upbringing from the earliest stages of life.[5]

Finally, there is the developmentalist heritage of Rousseau. This arises from his view of the human condition as one of growth, maturity and decay. Although this is a valuable insight, it also contains dangers. These arise from two sources, both of which can be found within Rousseau's thinking. The first is the contention that the sole, or at least the main source of motivation and hence of motivation to learn, is to be found primarily within individual human beings, rather than within human beings in the context of their social surroundings. The second is the idea of readiness, that certain things cannot be learned until the child is at the stage at which he is capable of learning them. The account of readiness poses a danger of over-dogmatic thinking about what children can or cannot learn at any particular stage of their lives, which may lead to a systematic underestimate of their capacities.[6]

Rousseau's epistemology

At a superficial glance, Rousseau's account of learning is quite similar to that of Locke. Like Locke, Rousseau starts with *sensation* as the source of human knowledge. The role of the mind in receiving sensations is passive. However, Rousseau asserts, unlike Locke and Hume, that what the mind does with sensations is a kind of activity, namely that of judgement, whose way of working is partly constitutive of our character. For example, Locke writes:

> By REFLECTION then . . . I would be understood to mean that notice which the mind takes of its own operations, and the manner of them, by reason whereof there come to be *ideas* of these operations in the understanding.[7]

Compare the Lockean account with that offered by Rousseau:

> At first our pupil had merely sensations, now he has ideas; he could only feel, now he reasons. For from the comparison of many successive and simultaneous sensations and the judgment arrived at with regard to them, there springs a mixed or complex sensation which I call an idea.[8]

Notice that it is the *pupil*, not his *mind*, that judges. Rousseau has little patience with the idea that the starting point for understanding the human intellect is to conceive of it as a disembodied spirit and he explicitly criticises Locke for taking this view.[9] It is far less clear, however, that he made a complete break with mentalistic individualism regarding personal identity and the possibility of disembodied existence after death.[10] Be that as it may, he does not regard the human mind as fully formed from birth, either through the possession of innate ideas or through being a *tabula rasa* ready to receive ideas. For Descartes and the empiricists, the mind has a structure that is complete from birth, waiting only for the particular experiences that the individual chances to undergo. In Rousseau's account, minds undergo changes that are directly related to maturation and to our experiences of the natural world and of other human beings. Furthermore, the way in which we judge is partly constitutive of our characters and, by implication, ways of judging can be learned.[11]

Although sensation is passive, *judgement* is a type of activity that we can perform more or less well and which, by implication, we can learn to do better. Our manner of judgement is partly constitutive of the kinds of people we are; poor judgement in one respect tells others that we are false, in another respect it tells people that we are superficial. On the other hand, we can be judged to have solidity of character by the quality of our judgements. We are not born with this ability to form judgements, according to Rousseau, it develops at an appropriate stage in human growth.

This seems to imply that the character and quality of human judgement are capable of developing for the better under the tutelage of other people. Our powers of judgement, one might think, can be shaped so as to promote thoroughness and exactitude and their corresponding personal qualities. It would be natural to think of the authoritative teacher as the person to cultivate judgement and character through explicit direction. However, Rousseau does not take this view, but insists instead on the generally baleful influence of society and of others on the formation of a young person's judgement.

There are problems with the epistemology: for example, the contention that perception is largely a passive reception of sensation is a great over-simplification. Since the work of Wittgenstein emerged, the complexity of the relationship between sensation, judgement and perception has just begun to be appreciated.[12] However, Rousseau is aware of the fact that judgement has a role to play in perception in his discussion of whether or not it is the clouds or the moon that are moving or whether or not a stick half-immersed in water is straight.

Not only is judgement involved in perception, but it can be either active or passive. Much of the judgement involved in our perceptions is passive; for example, that *this* is what we perceive. We cannot be misled about our sensations and so our judgements about these cannot be mistaken. We can, however, be in error about *what* we perceive through sensation, and in making judgements of this kind we are active and can get it right or fail to do so. For example, if I have never eaten an ice-cream before and the immediate sensation on doing so for the first time is one of discomfort, then my judgement that this sensation is uncomfortable is immediate and automatic; I do not do anything to make it and I cannot be mistaken about what it is that I am judging. Indeed, it could be said that my sensation and my judgement are only separable with some difficulty. On the other hand, if I cry out that the ice-cream is burning me, I have made a mistaken judgement about what the ice-cream is doing to me. My perception that the ice-cream is burning me is based on an uncomfortable sensation (which involves passive judgement) and an active judgement that this sensation is the same in character as others that I have had which have been uncomfortable and which have harmed me. In this case I have proceeded wrongly from an induction that past discomforts of a like kind were caused by heat, therefore so is this one.[13] In this instance, I have failed to learn through my inappropriate use of past experience. The implication is that I shall be able to make correct judgements through more accurate reflection on an increasingly wide range of experience. It would, again, in conventional pedagogic practice, be natural to think that the authoritative teacher could make good the deficiency in judgement through instruction, but Rousseau will have none of this.

Nature

Rousseau is thought of as the philosopher who extolled the state of nature as the condition in which men flourished best and which best expressed their species nature. This view is at best an oversimplification, at worst, seriously misleading. Was it his view that human beings should live as solitary beings, coming together only for purposes of reproduction or for other operations absolutely necessary for human survival? This does not seem to be the case, since Rousseau sees the capacity for social intercourse as an important part of personhood. The ability to use language to communicate with others is a significant constituent of that capacity. Rousseau shows himself to be well aware of the socially constituted nature of language learning.[14]

Therefore, some form of social existence appears to be part of man's natural being; it is, one might say, part of the human species nature to interact and communicate with other human beings. But if we accept this interpretation of what Rousseau meant, then we have to deal with an apparent paradox. The contrast between 'natural' and 'social' implies that there is a specific difference between these two states. This in turn leads us to the idea that the specific difference lies in what is distinctive about social as opposed to natural relations. We know that this cannot imply that man is naturally solitary and we know that Rousseau meant both more and less than that he was merely gregarious by nature. Less, because he was quite prepared to allow solitary existence for large periods as a normal mode of being for man. More, because in association with other men, there is far greater scope for relationships through a shared language and culture than is possible for other species.

But if this is so, then what sense can we attach to the notion that there is a natural state of human existence and that man finds his best expression in this natural state, whereas he stands in danger of corruption through entering into social relations? The answer is that Rousseau sees certain forms of social relations to be inimical to the proper development of human nature and that these relations can develop within the bosom of unavoidable and beneficial forms of human association. Such an interpretation allows us to see Rousseau as a consistent and logical thinker and this view is supported by a detailed examination of *Émile* and the *Discourse on Inequality*.[15] Rousseau appears to have believed that social association is natural when it does not involve the overt imposition of one human will upon another. The idea is that natural association is based on reciprocally free and equal respect between people.

This conception of the natural is allied with the more conventional notion of natural as meaning 'part of the natural order', in the sense of being part of our biological destiny. These two conceptions are not mutually contradictory. We all have impulses or passions that derive from our biological destiny; within the social frameworks that we construct, our response to this biological destiny can take two forms. The first form is beneficial and 'natural' in the first sense, namely it involves intercourse between humans based on the non-imposition of one will on another. Explicit denial of someone's need on the part of someone who is capable of fulfilling that need would be an example of the invidious imposition of one will upon another and hence of an 'unnatural' form of association. Likewise, the overt imposition of will on the part of someone who does not have a genuine need is also unnatural; for example, if I ask someone to do something for me merely for the sake of it. The claim that 'natural' excludes 'social' or that 'natural' merely means 'benign form of social association' will not, therefore, stand up to scrutiny. Neither will the idea that these two notions of natural are mutually contradictory; what is natural for humans is both what arises from biological destiny and what is beneficial for their flourishing in human relationships. The relationships themselves are founded on our need to satisfy the passions that arise from biological destiny.[16] It should be noted, however, that Rousseau does not consider that the overt imposition of one will upon another could be beneficial and hence 'natural' in his sense in precisely those situations in which it was done *not* to gratify a sense of power or domination but in order (as the teacher thinks) to further the interests of the individual imposed upon. Rousseau's failure to see that this could happen in a non-corrupting way is one of the major obstacles to accepting his account of learning or, indeed, of teaching.

We need to know why beneficial situations so rarely obtain and how the original (as Rousseau claims) natural state of association could so easily degenerate into the kinds of inimical and limiting forms that are so prevalent. The question is the more pressing as the very prevalence of 'unnatural' forms of association suggests that they arise from deep-rooted tendencies within human nature, not from rare circumstances. Although Rousseau's account of how these forms of association can arise is subtle and detailed, it does not properly meet the criticism made, namely that the invidious forms of association appear to arise as a prevalent human tendency whenever men form social institutions.

On Rousseau's own account, the urge to dominate and to subjugate, although unnatural (in the sense that it does not arise from the need to fulfil our biological destiny) can appear at the earliest stages of human life.[17] Unless the needs of a baby are carefully managed, therefore, the tendency to dominate will appear at a very early stage in life. So also will the suspicion and fear that arises from the frustration of the infant's will. The baby's impotence leads to its vulnerability and to the rebuffing of its nascent will. Here again, in another striking passage, one can find the sources of paranoid resentment of others which, according to Rousseau, are unnatural, seemingly arising in the most everyday of human circumstances, for example in the smacking of a crying baby.[18]

In this situation, the persistent crier feels the *injustice* of being smacked and all his rage and resentment arises from this. According to Rousseau, this imposition of the will by the nurse is an expression of injustice. From this kind of situation arises the suspicion, resentment and desire to over-compensate for real and imagined wrongs that is characteristic of inflamed *amour propre*. There is a clear implication in what Rousseau says that it is the overt imposition of will which causes the resentment because doing this is unjust, and it is the perception of actions like this being done to oneself that lead to social and psychological ills.[19] But if this is so, such situations are a virtually inevitable part of everyday life. The natural response according to Rousseau, namely to ignore the crying baby, is in fact a highly unnatural one for many people. A large proportion of adults placed in such a situation with a crying baby will react either with resentment, as does the nurse in Rousseau's own example, or with comfort. This latter reaction, as we have already noted, is also likely to lead to inflated *amour propre* in certain very common circumstances. Since both these reactions are in a sense 'natural' (that is they are part of the normal spectrum of human responses when confronted with this kind of distressing behaviour), the kind of response or lack of response that Rousseau suggests is appropriate to develop natural forms of human relationship is not only untypical, it would have to be cultivated in most people, since it would go against their 'animal' reactions to the situation. One would have to walk a moral and emotional tightrope in order to promote the kinds of reaction that Rousseau considers to be conducive to the development of natural (in his sense) relationships between people. Indeed, the strategy of the tutor in *Émile* is precisely to walk such a tightrope. But an important question is begged; namely why are the common reactions of resentment and comfort that we exhibit towards infants not 'natural' in his sense? That is, why do they not both arise from our biological nature and be such as to promote human flourishing? We are given no good reason to suppose that they could only arise from a gratuitous urge to dominate or be dominated.

One might consider the example above to be one of marginal importance, but Rousseau certainly did not. He writes of the relationship between baby and carer: 'These tears which you think so little worthy of your attention, give rise to the first relation between man and his environment; here is forged the first link in the long chain of social order.'[20] Rousseau intends this to be a comment about the growth of affective awareness of other human beings and its role in promoting the distinctive psychological characteristics of individuals, which in turn affect the relationships that they form with others. Whether or not he is right about this, there is however another point of great importance in this relationship, which is neglected by Rousseau and about which he has, in a sense, nothing to say. In these simple situations, where movements of resentment, sympathy and encouragement towards another are made at a spontaneous and unreflective level, there arises the infant's first awareness of the normative character of social life. His later awareness of the structure of society, of individual and social morality, of religious belief and of the intellectual achievements of mankind, all stem from his primary encounter with the affective awareness that others have of him. Through these encounters, he first becomes aware of the rule-governed nature of human society and all that this implies.

Rousseau appears unable to see that our reactive behaviour towards our offspring, and theirs towards us, is part of human natural history and forms the foundation of the rule-governed associations that constitute human society. The 'natural' reaction in his sense contains an evaluative component, namely the judgement that free and equal associations alone are beneficial. But if this is so, his conception of *natural*, although consistent, contains within it the very features of society that he wishes to recommend to us. A society without the possibility of the overt imposition of one will on another will not be a society in the sense in which this term is usually understood. Rousseau's conception of the natural in human relationships is not only implausible; if followed through, it would lead to the most artificial forms of human association.

His conception of what is natural is made less than convincing by an inability to distinguish between benign and malignant forms of the overt interaction of human wills with one another. His ideal is a co-operative one, but co-operation can only be secured through the mutual agreement of partners. However, partners can only agree with each other (as opposed to associate habitually) through a normative framework. Such a framework can only exist within the wider institution of language. Language itself involves authority as to what constitutes correct and incorrect forms of communication and, for a young child, that authority resides in the adults closest to him and their reaction to the child's early attempts to communicate. At their earliest and most primitive, these will involve the kinds of affective response of resentment, concern or encouragement that we have followed through the examples above.

There is, as Rousseau sees, a chain on which the social order depends, which runs from the cries of the baby to the most powerful political institutions. However, that chain has to have, as a vital link, the overt imposition of one will on another for even the kinds of beneficial and natural association which he favours to be intelligible, let alone to flourish. These occur in what Baker and Hacker have called the *normative activities* that constitute rule-following behaviour: correcting, approving, defining, interpreting and teaching, for example.[21] These do not just involve the exercise of power; they rely for their effectiveness on the *authority* of whoever is teaching; that is appropriate knowledge and skill, together with a recognition on the part of society that, for example, a particular parent or caregiver is a proper person to give such instruction.[22]

It is also a conceptual chain, one that traces connections between our concepts and hence describes part of the grammar of our language. Rousseau attempts to make this chain a causal one, which operates through individual psychology. The psychological account of how this causal chain issues in a malign set of psychological attributes and an unhealthy set of social relations is done with great subtlety, but in the end lacks any clear evidential basis. The grammatical chain is formed by the way in which concepts of rule and rule-governed behaviour, together with the normative reactions and practices associated with them, are implicated at every stage of human association, from the most domestic to the most public.

It can hardly be denied that there are malign as well as benign and neutral forms of authority or of the imposition of one will upon another, but it can be denied that such phenomena are *necessarily* malign. And of course, whether or not one finds a particular interaction malign will, to a large extent, depend on the judgement made about the likely outcome of that interaction and, in this respect, Rousseau's evaluation is but one among others that are possible.

Amour propre and *amour de soi*[23]

Each of us, according to Rousseau, has a sense of the importance of the preservation of his own well-being. We take care to ensure that we survive and are physically comfortable, guided by a sense of what constitutes our well-being. Not only is this a necessary feature of our lives but it is also a desirable one, allowing us and indeed motivating us to become active in the world in order to promote our own best interests. This tendency is called by Rousseau *amour de soi*. *Amour de soi* is, in a sense, an animal sense of self-preservation and flourishing, which does not, of itself, involve the consideration of other human beings.[24]

Amour propre, on the other hand, is *amour de soi* with a social and moral dimension, that is, it involves the standing which we have with other human beings.[25] Once again, there is nothing that is inherently undesirable about our having a sense of *amour propre*. At its most fundamental, *amour propre* is nothing more than a wish to be properly recognised as a human creature by other human creatures. Someone who is not recognised as a human, who is not capable of creating a moral space around himself which gives others pause is, to paraphrase Simone Weil, a member of the living dead.[26]

It is tempting to regard the contrast between *amour de soi* and *amour propre* as a contrast between benign and malign forms of self-regard. Dent, however, has argued convincingly that this is a major oversimplification of Rousseau's thinking and fails to locate the proper importance of *amour propre* in human life. *Amour propre* in its healthy or natural state (and 'natural' is used here in the sense intended by Rousseau) consists in a human being's desire to be recognised as a moral entity worthy of equal respect and consideration from others. As an aspect of *amour de soi*, the prime motivational factor in our lives, it is also the force that develops our dealings with the world, our satisfaction of animal needs, our relationships with others and our learning. It follows that learning will depend largely on the operation of *amour propre*, which in order to remain healthy and non-inflamed will need to be insulated both from the tendency to make imperious demands (the subordination of others' will to one's own) and from the tendency of others to dominate one's own will.

Since most human relationships in the world as it is actually constituted will involve the imposition of will on a non-mutually agreed basis, in a way that involves conscious awareness of the person whose own will is being imposed upon, it follows that the healthy development of *amour propre*, and hence the development of learning, must proceed independently of the *overt* influence of the will of others on the pupil or of his on other people's. Any other route runs the risk of producing in the pupil inflamed *amour propre*, arising from awareness of his own imperious domination on the one hand or from paranoid resentment and suspicion due to awareness of the imperious domination of another.

We have already seen how, for Rousseau, judgement is an active faculty which, in different forms, appears at an appropriate point in human development; a healthy *amour propre* will go on to ensure the proper development of judgement. The pupil will, through disinterested curiosity, develop judgement that is sound and exact rather than superficial, inaccurate or even mad. The latter characteristics are more likely to be present in judgement when it is driven by inflamed *amour propre*, through either sullenness and resentment or through an inordinate desire to show off amongst other people.

These considerations do not mean that a child must be educated outside any social context whatsoever, but it does mean that his encounters with the social world must be carefully controlled so that the development of *amour propre* is not diverted into harmful channels at the same time, thus distorting the development of judgement. Rousseau gives some examples of how he thinks this can be done in the various encounters that Émile has (e.g. with the gardener and at the fairground). In each of these encounters, the child is learning about, for example, the dangers of acquisitiveness and of pride as well as about the need to respect the *amour propre* of others. Later in the book, the development of sentiment, particularly in relation to the growth of sexual passion, is handled through the careful management of encounters with the opposite sex in the person of Sophie. During all these processes, *amour propre* is not only the driving force in learning, but also one of the attributes of Émile, which is itself being covertly shaped and guided in the right direction.

Rousseau's developmentalism

Rousseau's own particular conception of the natural, his view of the malign character of many social relationships, and his insistence on the active nature of judgement, have had very important consequences for our thinking about childhood, about how children learn, and about how they should be educated. Equally important is his view that the human life cycle, particularly in its early stages, passes through distinct phases on the passage to adulthood. Rousseau's stage theory of development is nothing like as systematically worked out nor as rigid as the systems of later stage theorists such as Piaget. Nevertheless, it contains many of the essential elements of some of those systems.

The main elements of Rousseau's account of human development consist in the following: first, a phase where knowledge is gained more or less solely through sensation; second, a phase where judgement is formed on the basis of the comparison of sensation and through induction on the basis of past judgements and past sensory experiences; third, a phase in which a cultivated awareness of others is gained. In this final phase, the exercise of reason becomes fully developed. Throughout each of these phases, motivation is provided by the individual's *amour propre*, which flourishes best when kept away from the possibility of dominating or being dominated by the will of others.[27]

However, this isolation cannot continue into adulthood, particularly when the individual's awareness of and response to others is at issue. *Amour propre* should be developed in such a way that the right responses should be possible, in order that invidious relationships based on domination and submission are no longer likely to occur. Instead, *amour propre* should be extended to become a concern for others, so that, for example, in pity, the person pitying takes on the concerns of the person to be pitied and makes them his own. For this to be possible, it is necessary both that *amour propre* is developed in a healthy way and that judgement is properly developed.

The growth of concern for others is necessary for our growth as moral beings. Our ability to recognise that there is a moral order, or indeed our failure to do so, or our tendency to respond to it in perverted ways, is a function of the way in which sentiments towards others have grown, in turn as a result of the development of our own *amour propre* and our ability to reason. According to Rousseau, sentiments are a species of idea; when we are directed to think of ourselves by the impression received from the senses, rather than the object, we experience a sentiment.[28] Judgement can work on sentiment in order to make it other-regarding as well as self-regarding; this is part of the process of growth of a healthy *amour propre*.

Thus, Rousseau's account depends on a sequence of stages whose pattern is invariant. It is teleological in the sense that there is a desired outcome which should emerge in early adulthood, and the motor of development is *amour propre* (which encompasses the more animal *amour de soi*), which itself undergoes growth and development. The progression from one stage to another is invariant not just for empirical reasons. That the development is as it is, is a matter of grammar. Judgement depends on sensation as its raw material and the growth of proper sentiments towards one's fellow human beings can only arise as a result of emotional responses in which a certain maturity of judgement is implicated through experience of sentiments relating to oneself in the first instance.

There is also in Rousseau a strong emphasis on the notion of 'readiness' or the idea that knowledge, skill and understanding can only be acquired when young people are intellectually ready for them. His views on readiness are quite firm; criticising the Catholic church for assuming that a child of 7 has reached the age of reason, he writes that even the age of 15 cannot be said to be the age of reason with complete confidence; this is not merely a matter of opinion, but of natural history.[29]

Elsewhere he asserts that one cannot reason with a child, as reason is the last faculty to develop and so cannot be used to develop itself.[30] These views have very important implications for education, and indeed Rousseau is not afraid to draw them out. It follows from his views about the development of reason that education must be placed on a primarily affective basis until well into adolescence. Not only should children not be exposed overtly to the will of others, they should not be exposed to certain kinds of educational processes that will place demands on a faculty that is not yet properly developed. The educational situations in which

31

Rousseau places Émile (the incident with the gardener; overcoming fear of the dark; the incident at the fairground; his finding his way back to Montmorency), are based primarily on an education of the emotional response; the Montmorency incident shows how Émile's use of reason will be spurred on by the desire to find his way home, rather than for any disinterested curiosity about navigational principles. The teaching of geometry, Rousseau recommends, should be based on imagination and memory rather than deduction.[31] The teaching of geography should be based on affective response to natural phenomena and on the curiosity that this engenders.[32] The learning situations that the tutor sets up do, however, also contain a very strong element of manipulation (see below).

A critique of Rousseau's views on learning

Despite the great strengths of Rousseau's anthropological approach to epistemology (which, in some respects, prefigures the work of Wittgenstein), his views of human nature and human growth contain misconceptions. These fall under two principal headings: one concerns the rejection of the normative in the dealings of adults with children and its confusion with tyranny; the other concerns the notion of development and his observation that developmental stages are based on the natural history of human beings. The two misconceptions are closely related.

We have seen how Rousseau regarded the development of a healthy *amour propre* as being conditional upon children and young people not being overtly subject to the will of others. Despite Rousseau's awareness of the fact that humans are essentially social beings, his failure to draw out the consequences of this in his educational theory leads to the implausible view, first, that most social encounters contain more malign than beneficial content, and second that comparative isolation is the best condition for a young person.

It is not difficult to concede to Rousseau the contention that many social encounters are malign, and that this malignity arises from the vainglorious human urge to dominate other people. It is also possible to concede that these sorts of encounters have long-term baleful consequences, both for individuals and for social relations generally. It is quite another point, however, to maintain that *any* overt domination of one will by another that is not sanctioned by a prior contractual agreement is malign. It is also speculative in the extreme to suppose that one can trace the ills of adulthood and of adult society through the bad experiences that a baby might have through being smacked for crying or for being allowed to dominate his mother. This is not to deny, of course, that adverse circumstances in a child's environment and family upbringing, particularly if these adverse circumstances result from pathological conditions in family life, may bring about the results that Rousseau describes. But his account needs to work not just for the extreme, but also for the most everyday circumstances, in order to carry conviction. And for these, Rousseau fails to produce any evidence.

The deep problem for the Rousseauian account, however, is not just the empirical implausibility of his claims, but his denial that the overt imposition of one will on another has any beneficial effects. This amounts to a denial of the possibility of forming any of the social bonds that constitute a human society. It is only within the nexus of correction, encouragement, approval and resentment that young human beings learn to become followers of societal norms. These sorts of primitive 'animal' interactions form the basis of our introduction to the normativity that characterises human society.[33] They cannot but involve the overt imposition of one will on another; this is part of what is meant by such terms as 'approval', 'correction' or 'discouragement'. These normative practices constitute the authoritative backdrop of normative behaviour; in their nature they have to be overt, otherwise the rules that they are used to prescribe would not be recognised as rules; one may learn to *follow* as opposed to *act in accordance with* a rule through training but not through conditioning. Rousseau's denial that any such exchanges can be beneficial not only excludes Émile from the possibility of growing up and learning in a society that is in any way normal, it precludes him from growing up in a society that is recognisably normative; i.e. human at all. It is important to realise, however, that the tutor constantly relies on the *covert* imposition of will in order to get Émile to learn. In some ways, the tutor's pedagogic technique resembles conditioning rather than training or instruction.[34] It is quite plausible to suggest that a child's discovery that it was being manipulated in such a comprehensive way would be far more likely to engender paranoid resentment than most normal forms of training and instruction would ever do.

The second line of criticism of Rousseau relates to his developmentalism. According to Rousseau, it is part of our natural history not only that different emotional and intellectual capacities become available to us at different stages of our life, but that they do so at specifiable times. As a general observation about human natural history, some of these remarks are trivially true, some more interestingly so. It is trivially true, for example, that the interests and intellectual capacities of a 5-year-old boy are likely to be different from those of an adolescent girl. It is less trivially true, but nevertheless not surprising, to learn that young children are incapable of the range of affective and emotional responses to members of the opposite sex that is normal for adolescents and adults. It is actually interesting, informative and valuable to learn about the likely normal patterns of growth in physical and perceptual capacity in very young children.[35]

It is far less clear that there are in all members of the human race patterns of perceptual, emotional, moral and cognitive development which fix in a predetermined and invariant way the ages at which the stages will occur. In this case it is no good appealing, as Rousseau did, to human natural history. The first reason is that the occurrence and the patterning of learning is often specific to individuals and to the contexts in which they are learning. The second is that cultural variation may play a very important role in learning. The third is that Rousseau's developmental account, like those that succeed it, depends on a form of intrinsic rather than extrinsic motivation in order to account for the fact that individuals develop and learn in the way that they do. For Rousseau, the need for a source of intrinsic motivation is pressing, since he cannot include in his account any motivation that arises from the overt imposition of the will of other human beings on Émile, since this is always liable to bring about a harmful development of *amour propre*, through the engendering of resentment.

It is true that the idea of *amour de soi* has some grounding in the observation of human natural history: human beings, like other animals, will seek to satisfy animal needs and to promote their own well-being without particular encouragement from others (although they may well need to learn from others in order to make these processes effective). *Amour propre* has to account for the human propensity to learn and to develop abilities, not merely in those attributes that promote 'animal' well-being, but also in those attributes that constitute the accomplishments of human society. Since Rousseau himself dismisses many of these accomplishments as nugatory, it is far from clear how *amour propre* could select the appropriate accomplishments to pursue, let alone provide the impetus to pursue them, given that, as Rousseau himself admits, the importance and value of these particular accomplishments is a matter of value judgement which may differ from person to person. In addition, *amour propre* as he describes it is at once too fragile and too robust to constitute a plausible psychological category. Too fragile because it can so easily be damaged; too robust because it is to provide almost the sole motivation for learning.

Even if an individual were motivated in the appropriate way, it is still an enormous leap of faith to suppose that strong motivation alone could provide sufficient resources for successful learning to take place. We are, in effect, asked to believe that the knowledge and skill that the human race has accumulated is of no use to a youngster; that he must recover what is valuable from it almost entirely through his own efforts. Given that this view is a direct consequence of Rousseau's unwillingness to countenance any forms of instruction and training (for reasons which should by now be clear), the justificatory burden that the educational prescriptions place on the speculative moral psychology on which the theory rests is pretty well intolerable, unless one is convinced on independent grounds of the plausibility of Rousseau's thesis.

Finally, Rousseau's own form of developmentalism leads him (like Piaget after him), to differentiate the different stages of human development very sharply and also implausibly. Certain things cannot be learned at all at certain stages: there is no point, for example, in giving children religious education as they are incapable of grasping the abstract ideas that religion expresses.[36] Rousseau appears not to subscribe to the view that one may partially grasp a concept at one stage and fully grasp it at another; learning seems to be an all-or-nothing affair.[37] However, a rule-based account of concept formation, of the kind that Rousseau would probably reject (for reasons that should be clear), would allow for the partial formation of concepts as a consequence of a growing, but incomplete, grasp of the rules governing the use of concept words.[38]

Rousseau's account of learning has been enormously influential. In the chapters that follow, the influence of his writings on learning theories will be readily apparent.

4

LEARNING IN A NORMATIVE CONTEXT

It is now appropriate to make more explicit and detailed some of the criticisms of Rousseau's account of learning raised in the previous chapter. At the same time, an attempt will be made to show how learning is possible in a rule-governed context, how it engages the emotional and affective side of human nature, and how it is necessarily social in character.

Emotion, learning and reactive behaviour

One of the strengths of Rousseau's approach is that he recognises that we are *embodied* as well as *thinking beings*. We learn through practical activity and through the engagement of our affections, feelings and emotions. Certain kinds of learning are not possible without the prior engagement of sentiment, he argues, particularly with reference to the complex issue of relations between the sexes.[1] Rousseau is also insistent that our aptitudes and tastes are, to some extent, shaped by our animal nature. In all these insights he advances beyond Locke and Descartes, while remaining recognisably within that epistemological tradition. Unlike them, however, he was not merely indifferent to the role of society in learning and growing up; he was more or less hostile to it. It is this feature of his thinking that has had perhaps the greatest and most unfortunate influence on educational thinking and practice. In what follows I shall try and redress the balance while acknowledging Rousseau's recognition of the importance of early childhood in forming our later experiences.

Our earliest experiences of others come through encounters charged with affection and reactive behaviour. We experience love through the comfort given to us by our parents and, as we start to make an impression on the world, we experience the reactions of others to our efforts. These reactions take the form of encouragement or discouragement, approval or disapproval. They are manifested through facial expression, gesture and tone of voice long before we are able to understand the meaning of anything that is said to us. Through these experiences, we learn to express our needs and wishes in such a way that these are taken account of by

36

others and so that our excesses are curbed. Gradually we learn to curb our feelings of rage and frustration and to express ourselves in ways more acceptable to our parents and to society. Wittgenstein was right to point to the elemental forces at work in the infant psyche and it is the taming, or at least the shaping, of these forces into more constructive paths that is one of the demanding tasks facing parents and other carers in the early months and indeed earliest years of an infant's life. The reactions of others to our own behaviour serve to shape that behaviour, so that we learn to control bodily movements, to feed, to play and to rest, in such a way that our lives begin to form a pattern.

At the same time, babies learn to make sounds and to gesture in such a way as to get others to recognise their needs. Not only are these needs met in a functional way, but we are spoken to, encouraged and discouraged and generally trained to make use of a more diverse repertoire of communicative acts. Gradually, we learn to adopt elements of our mother tongue in this enterprise and our efforts in this direction are further shaped and encouraged.[2] In this way, we learn the elements of our mother tongue, together with a pattern of behaviour that is acceptable to those around us. Through doing these things, by anticipating the reactions of others to our own activity and through attempting to shape their responses to ourselves, we learn to take responsibility for our actions and to make choices. The seeming paradox is that we are *trained* in certain actions and our training helps to give us the flexibility of behaviour that makes the vocabulary of choice and responsibility appropriate.[3] The paradox only exists if training is equated with *conditioning*; we are not conditioned to learn and to take part in society, but training plays a large part in the process.[4]

To say all this is to remind ourselves of some basic facts of human natural history; babies are subordinated to the will of those who care for them: they are trained through encouragement and discouragement and then, when they can understand enough of their mother tongue, their training is combined with instruction. None of this would work without a predisposition on the part of very young children to respond to voices, faces and gestures and to seek to satisfy their wants and needs in ever more diverse ways. In doing so, they are exercising that animal love of well-being that Rousseau calls *amour de soi*. But at the same time, they are learning to recognise and conform to authority, both in a personal form through the control that carers and parents have over them, but also in the form of a larger culture and society, through their learning of language and through the ideas, rules and values that are given to them by their parents and others. Thus, although their wills are subordinated to those of others, they are subordinated within a normative order with its own conceptions of right and wrong. They are subordinated, in short, and unless they are very unlucky, to the authority of those who are entitled to look on them with love and to attend to their present and future well-being. Through those individuals, the authority of the society of which they are a part also begins to exercise its hold, not in an overtly political way, but through the language and the culture, with its games, rhymes, routines and ceremonies. Nor is this entirely a one-way process. Young children are dependent on others and need to be able to influence others to get what they both need and want. As they are learning to act within a normative order, so are they also inciting those who care for them to act in a way that conforms both to their desires and to the expectations of society towards them as parents and carers.

Although all of this seems obvious enough in a purely descriptive sense, as an assemblage of reminders about human natural history, Rousseau saw these seemingly natural (to us) practices of child-rearing as both unnatural and harmful. Unnatural because they are not the association of beings on an equal footing and harmful because the effects of either an embittered or an inflamed *amour propre* have ramifications within the individual soul and throughout the social order. Rousseau was unable to distinguish between the *power* that parents exercise over their children from the *authority* that they have vested in them. Their exercise of power derives from authority vested in them by society and is thus properly exercised only within certain limits within any society. Rousseau only recognised the power and saw that as illegitimate, because it presupposed an unequal association. His concept of what is natural is value-laden, importing into itself notions of freedom and equality that are themselves only intelligible in particular societies. But in seeing all exercise of overt power as unnatural and therefore undesirable, he puts parents and educators in an impossible position; they have to bring a child into a normative order without allowing that order to impinge on him in any significant way.

Émile represents an attempt to resolve this conundrum by showing how education is possible through natural methods that do not involve the imposition of overt will or power, yet allow Émile to emerge as a civilised being. Not surprisingly, Rousseau does not succeed in avoiding the use of covert forms of power and will-imposition in the course of the educative process, while seeming to avoid the use of overt ones. This raises a number of points: first an ethical one – given that the use of power is unavoidable in education, is it not better to exercise it in an open way, backed by legitimacy, rather than through manipulation and concealment? Second, a practical matter – Rousseau issues an enormous promissory note on the education of Émile. We are shown, in a work of literary genius, how such an education could be made imaginatively plausible – we are not shown a practical possibility. Third, a logistical point: even if Émile's education is a practical possibility for that one individual, the prescriptions of Rousseau, relying as they do on wealth, leisure and privilege, can hardly be assumed to apply without considerable modification to the less fortunate vast majority of humanity. We are entitled, therefore, to look at the Rousseauian educative programme with a great deal of scepticism: on conceptual grounds (his confounding of power and authority), on pedagogical grounds (his cavalier dismissal of the importance of training and instruction), on ethical grounds (his lapses into deceit and manipulation) and on practical grounds (the privileged and untypical nature of the particular educational situation he invites us to consider).

Making a mistake

Rule-following behaviour in the broad sense in which that concept has been introduced in this discussion can be learned and taught. If there is a correct procedure for following a rule, then there must also be the possibility of incorrect application of a rule or of failure to follow the rule at all. Making mistakes, teaching, correction, explanation and practice are characteristic activities that go on when someone is learning to follow a rule. The mastery of a rule involves the mastery of a technique or array of abilities.[5] Learning a technique will very often involve making errors and having them corrected. Making attempts and having them corrected are part of the practice in which the technique is learned and later exhibited. If such techniques were not part of a practice, it would be difficult to see how learning to follow a rule could take place at all. One would either be applying the technique or one would not. Failure to apply the technique would constitute a failure to follow the rule and thus would be to fail to engage in rule-following behaviour with respect to that technique. Since we wish to characterise rule-following behaviour as involving the possibility of making a mistake, it would be paradoxical to describe incorrect attempts to follow a rule as non-normative (because non-rule-following) behaviour. We would have the further unwelcome consequence of being unable to describe how learning can be a normative practice. For if learning necessarily involves the possibility of making a mistake, and if making a mistake with respect to a rule means that one is not following that rule, then it becomes impossible to describe *learning to follow a rule* and *trying to follow a rule* as part of rule-following behaviour.

This apparent paradox is avoided once it is recognised that the techniques that are involved in rule-following are part of a *practice* or pattern of activity in which the technique is used, and that incomplete mastery of a technique need not exclude someone from the practice.[6] In particular, a learner will make mistakes but will be corrected; he will recognise the correction and will try to improve his performance. It is possible, however, that mistakes will be made, and that they will be corrected but systematically ignored by the learner. In these cases, we will often wish to say that the putative rule-follower has excluded himself from the rule-following practice and is not even attempting to follow the relevant rule. A child learning to calculate with pen and paper will often make mistakes, both with the use of arithmetical notation and with the calculations that he performs. In these cases, the child has an incomplete mastery of the technique, but takes part in the activity of doing arithmetic through his participation in the *normative activities* of instruction, correction, explanation and justification.[7] We assume that, as a result, the child will develop his technique so that he can practise it without further learning. We assume that the child has the ability and/or the commitment to improve his technique and to reduce the number of mistakes made. If the ability and the commitment are not there, and if the mistakes do not decrease and the explanations and examples do not result in an improvement in technique, then we may wonder if the child is really capable of taking part in the practice of calculation.

Learning that takes place within a practice in the way described above entails both that the learner has the ability to learn and that he has the commitment to do so. The first condition seems uncontroversial enough, but, at first sight, the second one seems curious. Surely uncommitted learners can succeed in learning techniques? This reply is true up to a point, since there can be varying degrees of commitment to learning or to any other activity and sometimes one can learn without making a great deal of commitment to the enterprise. But learning cannot take place within a normative practice unless the learner responds to approval and disapproval, correction, explanation and definitions and does attempt to acquire a technique. Learning to follow a rule involves recognising correct and incorrect applications and it thus involves at least some desire on the part of the learner to recognise and to avoid the incorrect applications of the rule and to practise the correct applications. As such, learning to follow the rule involves having intentions and making attempts. Commitment to some degree to a practice is then a necessary part of learning within a normative framework. What counts as commitment can, however, take very different forms for different activities.

Much of the learning commitment of young children is instinctive, which is to say that the young human has a natural predisposition to acquire certain abilities. Some of this learning is non-normative, such as the ability to walk, although even this statement needs qualification since our ways of walking, within certain biological parameters, are prone to cultural variation. Other abilities, among which the ability to talk is the most obvious, involve the child in human interaction. Most children make rapid progress in their ability to communicate through talk, but this progress is to a large degree dependent on their talking with other speakers, particularly speakers who are fluent enough constantly to extend the child's ability. By the age of 4, most children have acquired a speaking competence which, superficially at least, appears comparable to the ability of an adult native speaker.[8] This instinct is strong enough to survive the physical inability to vocalise and to hear. Deaf children, without instruction, will develop gestural languages comparable in complexity, although not perhaps in vocabulary, to those of normal children.[9]

However, the commitment to learn language is not wholly instinctive and may not be present at all with other aspects of language learning. Learning to speak a tongue other than one's mother tongue, for example, is an ability that many never acquire or even want to acquire. Neither does the ability to read and write arise from an instinctive commitment to the acquisition of these abilities. Nor does there seem to be an instinctive wish to learn to count in young humans. Nearly all young humans do, however, have a strong commitment to become moderately competent members of their community, and therefore are committed to learning a range of techniques that will make them able to play happily with their peers and attain a reasonable degree of independence.[10] The particular kinds of activity that are especially valued by different communities will also play a part in engendering commitment to learn and may even promote a desire to excel, if excellence is a path to prestige and respect. This point is not sufficiently attended to by those who maintain that our motivation is for our own immediate gain, as economic and public choice theory would have it. Others, following Aristotle, have recognised the importance of public esteem as a motivating factor and have incorporated this insight in a description of the complexity of learning in a social context.[11]

The connection made here between commitment to learning an activity and the value that is placed on that activity by a community is not a necessary one. But neither is it merely contingent. If the link between our usage of the concepts of value and commitment were to diminish or to disappear completely, these concepts would themselves alter and various connections that we now make in everyday inference would no longer be made, signifying a shift in the way in which we talk and think about human abilities. The kinds of fact about the connection between valuing something and being committed to learn about it that are being made here are background, general facts about human behaviour and attitudes, against which much of our various ways of dealing with other human beings is intelligible. In this sense, they are like the very general facts of nature which Wittgenstein sees lying in the background of our concepts. These facts do not directly determine our concepts, but they constitute the background against which they make sense and have significance.

The mastery of a technique is to be distinguished from the various degrees of skill with which that technique is handled. The ability to do F well implies the ability to do F, but not *vice versa*. Someone who is competent at calculation may still make mistakes from time to time and, even though the results of the calculation are incorrect, we are still inclined to say that he is taking part in calculation because, for example, he is capable of checking or he recognises an error when it is pointed out, he makes efforts to avoid such errors in the future and so on. It is possible to calculate badly and still to calculate, provided that there is some evidence of commitment to the practice of calculation.

Improvement of a technique is often not merely a matter of continued practice and reflection on practice. The ability to perform well is itself often subject to normative considerations.[12] Some rules prescribe what it is to practise a certain technique. When these rules are not followed or no attempt is made to learn them, the technique is not being used and such a person cannot be said to be taking part in the practice of following such rules. Other rules suggest or recommend a certain course of action as a means of the effective or excellent performance of a technique. We say of someone who does not pay heed to them that he takes part in the activity, even if he does not do so very well. Such recommendatory rules still involve normative practices such as teaching, explaining, evaluating and justifying; they therefore belong to the family of normative practices.

An example of the contrast between this kind of rule and rules that *constitute* an activity would be in the latter case the rules that govern the movement of pieces on a chessboard and what is to count as winning. Recommendatory rules, on the other hand, would relate to ways in which one might play chess well, such as an appropriate employment of the castling rule, sacrificing pieces, and the employment of certain strategies in the endgame. Such rules recommend what is appropriate for an effective employment of a technique; they do not constitute the technique itself. To fail to follow such rules is not to fail to take part in the activity, it is to fail to take appropriate measures to ensure as effective a performance as one could achieve.

On the other hand, the boundary between rules that constitute an activity and recommendatory rules is not absolute, but is to be drawn for particular purposes. A person who never did what was appropriate to winning in a chess game could hardly be said to be playing chess, even though he moved the pieces correctly and was not obviously following the rules of a different game, such as one where the object of a chess-like game is to be checkmated rather than to avoid being checkmated. We can say then that learning in a normative context involves not only some degree of commitment to what is to be learned, but also, where the activity learned has an end of some kind, a commitment to the achievement of that end as well. This is a grammatical point about what it is to follow a rule. But there is a further consideration, partly grammatical but partly psychological (although not in a scientific sense) about the role that affective commitment, including love, plays in our learning.

Learning through affective commitment

It has been argued that learning involves commitment to what is to be learned and to the purpose of the activity learned or engaged in. But how do we account for the striving for excellence and for the acquisition of knowledge and ability that have not been achieved before by anyone? Mastering constitutive and regulatory rules is a necessary condition for this but is not usually enough. Intense love of a subject or activity, combined with a passionate will to succeed, is more often than not a prerequisite of the achievement of excellence, even for people endowed with prodigious talent. The role that love plays in learning is not considered important by most psychologists, yet without a recognition of its place much human achievement is unintelligible.

Our earliest learning arises out of the bonds of affection between parent and baby. We go on learning through commitment, which is sometimes instinctive (as in the case of learning to speak), but which is more often than not without an instinctual basis (as in the case of learning to read). How do we acquire a commitment to learn in the absence of an instinct to do so? This question cannot be answered in any straightforward way. Sometimes the love of a subject or an activity is so strong and so visceral that it seems almost appropriate to speak of 'instinct' in this connection; the love of physical activity or of music-making seem to be examples that apply readily to certain individuals. On the other hand, there is something wrong with talking too glibly of instinctual urges to learn activities that, however physical or affectively charged they may be, are nevertheless socially constituted.

The reason for this is that, although considered generically, some kinds of activity appear to come naturally to humans: physical exercise, dance, competitive sport, music-making and the making of artefacts all come to mind – each of these activities takes place in a culturally specific context. It is true that language does as well; we do not have an instinctual basis for learning French, for example, but for learning our mother tongue whatever it may be. Unlike the case of acquiring language though, not everybody wishes to dance, to sing or to take part in competitive games, although these are all natural human activities. Each will take culturally specific forms and different cultures will accord different levels of prestige and esteem to different kinds of activity. Furthermore, they are very often linked with other culturally important activities: music with religion; art with commerce; physical exercise with military service; and so on.

This suggests that the sources of motivation for learning and excelling in any activity are likely to be complex and, to the extent that learning is encouraged by appropriate affective attitudes to the activity concerned, this will itself take different forms. Here are a few possible examples. Someone loves dancing and, as the main opportunities for following such a career in her society lie in the institutions of religion, she becomes a priestess and dances as part of religious ceremonials and rituals. It is important to note that she need not become a priestess *because* she likes dancing, but that the religious vocation is tapped and strengthened through the possibility of its finding a physical expression. It is a great mistake to think that our motives are unmixed; most of the time we do things quite sincerely for a variety of reasons of which we are not always fully aware.[13] Someone else enjoys military service and finds that it is also a satisfying way of playing music in a military band. A boy enjoys designing and making things and so becomes an apprentice in an engineering firm that specialises in high-quality products designed and made within the firm.

In all these cases, someone chooses to follow a path partly out of love for an activity that seems to answer an individual need within him or her, partly out of a wish to be recognised and respected by his fellow human beings, and partly out of a need to earn a living. The kinds of choices that are open are partly determined by individual preference and partly by the opportunities available in society, which are, in turn, patterned by the various activities that go on in that society, the connections between them, and the relative importance and prestige that each has. This is not to say, of course, that some people do things and apply themselves to learning out of purely instrumental reasons and not out of love for the subject or activity itself, nor that many people find themselves frustrated by the lack of opportunities that are available to them. Neither is it to deny that some people lack the love of something that would inspire them to do any of these things. There is no necessary connection between learning and love of an activity but there are, nevertheless, important conceptual connections.

These connections of a looser kind, if they were severed, would alter our perceptions of what it is to learn to do something, what it is to love something and the importance that society attaches to certain kinds of knowledge and ability. Many people learn about a subject or develop an ability out of esteem or love for it. Some of that love may come from within them and some of it may be engendered by the value attached to it by their society or culture. When this is an intense form of love on the part of an individual, either to do well in the chosen activity or to gain social approval or a mixture of both, then it is quite likely that such a person will strive for excellence in what they do, rather than just competence. We love things both for the satisfaction that they afford us and for the place that they give us in our society. We are inspired to learn and to do well because of both. If, as Wittgenstein remarks, love can be put to the test, then it is through the sacrifices that we make when learning about something that we love, that that love partially manifests itself.[14] It works the other way as well: activities that are not well regarded by society are less well regarded by individuals; and individuals are less likely on the whole to feel a burning love to take part in them and to succeed.

Were these connections to be severed, so that there was no longer any perceptible relationship between individual love of a subject, the striving for excellence, and the prestige attached to certain activities, then our concepts of learning, of trying and of social approval would change, with the connections between them no longer playing any part in the language game. One of the ways in which this would come out would be in the kinds of inferences that we are inclined to make: 'N learned to become a superb violinist because he loved the instrument from early childhood', for example, gives us a reason why such a person excelled, which is intelligible as a reason because of the background connections between learning, love and excellence that we take for granted. Without them the inference hangs in the air, a *non sequitur*.

Yet one of the problems with the theories of learning that we have considered so far and which we are yet to consider is that these kinds of loose conceptual connections have been systematically severed, with the result that those professionally concerned with teaching, training and education find it difficult to see them. Thus the epistemological tradition of Descartes and Locke ignores the social influence on learning as well as the affective, seeing the operation of the mind in quasi-mechanical terms. Rousseau and his followers, on the other hand, did recognise the physical and affective dimension to learning, but dissociated this from any social dimension, where affections can originate and be nurtured. Utilitarian approaches to training emphasise the social value of certain abilities but ignore the affective dimension which makes learning so effective through the operation of love and care for what is done. Like the Cartesians and empiricists, utilitarian-minded trainers conceive of learning as a somewhat mechanical activity, the progressive accumulation of competences which can be measured and graded by a largely external examination of performance in a limited range of settings.[15]

There are two tendencies that underpin this separation of learning from its social and affective connections. First, there is a scientistic desire to master and understand the often mysterious nature of human learning and the complex connections of talent, motivation, interest, social esteem, care and love that inspire it. Second, there is a fear of anything that could be considered authoritarian, with the learner in some way coming under pressure, either from other individuals such as teachers or trainers, or from society. There is an irony in this: the anti-authoritarian tendency is, to some extent, fuelled by the ability of some trainers and educators, inspired by behaviourism, to ignore the normative context of the direction that is often necessary in learning situations and to assimilate animal conditioning in experimental conditions to training in a recognisably human context. The behaviourally minded trainers are reinforced in their own conceptions by the sentimentality, inefficiency and ineffectiveness of much Rousseau-inspired discovery learning. The way back from such complex misunderstandings is to recognise both the normative and the affective nature of the way we learn and the ways in which it is bound up with the history, culture and ways of working of the societies in which we live.

Learning and private rule-following

In Chapter 2, it was seen that Wittgenstein's arguments against the possibility of a private language, while they are arguably damaging to empiricism, are not really relevant to cognitivism. Yet cognitivism is a solitary and asocial theory of learning *par excellence*. Modern cognitivism holds that individual brains, acting as solitary units from birth, possessed of representational structures and transformation rules, and receiving 'input' from the exterior, can account for the way in which we learn. Brain activity is not, however, necessarily private since neurological events can be observed. Furthermore, such activity is *shareable*, since individual brains can get together to communicate and share information. Cognitive behaviour, although initially solitary, is certainly not necessarily private; it is shareable and often shared. In order to demonstrate the inadequacy of cognitivism it is necessary to show how there is no possibility of an *ab initio* solitary engaging in solitary but shareable cognitive activities such as learning to follow rules.

As we have seen, rule-following is characterised by 'normative activities' which are an integral part of rule-following behaviour. Since these are pre-eminently social activities, it would appear to follow that rule-following could not be an *ab initio* solitary activity. In the considerable literature on this subject, the activity of *correcting* has been considered central, since correcting can only be carried out on a mistake and the possibility of making mistakes is essential to learning to follow a rule. If it makes sense to say of an *ab initio* solitary that he can self-correct, then it makes sense to say that he can make a mistake and subsequently recognise it. It follows that he has an ability to carry out the central normative activity connected to rule-following behaviour, namely correction. In Chapter 6 we shall see that the ability to represent entails an ability to follow rules. If an *ab initio* solitary cannot follow rules, then he cannot represent and, *a fortiori*, he cannot learn through representational means. The issues surrounding the possibility of solitary rule-following are, therefore, of the first importance for our understanding of human learning.

There is little doubt that it makes sense to say of a solitary, even a language-less solitary, that he can make a mistake and even that he can correct his mistakes.[16] The key issue, however, is whether or not he can make mistakes about his rule-following behaviour, and we cannot answer this question until we have established that he can follow rules. There are good reasons for thinking that a solitary could not invent a solitary language.[17] In order to do so, he would have to assign meanings to the terms of that language. The only way to do so would be through ostensive definition. But, to be successful, any ostensive definition must be already embedded in an existing practice. If it were not, then the *definiens* would be susceptible of interpretation and so could not be clearly defined. 'This is red' could mean this colour is red, or this sign is red, or this word is called 'red' and so on. Ostensive definition can only take place if a sign can be assigned a meaning without further interpretation, so that, for example, there are rules that allow me confidently to interpret 'this is red' as 'red is the colour of the patch in front of me' without the need for further interpretation. But it is the possibility of there being such rules which the practice of ostensive definition was meant to demonstrate. The solitary language theorist appears to have presupposed that which he wished to prove. As Wittgenstein puts it, the Augustinian account of how language is learned is constructed as if the child came into a strange country and did not understand the language of the country but could already talk to itself.[18]

However, this may not be enough to prove the incoherence of cognitivism since the claim is not that a solitary brain *invents* a rule-following language, but that he *uses* one that is already installed, the so-called 'Language of Thought' (see Chapter 6). It is critical to the claim that an *ab initio* solitary can follow a rule that he can check that he is following the rule and correct himself, otherwise we have no means of distinguishing between his behaviour being habitual and it being rule-governed; it is central to the claim that his rule is normative and not habitual that he can determine whether or not he is going on in the same way.[19] He must be able to say correctly to himself that he is doing x and that he is continuing to do x; that is, going on in the same way. But to be able to continue to do something in the same way is to be able to recognise that the instruction *and so on* or something very like it, is being followed correctly. So the *ab initio* solitary must be able to ask whether what he is doing counts as *and so on*. However, as Wittgenstein points out, the instruction to do x *and so on* is like ostensive definition. Everything depends on how *and so on* is taken. For example, someone may instruct me in painting a white line in the middle of the road; he may paint a section of line and say 'and so on'. If I am to take it as an instruction to paint in the middle of the road, rather than as an instruction to continue painting a white, rather than a yellow line, or a line of this particular thickness rather than another, then I must already have understood a great deal of the practice that underlies this activity. But if I am to do that, then I must already have a grasp of the rules that determine the practice.[20] The *ab initio* solitary cannot obey his own instruction to proceed in the same way, to do x *and so on*, without already having a practice that provides the context within which *and so on* can indicate the correct way of proceeding. So the *ab initio* solitary cannot have (let alone initiate) a practice without it being presupposed that he already has a background of practices against which *and so on* is intelligible.[21] But since the argument was meant to establish that he could, as a solitary, have a practice, it appears that he cannot have a practice without having a further practice, and so the attempt to show that he has one becomes viciously circular.

If this line of reasoning is correct, then the cognitivist project is effectively scotched in so far as it attempts to explain learning in terms of rule-following. It would, however, be hasty to conclude that it cannot be sustained in a form that allows rules to be *nomological* or *quasi-nomological* in character so that they are, effectively, mechanical while at the same time appearing to be normative. This move has some plausibility as the notion of a mechanical *ab initio* solitary language that mimics the properties of a natural language does not seem to be incoherent.[22] It will be argued, however, in Chapter 6 that such a move to reconstitute normativity is illegitimate.

5

LEARNING, TRAINING AND BEHAVIOURISM

'Any explanation has its foundation in training. (Educators ought to remember this.)'

(Wittgenstein 1967)[1]

Introduction

Training has a very bad press amongst most academic commentators on education. It is often thought of as the antithesis of education.[2] The unpopularity of training has deep and complex cultural roots, the full uncovering of which is beyond the scope of one chapter. Briefly these are: the belief that training is authoritarian and that authority is harmful; the confusion of training with conditioning; and the association of training with very narrow forms of vocational preparation. I shall try to show first of all that training is not the same thing as conditioning and, second, that the belief that either education or training can be accomplished without the recognition of authority of some kind is an illusion. Preservation of that illusion leads to a reliance on *covert* forms of conditioning. It would be better to recognise that the role of the teacher as someone who is *in* authority because they are *an* authority[3] on the acquisition of certain kinds of knowledge and skill, would lead to a more clear-sighted perception of what is necessary both for education and for training.

Although it is common for liberal educators to warn that education is in danger of being displaced by training of a narrowly vocational kind, comparatively little attention has been paid by them to the concept of training. Consequently, the role that training plays in education tends to be undervalued. The result of this neglect is that both liberal and vocational education have suffered. Liberal education has suffered from the influence of progressivism, which has tended to downplay the importance of training in learning generally. Vocational education has suffered by adopting the impoverished model of training that liberal educators have rightly associated with behaviourism.[4]

Training is a complex concept which is important for understanding many aspects of learning, from early childhood to adulthood. It is to be distinguished from concepts like *conditioning* on the one hand and *dis-*

49

covery on the other, although it has connections with both. Training is not an alternative to education because the two concepts belong to different categories: education concerns the long-term preparation of an individual for life; training is usually concerned with the shorter-term acquisition of abilities, attitudes and dispositions. But the successful acquisition of these is an essential aspect of education and so training should take its place at the heart of any worthwhile educational endeavour, whether it be liberal or vocational. On the other hand, a form of training that is sufficiently lengthy and broad in the range of knowledge, skill and understanding that it covers, may well qualify for the term 'vocational education' rather than 'job training'. The point is that although training and education are distinct concepts, the boundaries between the two are not clear in every instance. It is not part of my aim to argue that training should be a substitute for education, but to suggest that it should be recognised as having an important role to play in education.

One of the major problems inherent in any attempt to deal satisfactorily with the concept of training is its ramified nature. Training can be an important aspect of first language learning; of the acquisition of literacy and numeracy; of the acquisition of physical skills; of moral, aesthetic and religious sensibility; as well as of vocational education and preparation.[5] First of all, however, it is necessary to distinguish training from conditioning.

Training and conditioning

A major item on the charge sheet against training is that it is no better than conditioning and thus that it narrows human abilities rather than broadens them. Here is a typical complaint against training from P. Abbs, a well-known contemporary liberal educator.

> We talk about 'potty training', 'dog training', 'training an army', 'training engineers' or 'technicians'. It would seem that training invariably involves a narrowing down of the consciousness to master certain techniques or skills.[6]

Two highly questionable assumptions are made in this passage. The first is that dog training is comparable with training engineers, and the second is that learning skills and techniques involves a narrowing down of the consciousness. Both these assumptions are wrong and seeing that this is so is the key to understanding that training has far more to offer education than is often dreamed of by liberal educators.[7] Even the model of animal learning that behaviourist psychologists call 'operant conditioning' is quite inadequate to grasp what an animal learns when it is trained.

Associative learning theory concentrates on the relationship between

50

two events E1 and E2 and the way in which learners associate the two events. One of these events is known by psychologists as the 'important event' because it is capable of eliciting a response without previous conditioning. Such events are also known as 'reinforcers' because they strengthen other responses. For example, a bodily injury is capable of eliciting a response of flight without there having been any previous conditioning to flight. If an animal has been conditioned to flight by another stimulus, say a loud noise, the reinforcer will strengthen that response.

In *classical conditioning* theory, the important event is preceded by a stimulus, and the typical result is that the signalling stimulus comes to elicit the same response as the important event. For example, a puff of air induces blinking and will do so in the absence of previous conditioning. When the puff of air is preceded by a light, eventually the light will elicit blinking in the way that the puff of air does.

In *operant* or *instrumental conditioning*, the important event follows a response rather than a stimulus and the result is a change in the probability of the response.[8] In *reinforcement* the consequence is attractive and results in a strengthening of the response that was instrumental in producing the reinforcement. So, for example, if a child is given sweets each time he cries, he is more likely to cry in the future. When the important event is not attractive, it will tend to diminish frequency of the response. This negative reinforcement is sometimes known misleadingly as *punishment*, although it cannot have any of the normative overtones of what we ordinarily mean by 'punishment'.

Conditioning theory concedes that the behaviour of an organism is not completely determined by conditioning, by allowing for unconditioned response. But this should not lead us to think that the processes of either operant or classical conditioning in any way approach the complexity of training. In order to appreciate this, it is necessary to see that the behaviourist tradition, on which contemporary associative learning theory operates, models itself on a value-neutral system of observation and description. In order for a theory of associative learning to be built up, it is necessary that investigation of the theory be carried out in such a way that the values and beliefs of the researchers do not intrude on the research and its description. Furthermore, since it is necessary to study the effect of particular selected stimuli and the responses that they evoke, the variety of stimuli available to a subject have to be limited if one is going to find out how it reacts to particular stimuli. These imperatives mean that research into associative learning needs to be carried out under experimental conditions and descriptions of such work tend to be couched in a value-neutral 'data language'.[9]

These constraints have an important consequence. Since the theory of conditioning is concerned with the repeated application of positive and negative reinforcers, it is necessary to be able to identify and re-identify these on numerous occasions. This means that expressions such as 'the same reinforcer' have to be interpreted strictly so that they can be defined in experimental terms. This is to ensure that findings made in laboratory conditions are *reliable*, that is, can be replicated in future experiments. It does not follow that they are *valid*, that they can serve as general accounts of how the animals learn. In fact, the training of animals, although a much simpler affair than the training of humans, is more complex than the operant conditioning model suggests. To appreciate this, it is necessary to realise that the expression 'of the same type', when applied in non-experimental conditions, has to be interpreted much more loosely than when it is applied in the laboratory. An animal, when trained in a reasonably complex activity, has got to be flexible in recognising the stimulus and in responding. Neither of these possibilities is allowed for in the operant conditioning model.

For example, a dog who is trained to round up sheep is usually expected to respond to a variety of signals that tell it that certain manoeuvres are required. These signals are given in contrasting physical circumstances and will vary in volume depending on distance. They will also be related to a context in which the dog has to be flexible: it is expected to perform a manoeuvre of a certain type in connection with sheep in a certain configuration that will be unique to that occasion. This does not mean, however, that we are committed to saying that it entertains thoughts.[10] The dog has got to bring the sheep from one place to another efficiently, without causing them harm and without counting on the willing co-operation of the sheep themselves. It has to exercise perception, judgement, patience and audacity. In other words, its mental capacities are employed to the full.

The example shows us that successfully training a dog is a much greater and more complicated achievement than eliciting behaviour patterns in a rat in a maze through the use of operant conditioning techniques. Human training involves far more than dog training in many, if not the over-whelming majority of cases. Both the training process and the outcome of training are more complex in the case of humans than they are in the case of animals. Perhaps the most important differences are that *language* plays a part in human training; that humans learn according to *rules*; and what they do may be corrected and commented upon. These rules require interpretation and evaluation. They can be taught, but the person trained has got to be able to use them in a wide variety of circumstances as well, in which the associated activities of interpretation and evaluation may well play a key part. There are some activities that we are trained to perform which are like conditioning and which do not require a great flexibility of response; Abbs's example of potty training would be one such. But it would be unwise to conclude that this was in any way typical of a trained response. Dearden commented on the contrast between educational and training activities that, 'In each of these cases, the educational member of the pair particularly emphasises the importance of understanding as opposed to some specific kind of performance.'[11] This implies misleadingly that training in a performance does not involve understanding in the carrying out of a task. As we have seen, Abbs's example of dog training could be applied to a dog rounding up sheep, and a closer consideration of this example suggests that training can lead to the exercise of mental and physical abilities of a high order, given the general capacities of dogs.

It would be odd to say of a dog that had been trained to round up sheep that this involved a narrowing down of its consciousness. If a dog that had been trained to round up sheep thereby lost its abilities to do other things that required the exercise of skill and judgement, then there might be grounds for saying such a thing. But there is no reason to suppose this to be the case. The point applies to human training: a trained engineer, for example, has to follow rules, evaluate and interpret them and exercise skill, understanding and judgement in circumstances that are often unique to the occasion of their exercise. This hardly amounts to a narrowing down of the consciousness, particularly when we remind ourselves that, in becoming a trained engineer, that individual is not thereby precluded from doing things that he already does, or learning things that he does not already know.

The flight from training

We can now begin partly to answer the question: 'Why is training so unpopular with educators?' The manifest inadequacy of the theory of conditioning as an account of human, or even animal learning has already been shown above, and while it is right to be wary of conditioning as either an effective, or an ethically desirable way of getting humans to learn anything,[12] it has also been demonstrated that training is a concept quite distinct from that of conditioning and leads to the development of abilities that are more flexible than the responses evoked by conditioning. In addition, it carries no necessary connotations of ethical undesirability. One reason for suspicion of training on the part of educators is, therefore, quite unfounded.

It is now time to look at one of the other major reasons why training is viewed with suspicion, namely the influence of progressivism and the rise of anti-authoritarianism in educational thinking. It is appropriate to look again at Rousseau's educational prescriptions which, as we have seen in Chapter 3, are based on his desire to show how education should both promote and proceed in accordance with the maximum possible degree of human freedom. The rejection of authority is crucial to an understanding of the rejection of training as a form of learning and will be returned to later. But, as we shall see, it rests on a fatal confusion of authority with power. Successful conditioning depends on the *power* of the conditioner over the conditioned; in the human case, training involves the recognition by the trainee of the *authority* of the trainer.

However, in order to achieve the desired result, Rousseau sets up situations that essentially manipulate Émile into learning what Rousseau wants him to learn. There are numerous examples of this in *Émile* and, given that Rousseau does not think that a child fully acquires reason until the age of 12, and given also that he is averse to any use of training techniques, as these involve the submission of one will to another, it is difficult to see how else he could teach Émile anything. Thus the child is taught not to break things by learning what the lack of the thing broken will mean in his life: 'He breaks the windows of his room; let the wind blow on him day and night and don't worry about colds; because he's better off with a cold than mad.'[13] It is noteworthy, though, that if this lesson does not work, Rousseau recommends that the child be put in a room without windows in order better to appreciate what the lack of them means. Although formally the child is still learning through the appreciation of what the lack of something means, covertly the will of another has been imposed, since the child has been removed by an adult to a place where he can have this unpleasant experience.

A more famous example is the account of how Émile finds his way back to the house, Montmorency. Émile is told that the forest is to the north of Montmorency and the following day he is taken for a walk in the forest without having eaten very much beforehand. Presently he becomes hungry, thirsty and lost; it is midday and Émile begins to cry. Rousseau reminds Émile of what he knows in a manner reminiscent of the dialogue between Socrates and the slave boy in *Meno*.[14] Under questioning, Émile recalls that the north can be found at midday by looking at the direction in which the shadows fall. He works out, under questioning, that if the forest is to the north of Montmorency, then Montmorency must be to the south of the forest. By travelling in a direction opposite to that in which the shadows fall, he realises that he knows the way back to Montmorency.[15]

The example is meant to illustrate how a natural lack (hunger and thirst) can lead the child to begin to exercise his growing powers of reason in a spontaneous manner, in order to gain geographical knowledge that would otherwise be imparted didactically. But Rousseau's example will not do what he wishes it to do. Émile has already been given information that is vital to his subsequent discovery of Montmorency: that the forest is to the north of it and that shadows fall to the north at midday. There is no suggestion that he finds this out for himself. Second, he is placed in a particular situation by his tutor, he does not spontaneously put himself in there: if a human will has not actually been directly imposed on him, he has at least been manipulated into a certain 'learning situation'. Third,

Rousseau's style of questioning is designed to elicit from Émile the response that Rousseau desires. Far from demonstrating how learning can be spontaneous, the example of Montmorency illustrates how contrived the situation has to be in order to achieve the desired result of discovery learning, and this is with just one pupil.

Worse though from a Rousseauian point of view, Émile has been instructed already in certain vital pieces of knowledge and it could be said that he is being *conditioned* to put that knowledge to good effect by the manipulation of the situation by one human will effectively, although covertly, controlling another. Rousseau might reply that the *direct* imposition of one will on another is harmful and will lead to resentment. However, resentment might just as well arise from Émile's realisation that he has been put into a difficult position by the apparent irresponsibility of his tutor, and that he has been conditioned into making a response through the use of negative stimuli, namely feelings of hunger, thirst and fear. Rousseau's examples do not show that learning can most effectively take place without the imposition of rules or authority on a child. In the first case, one human will is imposed on another by the removal of a child to a windowless room; in the second, the tutor arranges a certain situation and Émile's learning relies crucially on knowledge that has been derived from instruction about certain geographical facts as well as the experience of unpleasant feelings. One could say that Rousseau has evacuated authority from his learning situations and substituted for them a covert form of *power*. It can hardly be claimed that this is morally superior to the traditional exercise of authority by a tutor, which is open and honest and which respects the dignity of the learner by not manipulating him.

Rousseau's own attempt then, to show that learning can take place effectively without either the imposition of one will on another or without the introduction of rules for deriving knowledge, is inadequate; he is constantly smuggling in elements of a kind of pedagogy he himself ought to reject in order to bring about the learning outcome that he desires. Worse still, he appears to be using operant conditioning techniques at times; the window example looks suspiciously like what we would nowadays call aversion therapy. The 'important event' which is to be negatively reinforced is the breaking of windows. Non-repair of the window or, more drastically, confinement, are negative reinforcers introduced to condition out the tendency to break the window. In the Montmorency example, the important event is the experience of getting lost, which is negatively reinforced by feelings of fear, hunger and thirst.

Neither ethically nor pedagogically does this seem to be an improvement on training techniques that aim to treat a person as someone who can understand what is happening to him and what he should be doing. This is all of a piece with Rousseau's reluctance to attribute the full possession of reason to children before the age of 12.[16]

Essentially, what Rousseau describes is a sham possibility; if it is true that human action is rule-governed, then learned human action will be rule-governed, no matter how it is learned. If engaging in rule-governed behaviour involves the recognition of authority, then the recognition of authority of some kind is a necessary and unavoidable feature of human life.[17] We are left with pragmatic judgements as to which is the best way to learn – discovery or training? Given that learning involves a submission to authority, at least in the minimal form of rule-following, then it cannot be a criticism of learning by training that it involves submission to authority in the form of rule-following. The argument becomes a practical one over which is the best way to teach and learn; does it involve drawing on human institutions and wisdom, or does it involve seeking to re-create them *ex nihilo*? Training can then be considered on its merits as a form of teaching.

The complexity of human training

The training of animals can be a complex affair which results in flexibility and plasticity of response. This already differentiates it from conditioning, which involves a rigid response to a single or very limited set of stimuli. There is no clear dividing line between conditioning and training; even some of the training that we give to infants is like conditioning (potty training, to use one of Abbs's examples). Although the experimental conditions required by true operant conditioning do not obtain, there is a fairly rigid set of responses to a restricted range of stimuli which makes the example closely related to operant conditioning in the strict sense. But the identity of training and conditioning cannot be settled by the use of a few isolated examples.

In fact, the range of activities into which humans can be trained far exceeds the scope of animal training. Training pervades language learning, early childhood education, primary education and vocational education, and it takes many different forms according to the stage at, and the context in which, it is used. Is there then, anything in common with this vast range of activities that allows us to label them all 'training'? The very fact that there are borderline cases between training and conditioning suggests that there is not.

There is, perhaps, a core use of the term 'training' which makes it more than just a variegated family resemblance concept like 'game', while remaining a concept with blurred boundaries. This core usage is connected to the idea of learning to do something in a confident way. The emphasis is more on action than knowledge on the one hand, and on *an unhesitating and confident action* rather than a hesitating and diffident one on the other. Putting it like this is not to deny that successful action requires a degree of knowledge, nor that confident action may issue from other forms of learning, like conjecture and testing, for example. It is simply to say that the kind of learning that is associated with training is more closely linked with the development of confident action than it is with knowledge and reflection.

Before it is said that it is precisely *reflective action* that is needed in many activities, let me point out that reflection is often most useful when there is effective action upon which to reflect. Training may well be, and often is, a stage along the route to quite complex forms of professional activity. Indeed, it is often the case that part of training involves the ability to stand back, reflect and check before carrying on; the concept of training is flexible enough to accommodate these cases. We do expect a properly trained airline pilot to act confidently, but not to disregard the particularities of a situation or to take no account of them in his actions.

Training and primary education

Discovery methods of learning are still fashionable in schools (at least in the UK), consequently the idea that training has an important part to play in primary education would be received with horror by most progressive primary educationists. It is, nevertheless, important to persist with this horrific assumption and to see where it leads us. In the first place, it is necessary to distinguish between the rhetoric and the reality. We know from various studies that the practice of primary teachers is varied and does not always conform to a progressive ideal.[18] Second, because something is a prevalent practice does not guarantee that it is the most effective or even *an* effective practice. The key question that we need to ask is: 'Does training have something to contribute to primary education and, if so, has it been neglected?'

There can be little doubt that primary education involves initiating children into a range of fundamental skills connected with becoming literate and numerate. In learning to acquire these skills, they need to engage in rule-following activities of various kinds. The question now arises: 'Does learning to follow these rules best take place through discovery or through training?' Although this is an empirical question, it is not without conceptual overtones. In particular, as in our previous discussion of Rousseau, we need to be careful about the nature of the discovery that is being proposed. If it resembles the kind of operant conditioning to which Rousseau is driven to resort, then this can hardly be a point in its favour. If conditioning is an even more autonomy-denying practice than training, then conditioning-masquerading-as-discovery will hardly escape the criticisms levelled against training, which, to the extent that they are valid, will apply with even greater force in the case of conditioning.

The case against training as an effective and flexible form of learning is certainly not proven. There are also a number of studies of primary school practice which, at the very least, suggest that some aspects of traditional primary teaching are superior to progressive, discovery-based forms of learning.[19] In addition, comparative international data suggest that countries with more traditional forms of primary education, in which training still plays a significant role, achieve better results in certain subjects, notably mathematics.[20]

But the dispute about the role of training, as opposed to other forms of learning in the primary school, has rarely been conducted on the empirical level, and empirical findings are always subject to dispute and misinterpretation. In order to understand why training methods have fallen into disrepute it is necessary to look at the ideological opposition to training as a form of teaching and learning. One aspect of this has already been identified, namely the confusion between training and conditioning. But the other aspect relates to the specifically human side of training, namely that it takes place in the context of a rule-system and therefore involves the recognition of the authority of the trainer on the part of the trainee.

As we saw earlier, progressivist forms of education, which ultimately stem from the work of Rousseau, rest on a rejection of authority in the context of education and child-rearing. The whole moral psychology of Rousseau and the progressivist movement is based on the idea that it causes harm for one human overtly to impose his or her will on another, both to the imposer and to the individual imposed upon. But Rousseau is unable to distinguish between cases where such an imposition is legitimate and cases where it is not, and he himself resorts to the covert imposition of will in order to achieve certain learning objectives. But it is the authority of the trainer in the human situation which makes training acceptable to the trainee. This authority is nothing if it just derives from being *in authority* by virtue of holding a special position; the trainer is in authority because he is *an authority*, that is, he has knowledge and skill that command the respect of the trainee, who stands in need of acquiring some of that knowledge and skill.[21]

This is true even in the case of mother tongue learning, where a young child relies on and defers to the linguistic knowledge of adults in order to develop competence in communication.[22] A primary school teacher, equipped with the knowledge and skill that children need to acquire, has the moral authority to use training methods where appropriate if he feels that this is the most effective way of getting children to acquire knowledge or skill, if he is in authority because he is *an authority* on the subject matter which he is teaching. No doubt this involves the imposition of his will on those of his pupils, since he, not they, is setting the agenda, but to see this as objectionable in itself is to fall into the confusion of Rousseauian moral psychology, where it is the imposition of will *per se* that is harmful. But, as we have seen, given the normative nature of human life, it is a confusion to think that this could be avoided. It is important to ensure that it is done in a proper way, through the legitimate exercise of authority.

Naturally, decisions about when, for how long, and with what other methods training should be used, are a matter of professional judgement. It will suffice to draw attention to the implications of the observation that human life is rule-governed. First, if recognition of and submission to authority are not in themselves morally harmful to children, then decisions about whether to use training or some other techniques to promote learning can be made on judgements about the efficacy of those techniques. In this way evidence about effectiveness becomes significant rather than just another ambiguous and disputable weapon in an ideological battle. Second, the potential importance of training extends across the curriculum, from activities like learning to read and write, to mathematics, learning to behave morally, and learning to create works of art.[23] In so far as these are all rule-governed activities, training can be considered as a possible technique for the promotion of learning.

Training and autonomy

I want now to consider the objection that if one of the main aims of education is the promotion of *autonomy*, then the use of training is inimical to that aim, since it encourages submission to authority rather than the growth of independent judgement. This objection might have some weight if it were to be proposed that all that children should be trained to do is to submit to authority. The use of training is best seen as a means to certain ends, one of which can be autonomy. A child who can use his mother tongue has more independence than one who cannot, even though learning to speak involves some training and some recognition of authority. An adult who is literate, numerate, reasonably knowledgeable and who possesses a craft skill, is more independent than one who does not have these attributes, even though the acquisition of them involves training at some stage. Training can lead to autonomy if it gives people the skill and knowledge to act independently and to discover things for themselves.

Learning by discovery is not an alternative to training: it is a set of techniques that can emerge from the skills acquired in training. The point is that the decision whether or not to use training or some other teaching techniques is not an either/or matter, it is a question of balance, and the balance of techniques may well change through the course of education.

Finally, in learning to follow a rule, one learns *to go on*. A child who has learned how to generate a number series through addition can then go on to generate further numbers in that series. Similarly, an adult who has learned to use woodworking tools can use his training to make and repair things. The very ability to follow a rule involves some degree of independence. In many cases learning to follow a rule involves judgement, interpretation and evaluation. For example, a rule-follower may need to *judge* whether or not some situation is one in which a particular rule applies; he may need to *interpret* a sign in order to determine which rule it is an instance of; and he may need to *evaluate* how well he has succeeded in following a rule. The ability to judge, interpret and evaluate in a variety of different contexts is an essential aspect of autonomy.

The learning curve

Behaviourism is a theory of *conditioning* rather than of training and, as such, it is of very little value in understanding human or, indeed, much of animal learning. One 'finding' of behaviourism has, however, entered everyday vocabulary and is thought to mark a genuine discovery about learning. This is the notion of the 'learning curve'; its relevance to human learning will now be briefly discussed.

Learning theory as a predictive science was apparently advanced by the discovery of what appeared to be general patterns under which stimulus–response associations are made. The Rescorla–Wagner model is popularly known as the 'learning curve' and purports to show how the pattern of learning (conditioning) develops.[24] Intuitively, it is based on the idea that learning is asymptotic in character – conditioning is subjected to diminishing returns as maximal learning is approached but never quite reached. While the Rescorla–Wagner model has a certain intuitive plausibility and appears to have had some predictive success, its success has not been complete: for example, it has been shown not to predict correctly in cases of both configural learning and latent inhibition.[25]

More startling perhaps is the *rationale* which is offered for the model, which is couched in terms of *surprise*. For example, in stimulus–stimulus learning, the first time that the subject is presented with the unconditioned stimulus, the association with the conditioned stimulus is unexpected and the subject is surprised. In subsequent trials expectation of the stimulus is increased and the element of surprise is consequently reduced.

There are two important points to be made about this aspect of the model. The first is that in describing its rationale in terms of expectation and surprise, the model helps itself to concepts that are intentional in character; one expects something, or one is surprised at something. While these concepts are not of themselves teleological, they do underlie some teleological explanations. An organism's goal-seeking behaviour can be partially explained in terms of patterns of expectations, and the disruption of those expectations can be described in terms of surprise. Certainly, in the data language, which is meant to describe pure movement and to be free of any mentalistic associations, such terms as 'expectation' and 'surprise' should not be directly available. It should be possible to explain the rationale for the Rescorla–Wagner model in somewhat different terms, as an empirical description of the relationship between conditioned and unconditioned response, for example.

But if this is the case, then it loses much of its interest, for although it is valid only as an empirical generalisation about *how* learning takes place, it is also intended to provide a kind of explanation about *why* learning is generally of that pattern. But it does this in ways that are generally illegitimate in behaviourist terms. In this role, however, it is less than exciting as a form of explanation. At first, an animal may be genuinely surprised by the concurrence of one stimulus with another; however, after repetition, surprise at the concurrence will diminish and the expectation that there will be a concurrence will increase. This explanation does no more than provide a restatement of a folk-psychological maxim which itself is by no means universally valid. Beyond this role, however, the only use that the model has is as a hypothesis about patterns of learning, to be provisionally corroborated in some cases and decisively refuted in others. It appears that the Rescorla–Wagner model cannot account for different forms of animal conditioning, let alone for the more complex forms of human learning. In fact, as has already been noted, the predictive value of the model has serious limitations.[26] The model has also been used as a predictive framework for the connectionist neural network research programme, where it is used to predict the development of neural connections under repeated stimuli. In this role, it can function perfectly well as a predictive theory, thus providing the framework for hypotheses about the behaviour of neural networks under certain conditions.[27] But in this case, it sheds its anthropomorphic characteristics and takes on the character of a working hypothesis or group of hypotheses.

Conclusion

It has been shown that training is to be distinguished from conditioning. It is a form of teaching that, if effective, leads to the confident deployment of skill and technique in a wide variety of situations. In the case of human training, it invariably involves the use of language and rule-following, thus making it more complex and qualitatively different from the most complex forms of animal training. It can, therefore, promote independence and autonomy. In so far as the case against training rested on a kind of anti-authoritarianism derived from the work of Rousseau, it has been shown to be confused. In most cases, conditioning rests on power or force and leads to an unthinking response in a limited set of situations; this is certainly the case in experimental psychology. There is a limited, but only a limited, set of situations in which it is morally justified to submit humans to conditioning. The first sort of case is where the conditioning is beneficial to the subject, but the subject is unable to give consent through extremities of youth, age or illness; in these cases a legitimate authority is required to consent on behalf of the subject. The second case is where someone in command of their faculties and not under duress consents to submit to a programme of conditioning which, he understands, will be for his benefit (as in some kinds of medical treatment). These exceptions do not cover any educational or quasi-educational uses of conditioning. Animal training rests on the power that humans have over animals but is capable, with the higher mammals, of leading to a variegated kind of response in a variety of cognate situations. The training of humans invariably involves the recognition of authority based on knowledge and skill, as well as institutional position, and can have a complexity of process and flexibility of outcome that the use of language and rule-following techniques are alone capable of giving.

Human training is, therefore, not merely more complex than animal training, it is of a different order and there is no reason to think that it is *per se* morally unjustified. Indeed, if it is an educator's duty to teach through the most effective means possible, then it may be stated that there are numerous occasions when training should be used.

6

REPRESENTATION AND LEARNING

Introduction

One of the dominant views about how people learn is derived from a complex of theories known collectively as *cognitivism*. It is particularly influential because it combines within it elements of the romantic view of learning associated with Rousseau and more explicitly scientific accounts of learning associated with Chomsky and others.[1] One of the main consequences of the influence of cognitivist theories is an emphasis on autonomous learning and a consequent devaluing of overt teaching as an aid to learning. If, however, cognitivism rests on a mistake, then the devaluing of teaching is no longer tenable on cognitivist grounds and the modern tendency in education of exalting the role of the learner at the expense of that of the teacher will need to be re-evaluated. That it does rest on a mistake and that the role of the teacher does need to be re-evaluated is the contention of this chapter. In this context I mean by 'teaching' the *active* transmission of knowledge and technique by an authoritative figure rather than the setting up of situations in which autonomous pupil learning can take place (the 'facilitator of learning' model).[2]

Cognitivism can be seen both as an alternative and as a response to behaviourist accounts of learning. It is a set of theories not only about how people learn, but also about how they think. Indeed, it is arguable that cognitivism claims that people learn through being able to think. It is maintained that the ability to think rationally, both consciously and subconsciously, amounts to an ability internally to manipulate symbolic representations of that which we think about.[3] Some versions of cognitivism emphasise the importance of the computer as a way of conceptualising such a system of internal representations, while others use neural networks. Cognivitist theories in both their 'classical' and their connectionist forms take the notion of *representation* to be the fundamental building block of their accounts, however, so there is a great deal in common between them. If we are to look at cognitivist accounts of

63

learning, then, we shall need first to look at cognitivist accounts of thinking since, if the account of thinking is inadequate, then so will be the account of learning in the absence of an alternative underpinning.

Representationalism

The main idea behind representationalism is that it is possible to show how physicalist explanations of mental activity are compatible with mentalist ones, so that our ability to talk about thought, learning, action and intention is not impaired by the possibility of explaining it in terms of mental or physical mechanisms. The representationalist, by appealing to mental mechanisms, is also able to show how representations can interact with one another to produce new representations.[4] Because these representations are, in a sense, *isomorphic*, they can also be *shareable*, if not actually shared. The isomorphy of different individual representational systems is not difficult to explain. In order for a representation to match reality, the elements of the representation have to stand in a one-to-one relationship with the elements of the reality represented. The relationships between the representing elements and those in reality also need to stand in a one-to-one relationship.[5]

If each individual representational mechanism is the product of natural selection for that individual, and the workings of natural selection are not significantly different for each individual who operates according to a representational mechanism (in particular requiring that individuals communicate with one another), then it is to be expected that groups of communicating individuals will use roughly similar isomorphic representational systems which can be shared with each other.

These individual representational systems fulfil much of the role of Cartesian innate ideas, and, together with the mental faculty of combining ideas, constitute distinctive features of the Cartesian account of mind. They combine a representational, conceptual and psychological role. They *represent* rule systems like languages through mappings of the structures of languages on to a representing medium like a tree structure or diagram. They act *conceptually* in so far as they provide rules for moving from one representational state to another. Finally, they provide a psychological mechanism which allows the mind to move from one representational state to another and from a representational state to an action.

The mind is also able to combine elements of the representational system in order to generate *hypotheses* which can then be tested against incoming data. So, for example, if an abstract mental representation of natural languages in general allows the possible combination of a certain string of words from a natural language (i.e. another tree structure representing how a natural language might be), whether or not this combination is possible within the natural language can be tested against data about the natural language either through producing utterances or through scanning input to see if the combination occurs in speech. Such data will determine whether or not the mechanism will then retain or reject the hypothesis that the string is a permissible combination in the natural language and will modify the representation of that language accordingly. This mechanism can be described in terms of rules such as those governing the propositional or predicate calculus so as to yield a *modus tollendo tollens* argument. The result of these procedures is a new tree structure if the hypothesis has been rejected and the same one if it has been retained. It is then possible to describe thinking in terms of symbolic manipulation of this kind and *learning* in terms of the operation of the hypothetico-deductive method on the symbolic structure.[6] This is why the learning of young children is described by cognitivists in terms of a very powerful and effective application of scientific method, much surer and swifter than anything a scientist could hope to achieve through the *overt* use of such methods.[7]

Cognitivism in all its forms makes use of both the concept of *representation* and thus of the concept of *rules*. Although these terms have varying technical uses, they are intelligible only in terms of their primary usage in non-technical contexts. A representation is a symbolic device that stands in place of something else, either possible or actual. The verb 'represent' is in fact *relational*, one represents *something* to *someone*. Examples include: paintings, maps, hieroglyphs and, arguably, sentences. They have a well-established use across the range of human life in different societies, cultures and contexts and are used for a variety of purposes. The institution of representation is primarily social and public. Cognitivists take the notion of representation and transfer it to the mental realm. The human mind, it is argued, operates by using representations, both internally and externally generated. The internal representations are theories about what the world is like, the external ones are data inputs from the world. *Thought* occurs when a transition is made from one representation to another. *Action* occurs when a representation gives rise to bodily activity. *Learning* takes place when internal representations become more accurate about what they represent.

In its everyday use, then, the concept of a representation is *normative* or constituted by rules. Representations need to be *complex* in order to reproduce the complexity of what they represent. But they are also *selective*, only representing those aspects of the world that are of interest to those using the representations. There are three aspects to the rule-governed nature of representations. First, there are rules that govern the relationship between the different elements of the representation itself. What makes a representation a representation of something actual or possible is that its elements are concatenated in a certain way and this way is the correct way or one of a number of correct ways. For example, if a map is to represent distances in terms of a scaling convention, and if that scale is 1 centimetre on the map to 1 kilometre on the ground, then the placing of a symbol for a windmill and a symbol for a church on the map 1 centimetre apart is correct only if the windmill and the church are 1 kilometre apart on the ground. The rule that determines the correctness or otherwise of the representation is, in this instance, given by the scale of the map.

Second, there are rules that regulate the way in which the elements of the representation stand for the elements of what is represented. Thus, on the map there is a key which fixes that a certain symbol stands for lighthouses, another for railway stations, and so on. The rule is incorrectly used when, for example, the lighthouse symbol is used to stand for a windmill, or the railway station symbol is used to stand for a bus station. Third, there are rules for getting from one representation to another. For example, if a larger-scale map is required than the one currently in use, then a rule would determine that all distances on the old map be doubled on the new. The use of representation can be taught, it can be explained, justified, interpreted and evaluated; in short, representation has all the features that we normally associate with rule-following practices.

Representation is *aspectual*: a representation is there to represent a particular aspect of what it represents, and this aspect relates to the purposes for which it was set up. For example, a road map will represent a road network, it will not represent geological structure, for it was not designed to do this. It is not difficult to see how the human ability to represent is useful to us in all sorts of ways. It underlies our ability to talk about what is not in the immediate spatio-temporal context; our ability to communicate through writing, and our ability to talk about possibilities as well as actualities. It also allows us to concentrate on particular aspects of the world relative to our purposes. Representation pervades our lives, including the artistic and religious aspects of life. Given that so much of human activity relies on representation, it is almost natural to see the workings of the human mind as representational, particularly if it is thought that people are really nothing more than minds. If one believes, like most cognitivists, that the mind and the brain are identical, it is a nearly compelling step to describe the workings of the brain as, in some sense, representational. Representation, as a characteristically human activity, is now the activity of brains primarily, and of people in the ordinary sense secondarily.

But it is important to note the shift that has now occurred. We started with a concept of representation that had its home in the rule-governed social world that, unreflectively, we take to be our primary mode of existence. Representation can be made to the representee, but it is still representation to *someone*, a user of representations. Representation is then transferred to a *secondary* use where it describes the workings of minds or brains. Then, since minds or brains are said to be the locus of thought, mental or neural representation is the more fundamental sort, since it governs our actions in the social world where representation in the original primary sense takes place. The final step is to make mental/neural representation the primary case and everyday representation the secondary one. But this is a sleight of hand: one cannot take a concept in use, redefine it and say that it remains the same concept, because it is through its *primary* use that it is that concept. But the cognitivist programme rests on this manoeuvre. In this case, the primary use of 'representation' applies to users (people); the secondary use, in most forms of representationalism, applies to a physical organ, the brain, of which it makes no sense to say that it is a user of representations in the primary sense. The secondary use only appears plausible as an instance of the primary use through a deliberate confounding of the concepts of *brain* and *person*. The point can be put in a more formal manner as follows:

1 The secondary use of a concept is derivative from and depends on the prior primary use of that concept.
2 The primary and the secondary uses are, therefore, not identical.
3 Since they are not identical, a secondary use cannot substitute for a primary one, it can only replace it.
4 The representational project depends on replacing the primary by the secondary use, since it proposes an alternative to the primary use.
5 But then, by (3) above, the secondary use expresses a different (albeit related) concept which replaces, rather than substitutes for, the primary use.
6 If the plausibility of the representational project depends on the non-recognition of the move that takes place at (5), then assertion of (5) is bound to undermine it, since (5) states that one concept has been replaced by another, rather than merely explicated.
7 Therefore the replacement of a primary by a secondary use requires *independent* justification, which shows how the secondary use is, in fact, a better use than the primary one; one that explicates and illuminates the primary use. This step is not provided by any version of cognitivism.

Such a strategy would require that the apparently normative nature of representations was, in fact, nomological and, since the secondary use of representation is nomological, then adoption of the secondary use as more appropriate would entail the *replacement* of the primary by the secondary use. The picture is, however, further clouded by a tendency in the literature to use the term 'rule' in a confusing way. On the one hand, it is not recognised that representations are rule-governed in the sense outlined above; on the other, it is also claimed by some that the way in which representations result in action is rule-governed. In one sense, there is nothing wrong with this way of putting things. For example, I am walking from the windmill to the lighthouse; I check the map (representation) and find that I need to bear to the north in order to reach my destination; I then turn and head north. I head north both because I wish to reach the lighthouse and because the map indicates to me that this is the way in which I should go in order to reach my goal. The representation (map) gives me a reason for what I do, given a further aim. The situation could be put like this: 'If you wish to reach the lighthouse, you should follow the route suggested by the map.' In this sense my following the map is a rule-governed activity. It does not cause me to do it, neither does my wish to reach the lighthouse *cause* me to head towards it.

When cognitivists talk of rules in relation to representation, they tend to talk about the relationship between representation and action, so that the rule determines what I do, given the representation. In the example above, there is nothing wrong with this, provided that the rule is seen to guide me in a non-causal sense (if you wish to reach the lighthouse then this is the correct way to do so). The term 'rule' is here used normatively as it is in the explanation of how representations work. But cognitivists who are committed to the view that the mind somehow *is* the brain take the relationship to be a causal one, albeit a 'soft' or defeasible causal relationship. But two notions have now been confounded, perhaps irreparably. The first is that the rule guides me (normatively), the second is that it *determines* what I do (nomologically) and the two senses are not just distinct, they are incompatible, for it is possible to be guided normatively only if not nomologically and vice versa. Normative behaviour involves following rules rather than just acting in accordance with them. But in order for us to be able to say that someone is following a rule, rather than just acting in accordance with it, it needs to be set in the context of *normative activities*, such as teaching, correcting, judging, evaluating and interpreting, which provide a disjunctive sufficient set of conditions for saying that it is normative behaviour. In the context of these activities it makes sense to say that the rule is or is not being followed correctly. These conditions cannot be provided for a brain (which does not operate in a normative environment) rather than a human (who does).[8] This confusion about rules lies at the heart of the cognitivist enterprise.

Cognitivist writers tend, then, to use normatively loaded terms like 'rule' and 'representation' in a nomological or quasi-nomological way, while allowing them to retain at least overtones of their primary normative usages. The results are incoherent concepts of rule and representation that have no clear use. But if they are inadmissible, then much of the cognitivist theory of the mind will be no longer tenable, since it is built on these concepts of *rule* and *representation*.

One way of countering this argument would be for a cognitivist to reply that we already have a well-developed example of a physically based representational system in which representations cause behaviour, in the shape of the digital computer. It is natural to talk of computers using languages in which they generate representations which then cause the computer to do various things in accordance with well-understood and definable rules. There is, then, not only no difficulty with the cognitivist account of rules and representations, it is one that is in ready use. It is to this contention that I shall now turn.

The language of thought hypothesis and representationalism

For cognitivists to talk about learning in the way that they do, as a form of logical deduction, a language in which sentential representations can be made and inferences carried out is required. This is the 'Language of Thought' hypothesis first put forward by Fodor.[9] Representational theories of mind require something like this in order to be viable. The alternative for cognitivists would be some kind of associationism or traditional empiricism, albeit linked to a physicalist account of ultimate explanation. There are reasons for thinking that some form of connectionism is such a theory, although it can be modified in a Cartesian direction through 'pre-setting' certain features of the neural network. When modified in this way it arguably becomes a form of distributed homunculus account with the multiple homunculi distributed *about* the system. It could thus be said to differ in *complexity* rather than anything else from more 'classical' versions of representationalism. For this reason, the critique presented here will concentrate on the form of cognitivism that postulates homunculi and a processing language.[10]

For reasons first advanced by Chomsky, it is claimed that empiricist accounts of language learning are bound to fail because they do not take account of the way in which language users can use and understand sentences that they have never heard before. Cartesian accounts of representationalism require that there is a mental device that is capable of mapping one representation on to another and this device is best understood as a representational device itself, in which the processes of natural deduction are perspicuously displayed.

According to Fodor, this 'language of thought' is required not just for representing and hypothesis-testing, but for the formation of concepts as well.[11] The Language of Thought Hypothesis (LOTH) is not a hypothesis about an internal language in any straightforward sense of 'language'. If it were, all the difficulties associated with the homunculus account would present themselves again. If it is a homunculus who uses the language of thought, does he too not need a language of thought in which to interpret the language of thought? And again, the user of this language of thought would need a homunculus to interpret this second language of thought, and so on, in a vicious regress. The problem does not apparently arise for language of thought theorists because, in truth, the language of thought is not a language to be used, even by a solitary homunculus. It is more akin to a control mechanism of the kind used by computers and, although the term 'language' is applied to this kind of mechanism, it is a misleading homology. If the language of thought is the 'software' available to run the brain, then it is a control mechanism for a biological computer, not a language in the sense in which that concept is ordinarily understood. However, the LOTH tries to have it both ways by claiming that the LOT (Language of Thought) is representational. If it is representational then it must represent to someone, and it cannot be representing to the brain because a brain is nothing more than a physical organ and not a possible subject of experiences. One might adapt Searle and say that representations are not intrinsic to physics, they can only be assigned to it. At first sight, then, it appears that the LOTH makes just the kind of error in relation to representation that was outlined above. However, it is worth looking at the attractions of the LOTH before considering in greater detail one of the most influential arguments against it.

Fodor's account of the Language of Thought circumvents some of the problems that bedevil reductionist accounts. Fodor and others like D'Agostino do not claim that the LOT carries with it any ontological commitments, although they do claim that it is quite compatible with token–token physicalism. The LOT does not need to be *reduced* to a physical language to be intelligible, instead the weaker claim is made that the workings of the Language of Thought supervene upon whatever physical properties support its operation.[12] This amounts to nothing more than the claim that any system employing the Language of Thought would not operate without the appropriate physically necessary conditions being in place and functioning; it is not the same as the claim that the Language of Thought has to be described in nothing more than the terms appropriate to the level of physical description of the workings of the mechanism that is its bearer. The Language of Thought is also one way of giving sense to the idea that we are intentional systems, that is, systems who act on held beliefs and desires. If it is rich enough to represent desires, beliefs, etc., then it can support a theory of action that couples beliefs with desires to *cause* action.[13] It is important to realise that the LOTH is not circular. Fodor does not claim that the Language of Thought is *learned*. It is innate and pre-exists the learning of one's native language. Fodor has a further argument for the LOTH: that concept learning would be impossible without it. Somewhat rhetorically, he claims that hypothesis-testing and formation is the only possible form of concept learning.[14] The only way in which a hypothesis about the meaning of concepts can be set up for testing is through a pre-existing language in which that hypothesis can be expressed which already contains those concepts. Because of these assumptions, concept learning is only apparent, it consists in learning the

terms of ordinary language that best match the innate concept. It is significant that Fodor ignores the possibility that humans may also learn through
training, practice, instruction and memorisation – many of the pedagogical
techniques recommended by non-progressivist educators. There is further
evidence here for a convergence of cognitivist accounts of the mind and
progressivist pedagogy.

However, the analogy between a computer and a mind endowed with a
language of thought will not work. The sense in which we talk of computers using languages is not the sense in which we talk of humans doing
so. It makes sense to talk of a computer language and of a computer
producing representations because the representations are made for us, not
for the computer. For the computer itself, the operating language, at whatever level, is nothing more than a control mechanism whose operations
can be explained in terms of the physical laws governing the operation of
the computer. The physical system is so designed that it can form a
representation for humans via various input and output devices, while at
the same time controlling the physical functions of the mechanism that
is the computer. The representational nature of the computer is, therefore,
man-made and is able to operate as a system of representation as opposed
to a purely physical system because *humans* have established rules whereby
they can interpret the physical output of the computer as representations
for themselves, and can input to the computer in a form that is intelligible
as a form of language to other humans. It is misleading to say that the
computer represents things to itself; it operates through a control mechanism that is able to represent things to humans.[15]

The best-known critique of a computational model of human understanding is that of John Searle.[16] Searle's arguments are directed against the
idea that understanding can be conceptualised in computational terms. The
inputs and the outputs may be genuinely representational for us (not for
the computer), but the process by which input leads to output is not. This
process could only misleadingly be described as the operation of a language.
We can represent to ourselves the mechanism as if it were a language with
its own system of rules, but the rules in question are in fact laws according
to which the mechanism works, not rules in the normative sense. The
computer does not learn rules through being taught, it cannot be corrected
and has no way of interpreting the system of 'rules'. Therefore it does not
operate by *understanding* what it is doing. These points apply to brains as
much as to computers.

Searle's own criticism of the LOTH is based on his analogy of the
'Chinese Room'. We are to suppose that someone who does not know
any Chinese is asked to operate a system whereby he responds to meaningful Chinese questions by giving meaningful and relevant Chinese
answers. This person sits in a room and is issued the questions in writing.
For him, they are squiggles. However these squiggles also occur on the

left-hand side of a list where they are matched on the right-hand side by squoggles. On consulting the list, the inhabitant of the Chinese Room matches the squiggle with its corresponding squoggle, finds the appropriate squoggle card and pushes that through the output letterbox. Although to a Chinese speaker outside the Room meaningful Chinese questions are responded to with meaningful Chinese answers, it is false to say that the inhabitant of the Chinese Room is using, let alone understanding, Chinese. This, according to Searle, shows that semantics is not intrinsic to syntax, that is, the possession of a set of rules is not sufficient to warrant the ascription of meaning and understanding to the agent. However, if we replace the inhabitant by a mechanical device, then the analogy with the way in which a computer uses language is complete; the syntactical nature of the Chinese Room is only apparent and the system becomes a purely physical one. Computational states mimicking rules are *assigned* to the physics, they are not intrinsic to it.[17]

The computer's internal workings, which account for the matching of input with output, are nothing more than the operation of a mechanism, even though that mechanism is so designed that it can convey representations to Chinese speakers. It follows that the inhabitant of the Chinese Room, if it is a mechanism rather than a homunculus, is not using a language of thought successfully to carry out its functions of representing to those who issue inputs and receive outputs. This remains true even if the operations of the mechanism in the Chinese Room run according to laws that are formally describable as a system of natural deduction. Whereas humans would follow the rules of the calculus of, say, propositional logic, the computer would be controlled by a mechanism that produced the same results as a human who diligently followed the rules of natural deduction for propositional calculus. The computer is therefore wired up and controlled in such a way as to mimic the efforts of a natural deducer.

One reply to Searle is to deny the analogy of a computer system with the solitary homunculus within the Chinese Room. Instead of a single homunculus, there is a division of labour within the Room, shared out between several homunculi. Although it still makes no sense to say that any single homunculus understands Chinese, it does make sense, according to Sterelny, to say that the Room as a whole does.[18] This reply misses the most important point about the example, namely that the operations within the Chinese Room are properly describable as *those of a mechanism*, rather than actions governed by rules. A mechanism that controls several different points of operation no more generates understanding within the system as a whole than does a mechanism that controls one single centre of operation.

It might be argued at this stage that, since the Chinese Room *as a whole* engages in meaningful interaction with other Chinese speakers, what goes on inside does not matter; to all intents and purposes, in the social world of Chinese speakers the Room is a Chinese speaker. But if this is so, then the example proves too much, for in so far as the Chinese Room (or a mobile and humanoid equivalent) is following the social and linguistic rules of Chinese and is treated as a Chinese speaker, then it *is* a Chinese speaker and understands Chinese just like any other Chinese speaker. But we can say this and make sense because now the Room is located in a normative framework in which it is intelligible to talk of understanding.[19] The actual physical mechanisms that constitute the physically necessary conditions of being able to take part in Chinese society drop out of the picture as irrelevant in explaining what the Room's ability to understand Chinese amounts to; that is described in the social and linguistic normative framework of Chinese.

What are the implications of Searle's critique of the computational model of intelligence for the LOTH? The workings of a mind could only be described as a language of thought in a figurative sense which would have two aspects. The first is that it could represent to other people, like a high-level computer language does. The second is that in its mechanical operations, it might mimic certain rule-governed languages or calculi. It would not, however, be a language in the sense in which that term is used to describe human natural languages or even the artificial calculi like those of formal logic, which are constructed for particular purposes and used by people. It is, therefore, misleading to describe the language of thought as a language in any other than a figurative sense. All that Fodor can coherently be claiming is that, in order to use natural language, the mind employs a mechanical system that appears at one level to mimic the operations of a norm-governed human natural language. Seen this way, the thesis becomes a testable one which can be resolved by investigating whether or not the LOTH gives us the best description, at some level, of the workings of the brain. LOTH becomes a genuine hypothesis, capable of refutation. There is no *a priori* reason to suppose that is the best description.

However, even if the claim that the language of thought is a genuine language is taken seriously, does it make sense to describe the activity of learning as a process of unconscious hypothesis formation and testing? In other words, can the language of investigation, which involves the construction and testing of hypotheses, bear transposition into a situation where it is done unconsciously and automatically? To what extent is one still talking of the same phenomenon in this situation? In everyday life, the forming of hypotheses and the testing of them are conscious, deliberate and reliant on previous experience to work properly. Experience, as well as intuition and creativity, tells us what is a plausible hypothesis and what is not. We also use experience to specify the kind of predictions whose occurrence or non-occurrence we would wish to monitor; none of this applies in the innatist case.

One central problem for the cognitivist case is that mental operations, in the sense in which these are understood by cognitivists as workings of the mind, are assumed to be primary cases of what we ordinarily call, for example, the framing and testing of hypotheses. Concepts such as *hypothesis*, *prediction*, *test*, *corroboration*, *refutation* and *proof* all have a place in our everyday talk about learning, finding out and investigating. It is possible to extend our talk using these concepts to situations where they are applied inwardly, without participation in the social milieu where the application of these concepts has its primary life; some conceptual threads will be broken but enough will probably remain between the old concepts and the new for it to make sense of the extended use of the concepts into the 'private' domain. But if this is acceptable, then it cannot at the same time be acceptable that the inner or private use of concepts is the primary one and the social, public use is a secondary derivation. One has to be derived from the other and since the *sense* of the idea of hypothesis-testing arises from its social role where it is associated with normative activities like testing, *rejecting*, *modifying*, etc. which have their primary employment in a social milieu, the non-social usage cannot be the primary one. If one wished to make it so, that would require independent justification. The position here is the same as that of the primary and secondary uses of representation that were discussed earlier.

Conclusion

If cognitivism is not coherent, then its influence on theories of learning and hence on education needs to be questioned. Cognitivism supplies plausible-looking reasons for thinking that learning can take place without instruction, practice, memorisation or training; moreover its prestige as a theory of learning devalues those activities within education.[20] Its rejection should, therefore, lead us to re-examine our need for explicit, teacher-oriented pedagogies. While most varieties of connectionism do emphasise the importance of 'training up' neural networks and are thus not hostile to the use of explicit teaching techniques, its reliance on the notion of internal representation leads it to stand or fall with classical cognitivism as a coherent theory.[21] Any convincing account of learning that relied on the idea of representation would then have to move outside the brain and take account of the irreducibly normative nature of human learning and all that is implied by such a shift in perspective.[22] The Fodorian conception entails that each person has access to a solitary rather than a private language[23] and it can be maintained (although it is beyond the scope of this chapter) that such a language can only be understood as a mechanism. But if it is a mechanism then, as I have shown, it cannot be representational in any philosophically enlightening sense.

Such a shift would involve looking at the way in which we learn to follow rules and the importance of training in the acquisition of the ability to follow rules, particularly in the early stages of learning. If this shift is made, then the consequences for primary school pedagogy in particular could be profound. Training will need to be emphasised more and discovery-based forms of learning may need to be considered in the context of prior training.

If, contrary to cognitivism, concepts are not innate, then learning new concepts is not a matter of matching words to innate concepts; children need to be able to master concepts through acquisition of the rules governing their use and this is likely to be a gradual process.[24] It will involve instruction as well as training prior to the experimental working out of the full range for the correct application of concepts.[25] Note that on this conception discovery and hypothesis-testing are not ruled out but they take their place conceptually behind instruction and training in technique and form, which together provide the necessary technique and knowledge for their secure application.

If human learning is largely a normatively dependent activity, then the importance of the interaction between teacher and class needs to be attended to as one of the primary ways in which knowledge and technique are transmitted and reinforced. The notion that class teaching should be interactive is also congenial to the position that I have been outlining, in the sense that a process of trying out and testing in the presence of a knowledgeable authority allows for participation in the learning process: concepts are acquired and developed in use through instruction, correction, interpretation and evaluation. The confluence of progressivism and cognitivism poses a considerable challenge to those who maintain that the role of the teacher is, among other things, to instruct, to train and to correct. If cognitivism is shown to rest on a mistake, that challenge is significantly weakened.

7

DEVELOPMENT

Introduction

In this chapter theories about the relationship between the growth of young humans and their learning will be examined. It will be maintained that there is no such thing as *psychological development* in anything other than the biological sense, but that there are constraints on learning of various kinds, some of which, because they are connected with biological immaturity, may be classed as 'developmental'.[1] However, there is no well-developed theory of what those constraints are, nor should we confidently expect to see a well-grounded theory arise, let alone a well-grounded theory of *psychological* stages of development. Neither am I interested in educational theories of development, such as those of Whitehead and Egan; it seems to me that these are largely normative accounts of what education should be, rather than theories about learning.[2] Learning as much as possible about constraints on learning is extremely useful, even though there is no theory of development underpinning our knowledge. Indeed, large-scale theories of development, when they are based on inadequate evidence, may actually hinder our knowledge of such matters.

Some of this is uncontroversial. A 1-year-old cannot speak, an 8-year-old cannot properly understand the affective responses of the sexually mature, but beyond this, not much is clear. The claim that development of the *general capacity to learn* takes place in sequential stages associated with age is very hard to sustain. There are two massive problems associated with most developmental theories; the first is that they seek to show what children *cannot* learn at certain ages. The second is that, rooted squarely in the metaphor of organic growth, they find it difficult to account for motivation. The growth metaphor usually has a covert evaluative component built into it, which of itself is not necessarily wrong, except that it is usually the case that this evaluative component requires independent justification which it never receives. The persuasiveness of the growth metaphor arises largely from a neglect of the social aspects of learning.[3]

The first problem is a logical one, namely that of proving a negative. If one asserts that anyone of age A cannot learn L, then a single instance of someone of age A learning L damages the theory. There are two possible responses to this: the first is to say that any developmental theory is about *stages* rather than ages; the second is to say that whether or not one learns anything at any given age will depend on other characteristics like culture and context of learning. The first response is not very convincing because, unless ages are tied closely to stages, the revised theory is little better than a tautology. Suppose that it is claimed that children cannot reason until they reach stage 3 of a developmental schema. Then any child who cannot reason is *ipso facto* not at stage 3 of development. But this tells us little except that stages 1 and 2 are so defined as to exclude reasoners.

The second response is more nuanced and apparently takes account of the need to provide conditions under which the theory can be tested. It says that the acquisition of abilities is dependent on context and on culture as well as on developmental maturity. But there is a serious risk of such a theory dying the death of a thousand qualifications; there are so many different cultures and so many ways in which context may affect under-standing, motivation and interest, that the promised generality of a developmental theory threatens to disappear very rapidly as it becomes contextually and culturally qualified. Nevertheless, there are at least some physiological and logical constraints on the sequence in which learning can occur. This chapter will explore the extent to which it can be said that there are likely further constraints of a *psychological* character.

In most theories, development is something that happens to someone. For example, if one acquires language through a developmental process, then one does not actively work at learning the language, it is, in a sense, 'switched on' at the appropriate stage in the developmental sequence.[4] We need, therefore to distinguish carefully between learning *through* develop-ment and learning at an appropriate developmental stage. In the latter case, the arrival of a certain stage of development only provides the necessary conditions for learning, in the sense that the learner has still got to engage actively with what is to be learned in order to succeed. This distinction between two senses of developmental learning is not always closely observed in the literature.[5] Sometimes the issue is further clouded by the fact that *motivation* is said to be supplied with the developmental stage, as an internal force, so that extra-personal motivation is superfluous.

The analogy between human and plant growth operates very powerfully in this area.[6] Its hold can plausibly be ascribed to a number of factors. First, the drawing of an undoubted parallel between humans and the rest of the organic world in terms of the existence of a biological life cycle with different stages. Second, the poetic attractiveness of the plant/growth metaphor in relation to children. Third, the fact that the metaphor also holds scientific promise; just as the growth mechanism of plants can be scientifically studied, so too can the growth/learning mechanism of human beings. Fourth, just as a plant grows when given the right nourishment, so the analogy with human learning suggests that this will occur automatically in the right conditions; there is little or no need for training, instruction or authority in the learning process.

Development and constraints on learning

Developmental theories maintain that there are constraints on when, in the human life cycle, different kinds of learning are possible. However, the senses in which learning might be constrained are quite different, and it is important that they be distinguished if we are properly to understand and assess the claims of developmental theory. The following are useful distinctions to make.

1   Logically speaking, some things cannot be learned before others. You can't learn that all whales are mammals before you have learned what mammals are, although these things may be learned contemporaneously.[7]

2   Conceptually speaking, some things cannot be learned before others: this is a looser and more disputable constraint than the logical one mentioned earlier, but if accepted, gives *a priori* limits on what can be learned and acquired and when. Although one cannot learn that all whales are mammals before learning what mammals are, it is possible to acquire a partial concept of whales before learning that whales are mammals.[8] It is quite likely in fact that our concepts do not come all at once, but develop as we increase our grasp of language (see Chapter 9).

3   Depending on one's epistemological position, there may also be theoretical constraints on learning. For example, if it is believed that one cannot remember facts before one acquires language (something that most empiricists would probably dispute), then a limit has been placed on what learning is possible.

4   Physically speaking, some things cannot be achieved without the appropriate physical state being reached. Thus, it is impossible to jump 6 feet when you are 3 feet tall. Well-established principles of biomechanics make this extremely unlikely.

5   Neurologically speaking, some things cannot happen until neurological organisation has reached a certain point. This is more difficult to maintain, owing to the plastic nature of our neurological organisation and our imperfect understanding of how our neurological nature constrains what we can do. There is some evidence however from animal studies, that the phenomenon of *imprinting* – when a young animal identifies and stays with a putative or real parent – is linked to a state of neurological receptiveness that lasts for only a short time.[9] There is

some reason to think that our ability to acquire a mother tongue may be subject to constraints of this sort as well.

6   Psychologically speaking, a human at a certain age or stage is incapable of learning certain things. This means something other than (1)–(5), unless mental structure is identified with neural structure. But since such an identification is programmatic rather than actual, the claim that there are psychological stages of development is, to all intents and purposes, a distinct claim from the one that there are neurological ones. The claim that the mind goes through distinct, fixed and sequential stages in each of which the nature and kind of learning that takes place is radically different from that in each of the other stages, is the central claim of most forms of developmental theory. They offer themselves as scientific theories about the nature of and limits to learning, but, as we shall see, they are scientific theories with some odd features.

The first of these is their apparent vulnerability to refutation, through counter-instances of learning taking place during a period when such a thing is allegedly impossible. The second is the mixing up of value-free and evaluative elements. In one sense developmental theories offer an account of the organic constraints on learning due to the slow process of physical maturation in humans. But since the time of Rousseau, developmentalists have seen their theories as more than just claims about when it is *possible* for learning to take place: they make claims about when it is *desirable* for it to do so as well.

Development is usually seen as a process by which an organism matures to a point where it is capable of acquiring a capacity or an ability through interaction with its environment.[10] There are two necessary conditions for acquisition on this model: one is that the organism has reached the right stage of maturity (itself a question of interaction with the environment together with pre-existing biological structure), and the other is that it is exposed to those sorts of experiences that will enable it to acquire a given capacity or ability. This sounds uncontroversial, but the choice of words to describe development is nearly always significant. 'Maturity' can be given a purely descriptive sense in which it denotes the achievement of a certain phase in development.

X has matured to state A

then asserts nothing more than that X has reached state A (which may be a necessary condition for the acquisition of a capacity or an ability). When applied to human beings, however, the term 'mature' can often take on an evaluative sense. For example, if I were to assert that Rosina is not mature enough to go to university, I may mean that she is physically unready to do so (although this is an unlikely interpretation of what I mean). It is more likely that I wish to draw attention to her inability in relation to sets of norms such as those followed when acquiring knowledge, organising one's life and getting on with other people. Therefore, to say that Rosina is not mature enough to go to university is to evaluate her abilities against a set of norms and, at least implicitly, to judge her as a member of her society. When the term 'mature' is applied to a human being in a developmental context, its meaning should be examined carefully.

A similar point can be made about the phrase: 'those sorts of experiences that will enable the organism to acquire a given capacity or ability.' As it stands, it does not appear to contain any hidden evaluative content. But the use of this phrase is rather longwinded and it is tempting to use the phrase: 'the right sorts of experiences for acquiring a given capacity or ability.' However, 'right' could be even more tendentious than 'mature'; it may mean no more than the first phrase, but it may also mean 'those sorts of experiences that are valuable or approved of' and here, once again, the possible experiences that a human may have are evaluated against norms established for classifying and judging the quality of human experiences.[11] It should be clear that at the very least, talk about development, when transferred from the biological to the human context, may acquire some accretions which subtly alter the terms of the discussion. When it is claimed that there are cultural variations in developmental speed or sequence, this question of the right sorts of experiences becomes critical. This is, however, no accident. Developmental theories are about *human* development and, as such, they have to show that it takes place in a morally desirable direction. There is no educational attraction in a developmental schema that leads to criminality, for example. So in order for developmental theories to have any educational rationale, which they must have in order to be of any educational interest, they need to have inbuilt normative constraints, even when, because of the biological paradigm adopted, these are *covert*.[12]

The matter becomes even more obscure when the ambiguities around 'growth', another central and related organising concept of developmental theory, are added to those about 'maturity' and 'experiences'. The growth metaphor, although influential, is in fact muddled. On the one hand we are invited to consider growth as a process closely related to the life cycle of plants in a garden, and on the other hand we are assured that growth and effective learning can only take place through *active* engagement rather than through the *passive* absorption of nutrients, water and sun.[13]

The two aspects of the growth metaphor are encapsulated in the following quotation from Chomsky.

It is a traditional insight, which merits more attention than it receives, that teaching should not be compared to filling a bottle with water but rather helping a flower to grow in its own way.

As any good teacher knows, the methods of instruction and the range of material covered are matters of small importance as compared with the success in arousing the natural curiosity of the students and stimulating their interest in exploring on their own. What the student learns passively will be quickly forgotten. What students discover for themselves when their natural curiosity and creative impulses are aroused not only will be remembered but will be the basis for further exploration and inquiry and perhaps significant intellectual contributions.[14]

It is difficult to know where to begin in picking out the evaluatively loaded aspects of the growth metaphor in this passage. One could point to the use of phrases like 'as any good teacher knows' to make the point that a certain kind of pedagogical approach is the right one, providing the 'right' experiences to enable development to take place. Presumably a good teacher is one who, by definition, adopts such an approach. While the growth of a plant is in some fairly obvious sense 'natural', that is, it takes place in accordance with laws of nature, it is far from clear that there is anything like 'natural curiosity' on the part of human beings that is law-governed in the same way. In effect, the ambiguities in the Rousseauian concept of *natural* resurface in this passage; the nomological sense of 'natural' is combined with an evaluative sense of 'free' or 'unconstrained'. But the use of 'natural' in this sense is precisely as a term of approval; what is natural is what Chomsky approves of: that is, teaching without instructing or the use of prescribed material. There is nothing logically reprehensible about using the term 'natural' in this way, but such a usage requires independent justification, which Chomsky, like Rousseau, is unable to give.

The growth/plant metaphor tells us that individual human growth is a natural (i.e. nomological) process. But a natural (in its quasi-normative sense) process is something that generally we approve of; therefore we cannot but approve of a nomologically governed process of growth. But if learning takes place through growth, and maybe only through growth, then the impact of society on the process of learning will be minimal. This will be a good thing for developmentalists because growth for them is 'natural' in the evaluative sense. It is also significant that motivation to learn has also been incorporated into the growth metaphor. Curiosity is 'natural' in both senses; it will occur according to nature and it is to be approved of. The problem of how growth alone might account for why anyone should want to learn anything is dealt with; all learning takes place through instinctive drives and there is no place for reactive behaviour, training, commitment, social approbation, or the development of love for a subject, in making successful learning possible. Developmentalists, especially in their romantic mode, emphasise more the *constraints* that

81

society places on motivation and learning rather than the *impetus* that it can provide.

Piaget's developmentalism: a case study

Although Piaget's developmental theory is not the only one, it is probably the best known and most influential.[15] Because of its influence in the earlier part of this century, it has come under increasing criticism over the last two decades, but the criticisms have usually been of the empirical claims made by Piaget and his associates, rather than of the conceptual structure and research programme that he developed.[16] Enough has already been said in the previous section to suggest that developmental theories have potential conceptual problems to do with: the nature of their claims; their covert mixing of description and evaluation; the way that they deal with motivation. Without ignoring the empirical evidence, however, this section will focus primarily on the structure of, and assumptions behind, Piaget's theory.

Piaget describes his epistemological approach as constructivist. By this he means that elements of empiricism and rationalism are required in order to provide an adequate conceptualisation both of the mind and its growth and of the nature of human learning. According to Piaget, learning cannot take place without the possibility of the integration of experience into pre-existing mental structures. On the other hand, without a contribution derived from outside the mind, there is no possibility of knowledge. There is a dynamic relationship between the structural features of the mind and factors external to the mind. Information reaching the mind, together with an internal maturational process, progressively alters the structures through which the mind recognises the world and organises contributions from the world into knowledge. The different structural forms that the mind goes through are characterised as the *developmental stages* through which the mind of the infant matures into the mind of the adult human.[17] Knowledge is organised into specific structures. At each stage beyond the sensori-motor, which is the initial developmental stage of infancy, the mind has available to it a set of inferential operations describable in set-theoretic terms.

Piaget's account is completed by a theory of motivation that postulates an internal drive to master each developmental stage and then to move on to the next. It is not unlike the *amour de soi* of Rousseau. But whereas *amour de soi* can be seen as an impulse for the promotion of well-being, Piagetian motivation is an impulse for the promotion of development and learning. The existence of the stages as real structures of the mind is inferred from the inability of children at certain ages to carry out certain kinds of task. Their failure to carry out these tasks is taken to be indicative of the fact that their minds are still at a stage at which the cognitive operations necessary to carry them out successfully are not yet available. The evidence for this view is weighty. However, disconfirming evidence is also weighty.[18] As remarked earlier, there is a general logical problem with any attempt permanently to prove a universal negative thesis, namely that it is always possible for a counter-example to be produced, which renders the thesis in its universal form no longer tenable. More specifically, the problem can be located in the fact that any demonstration that a task cannot be achieved by a child of a certain age necessarily takes place in a certain context. The problem then becomes one of the inductive soundness of generalising from that particular context, and it is a pressing problem when the context of data collection is an experimental one where the task is unrelated to any practical interest of the subject and where the purpose of which is also poorly perceived by the subject.

For developmentalists, context should not affect motivation, which is the key factor promoting learning, unless there is something in that context that specifically disables the motivational process underlying learning. The context will either present a learning task that is not sufficiently demanding or one that is too demanding. It is frequently alleged that such a disabling factor is likely to be found in educational contexts where the work presented is said to be either above or below the developmental level of the child (the child has not reached the required state of maturity), or where it is presented in such a way as to stifle the child's natural creativity and curiosity, which are themselves the manifestations of intrinsic motivation. Alternatively, some features of the environment, particularly cultural background, are held to discourage the manifestation of curiosity.

But the inability of context to affect motivation, except in the ways described above, is only plausible if the developmentalist conception of motivation is accepted, and this conception is something to be argued for rather than taken for granted. In fact, the innatist notion of motivation runs counter to 'folk psychological' views of action and indeed to any conception of action that takes seriously the social nature of most human activity. This point is crucial to understanding the defects of developmentalism. As we have already seen, it stems both from an asocial or even, in some respects, *antisocial* idea of human flourishing and from a natural scientific view of human activity which sees people much as any other kind of organism, governed solely by innate biological drives. But these views are programmatic, they underpin developmentalism rather than provide evidence for it. They ignore the social nature of humans and the way in which this social nature affects their psychology. However, this is a crucial omission since it is largely through various kinds of extrinsic motivation that people act, and a recognition of this is written into the way in which we regard and talk about action (see Chapter 4).

As we have seen, the difficulty of proving a negative has already led to major re-evaluations of Piagetian theory. But there are also good reasons why a Piaget-type account of human maturation and learning must be wrong. The contexts in which humans are motivated are social; they are so even for a solitary individual. In such a situation, the physical context is one that is individuated within the complex of institutions in a society. For example, a solitary writer sharpening his pencils is working for an audience whose attitudes and expectations affect the way in which he goes about his work or even whether or not he is able to go about it. Both his perception of his own situation and the attitudes and expectations of his potential readership can only be understood within the complex of institutions within which a professional writer and his readers exist and relate to each other.

This is not to say of course that the springs of action and activity have no individual characteristics. Motivation varies greatly from individual to individual; it is the individual's own conception of the value of an action to him, as a member of a society, together with his own perception of the nature and feasibility of that action which are likely to be decisive influences on whether or not he takes that action. But the value of an action as it is perceived by an individual is quite likely to be influenced by the worth and prestige of the action as it is perceived by others.

Whether or not someone carries out an action or pays attention so as to learn, also depends on how they understand the situation they are in, or even whether or not they understand it. Very often this is affected by what they judge is being expected of them. Where this judgement is unclear or if they do not feel like doing what they think is expected of them, they are unlikely to do or to learn as well as they might.[19] This is nothing to do with natural curiosity or creativity, but with their perception of themselves in relation to others and to the society in which they live. There is ample evidence that Piagetian developmentalism has systematically underestimated human learning capacity. Since learning capacity, according to the theory, is a biological given activated by experience, which should be common to all humans, the apparent discovery that there are cultural differences in the *rate* or even the *end point* of development, suggests that some cultural environments fail to trigger stage development in the way suggested by the theory. There is, though, another possible explanation for the results of these cross-cultural studies, namely that the Piagetian tests are in fact culture-specific.[20] This possibility, which was first noted by Vygotsky, poses a grave threat to the possibility of generalising such theories beyond certain very specific cultural parameters.

The final criticism of developmentalism which I wish to discuss is just as damaging as any of the other points raised so far. It applies not just to the work of Piaget, but to any developmental theory that represents certain modes of thinking at certain developmental stages as yielding false information to the subject at that stage.[21] At the pre-operational stage, judgements about quantity, shape and distribution seem to be systematically false if developmental theory is right. A little reflection reveals the absurdity and implausibility of such a claim. There can be no point in a child possessing an epistemic strategy that systematically yields false information. Such an idea would not be entertained but for the alleged scientific authority with which developmental theory has been endowed. But the paradigm within which most scientific theories would look, especially biologically based theories such as that of Piaget, would be that of evolutionary biology. But evolutionary theories are predicated on the idea that the particular epistemic apparatus that we have enables us to maximise our chances of survival, or at least of propagating our genes.[22] It is hard to see how an epistemic apparatus of the kind that is supposed to occur with pre-operational thinking would fulfil such a condition, since it would minimise the survival chances of the immature. At the very least, one would expect to see a complex evolutionary explanation of why such a strategy would be beneficial to a species; as far as I know, none has been forthcoming.[23] But until developmentalists can address such difficulties, their claims lack plausibility at the most fundamental level, by lacking one of the most important features of any putative account of human learning; namely giving us an account of how we get *knowledge* of the world rather than false beliefs.

Conclusion: the craving for generality should be resisted

Developmental theories rest on a truth: there are certain biological constraints on learning. The danger lies in moving from an examination of these constraints in a variety of contexts and cultures to an over-ready reliance on the experimental method to examine them in a general way. The experimental setting is itself highly culture-specific. It is a mistake to think that, for humans, it is context-free and likely to provide high validity. All that one can safely infer from a performance in an experiment is strictly related to performance under experimental conditions, unless there are independent grounds for thinking that experimental situations are generalisable. This is unlikely to be the case where the subjects of the experiment are unsure why they are being asked to do something (as they usually are), because, in most cases we act on practical reasons of which we ourselves have a grasp. Even a context such as examination or testing is understood as a practical means to an end, and the examinee knows what is expected of him and can act accordingly.

There is no doubt that much of great value can be learned about the different conditions under which people are capable of learning and the *biological* stages at which they are capable of doing so. But this information will only be valuable if the urge of psychologists to provide generalised theories of development can be resisted, as it muddles a modest but useful line of enquiry with a grandiose and ill-founded one. The temptation comes in two forms: the first is to import crucial assumptions into the explanatory framework without any empirical basis, like the theory of internal motivational drives, abstractionism and an account of underlying psychic operations;[24] the second is to infer the existence of a related series of structures that are, in some sense, instantiated in the human mind, on the basis of very little evidence.

The conclusion of this discussion is that there are biological constraints on learning of which we have some incomplete knowledge. The incompleteness of this knowledge relates largely to our ignorance of the ways in which context and culture interact with biological maturation. There is, therefore, as yet no general theory of how these constraints operate, let alone a general theory of how *psychological* development affects learning. Indeed, the discussion has shown that so far psychologists have failed to produce a convincing argument that there is any such thing as psychological development in a very general maturational sense, as opposed to producing some useful observations concerning changes in functioning and capacity, particularly in the earlier stages of human growth. Developmental psychologists should heed the advice of Francis Bacon, when he wrote;

> There are and can be only two ways of searching into and discovering truth. The one flies from the senses and particulars to the most general axioms, and from these principles, the truth of which it takes for settled and immoveable, proceeds to judgment and the discovery of middle axioms. And this way is now in fashion. The other derives axioms from the senses and particulars, rising by a gradual and unbroken ascent, so that it arrives at the most general axioms last of all. This is the true way, but as yet untried.[25]

It would be sad if much of developmental psychology were to remain at a pre-Baconian state of methodological sophistication by failing to observe some of the simplest principles of sound inductive generalisation. Indeed, if the argument of this chapter is correct, they need to question whether there are any 'most general axioms' to be arrived at in this area.

8

LEARNING LANGUAGE

Introduction

It is very often said that our mother tongue is acquired rather than learned. I shall use the term 'acquisition' for mother tongue learning to distinguish it from learning to be literate and learning a second language, which require greater degrees of attention, memorising and instruction. Early language learning apparently takes place without much conscious effort or the need for extrinsic motivation; instead children have a powerful instinct to communicate. While there is a biological basis to language acquisition, it is not itself a biological process, but a social one. The view that language acquisition occurs without the need for any conscious effort or extrinsic motivation is much exaggerated; in fact, both children and caregivers have to apply themselves, even though they are aided by strong instinctual motivation.

The cognitivist account

One tradition of explaining language acquisition comes from the earlier work of Piaget. He explained language learning as the transition from imagery to inner speech where images receive symbolic representation, through the egocentric use of language to, finally, its social use.[1] Vygotsky's criticisms of this theory are by now well known. They centred on Piaget's faulty method of generalising from unusual situations, like a child nursery, to a range of other situations in which young children start to use language.[2] It might be added that the Piagetian model of language development also derived from a dogmatic model of stage development outlined in the previous chapter. Quite apart from this, however, is the fact that Piaget's account is vulnerable to the arguments of Wittgenstein regarding the impossibility of a private sensation language (see Chapter 4).

The most influential current theory about language acquisition derives from the work of Chomsky and his associates. They, too, provide an account of mother tongue learning that starts from the child as a solitary.

Does the cognitivist account avoid the kinds of difficulties that attend the early Piagetian one? Although the cognitivism of Chomsky and Fodor avoids the arguments against a private sensation language,[3] it does not avoid the arguments against *ab initio* solitary languages advanced in Chapter 4, nor those against the problems of representational theories advanced in Chapter 6. Let us, however, leave these aside and consider the account on its own merits.

It is proposed that the basis of human natural languages is an innate individual faculty an infant possesses which is then adjusted or tuned to the rules of the particular natural language which happens to be the mother tongue of the infant's community. The innate individual faculty which each human neonate possesses is a rule system that is largely common to the human species, which is 'wired in' to the human nervous system. Exposure to the mother tongue allows the child to adapt this innate faculty to the parameters of the particular language community into which he is born. This process of adaptation is sometimes described in homuncular fashion, as if the neonate is a 'baby scientist', forming and testing hypotheses about the nature of the local rules that are used by his own language community. Alternatively it is described in more impersonal terms as an electronic network.

> We may think of the language faculty as a complex and intricate network of some sort associated with a switch box consisting of an array of switches that can be in one or two positions. Unless the switches are set one way or another, the system does not function. When they are set in one of the permissible ways, then the system functions in accordance with its nature, but differently, depending on how the switches are set. The fixed network is the system of the principles of universal grammar; the switches are the parameters to be fixed by experience. The data presented to the child learning the language must suffice to set the switches one way or another. When these switches are set, the child has command of a particular language and knows the facts of that language: that a particular expression has a particular meaning, and so on.[4]

Despite this alternative way of describing how language is learned, the neonate is still described as possessing a body of knowledge about language, albeit a special kind of knowledge.

> The child learning Spanish or any other human language knows, in advance of experience, that the rules will be structure dependent. The child does not consider the simple linear rule R, then discard it in favor of the more complex rule R-Q, in the manner of the

rational scientist inquiring into language. Rather, the child knows without experience or instruction that the linear rule R is not a candidate and that the structure-dependent rule R-Q is the only possibility. This knowledge is part of the child's biological endowment, part of the structure of the language faculty. It forms part of the mental equipment with which the child faces the world of experience.[5]

D'Agostino has argued that the requirement that the child knows the rules is not necessary to the cognitivist account. It is enough to maintain that, in some sense, the child possesses the rules of language.[6] While it is true that this alternative formulation allows the cognitivist to dispense with the kind of knowledge that is held beyond the possibility of conscious inspection and which is neither propositional nor practical in the ordinary sense, it does raise questions of its own. Cognitivists are keen to argue that the neonate already possesses a system of rules. This seems to be central to the claim that the child knows a language, for languages are systems of rules. But to possess a system of rules is to *know* that rule-system in some sense. One could allow that the neonate is guided by mechanisms that are describable as rules by observers, but this is not what the cognitivists really wish to say. Their central point, as we saw in Chapter 5, is that the mind operates with systems of representations and, as it was argued there, a mechanical guide system is not a system of representations any more than an internal combustion engine is. For a system to be a system of representations, it must represent *something* to *someone* and this someone is the mind/brain of the neonate who is thus acquainted with the rule system. It does seem, then, that it is not so easy to dispense with the idea that the neonate is in some kind of *epistemic* relationship with the representational system, if the broader aspects of the cognitivist programme are to be preserved.[7]

Given this initial implausibility, what are the advantages claimed for the cognitivist account of language learning? The scope of the theory extends to syntax and semantics; it does not apparently include pragmatics, phonology, prosody, gesture, posture, facial expression or context. The principal advantage relates to syntax. We are asked to believe that *ab initio* possession of a language acquisition device is the only way in which a child could build up a knowledge of the syntax of his mother tongue so quickly and with so little apparent effort, and could come so quickly to understand and to use sentences that he has never heard before.

Language learning is not really something that the child does; it is something that happens to the child placed in an appropriate environment, much as the child's body grows and matures in a predetermined way when provided with appropriate nutrition and environmental stimulation.[8]

But is this ability, remarkable as it is, only to be explained in terms of an innate language faculty? The claim that this is the only plausible hypothesis available to explain the phenomenon is a very strong one, coming from individuals engaged in a scientific research programme. Its strength is all the more surprising given the evident weaknesses in the cognitivist approach. It is now time to cast doubt on the idea that some form of innatism is the *only* available and plausible hypothesis for explaining language learning. After this, it will be appropriate to dwell on further shortcomings of innatism.

Chomsky admits that the phonology of a language is learned by imitating other language users.[9] He does not claim that vocabulary is innate, only that concepts are. Neither is it claimed that children use *sentence structures* that they have never come across before. The truly remarkable and mysterious feature of language is said to be the fact that they are able to use sentences which they have never encountered before. Upon this simple observation rests the whole edifice of the innatist programme of accounting for language acquisition (language development would actually be a more accurate description for their account). All that is claimed, however, is that young children are capable of using sentences whose structures they are likely to have come across before, containing words, not all of which they will have used before. They will have heard sentences with these structures and they will have heard the words that they then go on to use.

In many circumstances, using a sentence one has never heard before could very largely be a matter of using a sentence (or components of a sentence) that one *has* heard or used before. The parts of any sentence can be represented as sentential functions. Strike out one word or phrase and you are left with a functorial expression which can take as its arguments a range of words or phrases of the same or related syntactic categories, yielding as a value a new sentence of the same logical category as the original sentence. Thus;

Mummy, fetch me some milk

yields the sentential function:

Mummy, fetch me some——

which could be filled by a range of possible arguments such as: *bread, sweets, toys,* etc.

A little reflection shows that the original sentence can yield a whole range of different sentential functions, each with its own range of appropriate arguments. It seems much less mysterious to claim that children are able to use sentential functions to utter sentences that they have never heard before, using elements and structures that they *have* heard or used before, than to claim that what they use is, in some sense, completely novel.[10]

Should we be surprised at even this apparent capacity for novelty in the child's acquisition of the ability to construct sentences? It would be surprising if our abilities were so rigid that we were incapable of coping with and even exploiting novel situations. Most situations that people encounter are different in some respect from similar situations that they have previously encountered. If human beings were not able to adapt their abilities to take account of novel situations, the prospects for the human species (and indeed for most other species) would be bleak indeed. Consider how implausible it would be to say that someone must have an innate faculty for driving a car because, as a driver, he continually has to perform manoeuvres that, in their detail, are different from any manoeuvres he has ever performed or encountered before. We do not consider this to be mysterious; we recognise that, in driving, we make use of a stock of standard techniques that we have been trained to use. We use these techniques in circumstances where they have to be deployed and combined in ways that we have neither observed nor used before. Were we not able to do so, we would be confined to driving on the same roads in exactly the same way as the way in which we had been originally trained.

The situation with language learning is no different. At a certain age, the young child acquires the technique of using a range of vocabulary in a series of grammatical structures. He learns to apply these techniques in a range of circumstances that are different in certain respects, sometimes in significant respects, from those circumstances that he has previously encountered. Sometimes he uses the same words and the same sentences in different situations; in other circumstances, the same sentence may be accompanied by different prosodic and paralinguistic features. On other occasions, he makes use of sentential functions that he has used before with vocabulary he has used before in a different combination.

How does a child *understand* sentences that he has never heard before? The same points apply as to the production of new sentences. The child encounters structures and vocabulary that he has encountered before, albeit in somewhat different combinations. However, he will encounter vocabulary and sentence structures he has not previously come across. In these circumstances, he may need help and explanation if he cannot understand straightaway. Very often, however, there will be cues to help him, such as the context of utterance and gestural, prosodic and other paralinguistic attributes of the speaker. The natural reactive behaviour of humans to their children is essential to this process. He may also have observed similar situations and noticed the behaviour of the participants in those situations and what the outcomes were. For example, he may understand,

Have you fetched the milk?

as a request for information when addressed to himself and may also have observed his sister being asked

You haven't brought your teddy, have you?

and have noticed her taking this as a request for information. On other occasions he may notice that his sister is asked,

Have you fetched the milk?

in a different tone of voice in a different context, and may have observed her looking sheepish and then going to the refrigerator to get some milk. On subsequent occasions, he is able to understand certain sentences which have the grammatical form of negative questions as requests for something to be done, because of the manner in which the request is made and the context in which it is made.

Chomsky dismisses such accounts of how children learn language as *analogical,* and argues that they rest on a confusion of the concepts of *ability* and *knowledge.* On this account we can never explain a child's knowledge of his language, which we need to do in order to account for his ability to speak and to understand his native language. However, a speaker's knowledge of his mother tongue is precisely that kind of knowledge, namely know-how, to a large extent. That this is a confusion is supposed to be shown by the following example:

> Consider two people who share exactly the same knowledge of Spanish: their pronunciation, knowledge of the meaning of words, grasp of sentence structure, and so on, are identical. Nevertheless, these two people may – and characteristically do – differ greatly in their ability to use the language. One may be a great poet, the second an utterly pedestrian language user who speaks in clichés. Characteristically, two people who share the same knowledge will be inclined to say quite different things on given occasions. Hence it is hard to see how knowledge can be identified with ability, still less with disposition and behavior.[11]

This is to make a mystery out of the banal observation that some speakers of a language are more skilled at using that language than some others. The problem with knowledge only arises if we accept Chomsky's own account of innate linguistic knowledge, but that is precisely what he wishes to establish; he cannot trade on it to criticise alternative accounts to his own. What is added to our understanding of the two people in Chomsky's example above by saying that they share the same knowledge? All that needs to be said is that they both speak and understand Spanish, but that one speaker is more *skilful* than the other. Granted, one might possibly find that the great poet has knowledge that does enhance his skill: for example, he may know a great deal of the history of the language, be well versed in its formal grammar, have a wide vocabulary, know a great deal about verse structure, etc. But none of this is the kind of *tacit* knowledge that Chomsky claims is so important, it is simple propositional knowledge about the language.

Why, then, has there been so much speculation as to the mysterious nature of language acquisition? The answer probably lies in an excessive concentration by some influential researchers on one or two aspects of language acquisition to the detriment of an understanding of the broader picture. In particular, concern over the fact that a speaker learns to produce and understand new sentences, and concern over the evident inability of classical behaviourism to explain this phenomenon, have led researchers to conclude that there must be an innate body of knowledge which is, in some sense, already 'known' by the neonate. We have seen, however, that the novelty is not as great as might be thought, simply because new sentences bear substantial relationships (in terms of phonology, syntax and vocabulary) with ones already encountered.

But there are other, very important aspects of language that are both learned and attended to in language acquisition which, when they are noticed, again make the ability to deal with novelty less surprising than it might seem on the first encounter with the cognitivist thesis. Speech is an encounter between two or more embodied animals. This simple observation brings in its train a wealth of consequences. First of all, our vocal apparatus does not just yield grammatical structures filled with vocabulary, we express meaning through intonation, stress, volume and pausing. Thus a child learns to appreciate the nuances in a speaker's prosody as well as to appreciate vocabulary, phonology and syntax. Second, the child learns to 'read' the speaker's facial expression, gesture, positioning and body posture as part of the message. Third, both the immediate physical context and the wider background of shared experiences and culture contribute to the understanding of particular utterances. It takes experience and a lot of assistance to be able to handle all these different elements, both of listening and of talking.

The sharing of cultural assumptions and personal experiences makes the need for textbook grammar superfluous in many speech situations. Meaning is often conveyed in an effective way through implicit reference to the immediate physical context, to shared previous experience and to shared cultural assumptions and knowledge. This is one, although not the only reason why Chomsky and his followers draw a contrast between *competence* and *performance* in language capabilities. Because most of what we say does not receive full syntactic articulation, he argues that our competence (our innate and acquired knowledge of linguistic structure) is not matched by our actual performance in real-life situations.[12] For Chomsky, competence is an epistemic relationship to a body of knowledge, rather than a disposition to behave in certain ways in certain circumstances.[13] This is required by the *representational* nature of deep language structures, which, in turn, explain our ability to use and understand sentences that we have not heard before. As such, it bears no relationship to competence as that notion is ordinarily understood, and it is not needed to explain the phenomenon of implicit meaning that we are here discussing.

Any grammar (morphosyntax) of any language that is found in a textbook is nearly always a codification and idealisation of the practice of speakers, put together for a particular purpose. It does not directly prescribe usage (except in specialised formal circumstances, for the purposes of writing or for second language learners for example), but codifies and tidies up the informal rules employed by speakers. For this reason it is not a description of the actual rules used by most speakers. The competence of speakers in this sense is their ability to use the rules that govern effective speaking and listening in a variety of speech situations. An ascription of competence to a speaker does not require us to ascribe propositional knowledge of the morphosyntax as it might be found in a grammar book to that speaker. But neither does it follow, as some cognitivists (including Chomsky) would maintain, that this knowledge is held beyond the limits of conscious awareness. All that follows about competence is that it does not require the production of fully articulated sentences prescribed by a primer of the grammar of the language at all times, but that it does require a matching of grammar and vocabulary to context and personal features of speakers and listeners. Competence is thus an ability to perform in appropriate ways in appropriate circumstances. In Chomsky's sense of 'competence' one can be competent but never perform in appropriate ways in appropriate circumstances, since 'competence' refers, in this sense, to the grammatical knowledge held beyond the level of conscious awareness. But the requirement that we must have such knowledge in order to learn to speak is just what needs to be shown by Chomsky and his followers.

Competence can be extended and there are aspects that require acquaintance with a more formal and codified grammar. Some types of formal speech situation make such requirements. In most languages, mastery of the written form requires that writers have to attend to formal grammar before competence can be achieved. But this does not mean that they then come to rely on a special kind of knowledge that exists beyond the limits of conscious awareness. Rather, they acquire a certain amount of 'knowledge that', and this enables them to become effective writers.

In terms of scientific methodology, the cognitivist explanation of mother tongue language learning is unusual. Since the claim is that knowledge of language is held in the 'mind/brain', one would expect evidence that it was located there. Instead, we are told that phrase structure grammars with a transformational component give a perspicuous representation of certain features of the rules of natural languages.[14] But this is not scientifically acceptable evidence. The theory of the innate mental representation of universal grammar is consistent with a range of possibilities as to what that grammar might be. Chomsky points to certain features of Spanish, for example, that suggest that an inverted tree, rather than a linear structure, is a better representation of some of its features. But these observations cannot lead us to even the tentative conclusion that such structures are actually in some sense representationally instantiated in the brains of individual speakers, without a range of other assumptions being made which effectively rule out alternative explanations. One of the most important of these further assumptions is that a speaker needs already to know a language in order to learn his native language; but, as we have seen, this assumption has serious difficulties associated with it.

What, then, are we to make of the claim that children learn their native language effortlessly and very quickly and that only the presence of innate structures can allow this to happen? That there is some kind of instinctual basis for language learning, which is related to our biological nature, and that this may be particularly active at certain phases, is not particularly controversial. The following two claims made by innatists are, however, more so. The first is that learning language is more a matter of *development* than it is of *acquisition*. Chomsky says, for example,

> Acquisition of language is something that happens to you; it's not something that you do. Learning language is something like undergoing puberty. You don't learn to do it because you see other people doing it; you are just designed to do it at a certain time.[15]

The second controversial point is closely related to the first and implicit in the claims of the quotation above, namely that language learning is something that happens to you 'at a certain time', typically by the age of 4 or 5.[16] Neither of these claims bears much scrutiny, except when interpreted in a very simplistic way. Early language learning requires that infants are trained in certain ways, through, for example, the use of ostensive definition to explain the meanings of some words. The reactive behaviour, which is a response to their early attempts to communicate, first conditions and then trains responses. Later, children learn more actively by asking for the meanings of words.[17] But even at the conditioning and training stages, language learning nearly always involves the learner's active participation through speaking and listening to other people. Were this not to happen, the child would fail to learn to speak. To say that the child makes no effort is simply to misrepresent the process. For a child with limited linguistic resources and competing demands for the attention of his inter-locutors, to make himself understood sometimes requires great efforts. It is perfectly true that a young child seems to be particularly attuned to imitate the phonology of his native language and that he can do this with far less conscious effort than is needed by an adult. But he does not make any conscious effort to learn the grammar of his native language, not because most of it is already there in his mind, but because he does not need to make an effort consciously. But this does not mean that he does not need to make an effort, indeed, and there is plenty of evidence that he does, as can be seen by his hesitations, pauses, mazes and self-correcting behaviour as he learns new vocabulary and structures.

Of course learning something that one does not really learn is going to be effortless, but this is an uninteresting claim. The child learns the rules that govern the language that he is trying to speak and he does this by *participation*, which requires variable degrees of effort. He does not modify an existing body of grammatical knowledge as Chomsky claims, because he does not possess one. We still need some convincing arguments or evidence to the effect (a) that a language acquisition device is a necessary precondition of language learning and (b) that it exists. The claim that language learning is effortless gains its plausibility from concentration on phonology and syntax and even then will not stand up to scrutiny.

It is now generally accepted that although there is a fairly short critical period of language acquisition, it continues up to and including the teens. However, Chomsky seems to want an *a priori* explanation for this, but this explanation is incorrect. He argues that since development of the nervous system takes place until puberty, and since language development is a function of development of the nervous system, then language develop-ment takes place until puberty.[18] But this is a *non sequitur*; it does not follow from the proposition that *a is a function of b*, that whatever occurs in b must occur in a. It is quite possible for an innatist to claim that language development is a function of some aspect of the development of the nervous system which is completed around the age of 5. It could be argued that the long time-scale required for the full acquisition of even the syntactic resources of the mother tongue casts doubt on the innatist hypothesis. For their hypothesis is that the grammar of the language is, in a sense, pre-formed. Therefore, it should be possible for a young child to have acquired all the 'switch settings' after exposure to the range of syn-tactic structures available in the mother tongue. But this does not seem to happen. There is plenty of evidence that language acquisition is a long, drawn-out process which includes periods of regression as well as rapid growth. Fluency and confidence, as well as basic grasp, grow over a long period.[19]

An innatist could argue that certain structures only become available to be 'switched on' as the brain develops over the years to puberty. There is no evidence for this and the claim remains vulnerable to cross-cultural research which could show differences in rates of grammatical development. This is quite likely to be the case when literate and non-literate societies are compared, since the use of many spoken structures (e.g. the passive) tend to be related to their relatively frequent occurrence in writing. In any case, the innatist hypothesis cannot explain regression and slow growth in expertise in a convincing way. He can always appeal to the competence/performance distinction but the more he does so, the more otiose the distinction appears, since the interest in language acquisition relates to performance rather than to competence in the innatist's specialised sense. Any account of language acquisition that is unable to account for specific aspects of the growth in ability to perform (i.e. 'competence' in the everyday sense) is seriously inadequate and there is evidence that the acquisition of grammatical structures is marked by hesitation and a gradual growth in fluency.

> Another process that continues for many years after the age of five is the gradual increase in fluency, with a reduction in the number of mazes and hesitations. In addition, errors of immaturity are slowly eliminated. They include: complex NPs (noun phrases), particularly in subject position; some modal auxiliaries, e.g. *shall, may, ought*; nominal clauses as subjects; adverbial clauses of place, manner, concession and hypothetical condition; non-finite adverbial clauses (apart from those of purpose); relative clauses introduced by *whom, whose*, or a relative pronoun plus a preposition; clausal substitution; some types of ellipsis and all but the commonest sentence connectives.[20]

How does the innatist case fare for the other aspects of language acquisition? Phonology, as we have seen, is largely acquired by imitation. For vocabulary, innatists generally claim that the conceptual structure with which the human mind works is innately given and that we acquire words that are, in most cases, matched with meanings innately acquired.[21] The difficulties about accounting for concept formation from an innatist point of view will be left to the next chapter.

Innatists, developmentalists and behaviourists alike have little of interest to say about the development of *pragmatic* ability, that is, the ability to take part in specific acts of communication. There is, it is true, a certain artificiality in making distinctions between syntax, semantics, pragmatics, etc., as if they were aspects of language that children learned in discrete boxes. Nevertheless, learning to talk and listen in different circumstances is a fundamental part of our ability to speak, and any account of language development that fails to say anything about it is gravely flawed. Innatists could point to a device for the tuning of innate paralinguistic and prosodic features to particular natural languages, and developmentalists could cite the growth of social awareness at particular stages as preconditions for the development of certain kinds of pragmatic ability. But the truth seems to be that neither school really has any evidence to contribute to the debate. Behaviourists can argue that pragmatic and prosodic repertoires can be acquired through imitation and reinforcement, but this claim would be difficult to reconcile with the relative novelty of most of the situations in which we speak to other people. There are simply not enough similarities between one speech situation and another in most cases for it to be possible to say that one is encountering the same situation as one that had previously occurred, although there are enough similarities between them to enable speakers to deal with novelty without too much difficulty. Speech situations have all kinds of subtle variations in terms of personnel, physical surroundings, the history that leads up to the encounter, and the particular social conventions that apply in particular situations, which make the notion of 'the same situation' too vague to be of much use to the behaviourist, who needs a rigorously specified notion of 'the same situation' in order to provide his kind of explanation.

Much can be said about language acquisition and it is easier to say once the mysteries of behaviourist, developmentalist and innatist theories have been dispelled. The apparent novelty involved in understanding and producing sentences not heard before need not be a mystery requiring an innate device to explain it. If we return to the view, argued for in Chapter 4, that human life is social and rule-governed, and if we remind ourselves about some of the biological limiting features of human life that are to be found in all communities – namely the need for comfort, shelter and food – then the observable features of language acquisition that we can gain by prolonged and careful observation will not seem particularly mysterious. There is now a large body of observational data on the history of how children actually go about acquiring their native tongue and, if we look at it, we will see that it is readily accommodated into a general picture of human beings as social, rule-following creatures with a certain biological nature, who learn to communicate by participating in the rule-governed social world into which they are born.[22] It does not yield us a theory of language acquisition but does provide a reasonably reliable account of the process for most children.

9

LEARNING AND CONCEPT FORMATION

Introduction: the importance of the question

As we learn to make our way in the world, we learn to recognise individual things as instances of certain *kinds*. Animals can do this as well; their ability to recognise sources of food, danger and so on is essential to their well-being and survival. But in human beings this recognitional ability is not only more complex, it is also largely bound up with the use of language. In acts of judgement, questioning, wishing, promising and so on, we make distinctions that underpin our ability to distinguish between truth and falsehood, between compliance and non-compliance, between fulfil-ment and non-fulfilment and between sincerity and insincerity. Animal recognitional abilities, together with non-discursive agreements in judge-ment, form the bedrock of the complex of discursive concept-using abilities that are exercised in everyday life.[1] Learning, then, involves the acquisition and the exercise of these complex recognitional abilities, both dis-cursively and also in non-linguistic acts of judgement, etc. which are nevertheless language dependent. These abilities are essential to both the practical and the theoretical side of our life.

These recognitional abilities are called *concepts* and it is the acquisition of concepts that forms the subject of this chapter. On this matter there is a significant divergence between Cartesianism and empiricism, although both traditions locate the acquisition of concepts within the mind of an *ab initio* solitary, rather than an individual born into a social milieu. Both traditions remain influential, although they have been challenged, notably by philosophers working in a Wittgensteinian tradition.[2] More recently, there have been attempts both to revive the Cartesian tradition and to redefine empiricism with some help from the Cartesian tradition.[3]

Abstractionism

According to Locke, ideas originate through the senses and we then form more general ideas of classes of things on the basis of working with the material provided by ideas derived from the senses. We thus acquire the concept of F-ness first by being acquainted with a range of particular ideas that are F, then by noticing what they have in common, and finally by taking what they have in common and making that a distinct idea. When, for example, I am presented with red things, I notice that they have something in common and form a distinct idea of that common feature which I can then label 'red'. Thus I form the concept *red*.

It is by now fairly commonplace to say that abstractionism is a non-starter as it presupposes the very ability that it seeks to account for.[4] The objection runs as follows. It is alleged that the concept F is formed by attending to a, b, c, etc. and noticing that they are all F. The common feature of F-ness is then abstracted from them and is formed as a distinct idea. The concept of F cannot arise without prior exposure to instances of particulars that are F, the presentation of which are necessary conditions for the formation of the concept F.[5] But how could someone notice that a, b and c were all F unless he could already bring them under the concept F? If he could do this, he would already possess the concept F and the claim that abstraction could yield the concept would be superfluous, since it would have to be held innately for such a claim to hold true and a vicious regress avoided.

The objection, however, is a little hasty. It presupposes that the concept F is formed by someone *attending* to particulars that are F and then *noticing* that they have a certain quality in common. If that is how abstractionists were committed to accounting for how F was formed, it would be a decisive objection. For in attending to particulars and noticing that they are similar in some respect I would have to be exercising an act of judgement (in Rousseau's sense of passive judgement). I would notice that a is F, b is F, and so on, and then judge that they were all F. In making that judgement I would be exercising the concept F, and if I were doing so, I would already possess the concept. But it is not clear that the empiricist is committed to this account of abstraction. He is committed to the view that a necessary condition for the formation of a concept is that instances of it are presented in experience and that the concept is acquired as a result of that experience. But these two commitments do not of themselves compel him to a circular account of concept formation.

If the possession of a concept is, at the most basic level, possession of a non-discursive recognitional ability, then it can be acquired through the possession of an innate *capacity*. This is something that no empiricist has denied: indeed, Locke insists that the mind does have innate capacities in order to work on the raw material presented by sense data.[6] All that is then required is that the mind is presented with a, b and c which are all F and then, *without any act of judgement, let alone conscious judgement*, forms the concept of F by abstracting what is common to a, b and c. An innate capacity for abstraction is brought into play and, as a result, a recognitional ability that previously did not exist has now been acquired.[7] Such a capacity need not itself be conceptual, although on a representationalist account it would have to be. If it is a conceptual process, then abstractionism would require innate concepts which would undermine its value as an account of how concepts can be formed from experience. If abstraction is conceived of as a mechanical process, it would not have to be conceptual. In that case, not only would abstractionism not be viciously circular, it would not presuppose any conceptual ability either.[8] Only in the noticing of ideas already formed would the recognition of concepts occur.[9]

Yet this story comes at a cost. It has difficulty in accounting for the formation of concepts that are not derived in any obvious way from sensory experience. Neither is the postulation of an innate recognitional capacity without its difficulties. The most obvious of these relates to a principle to which appeal was made by D'Agostino in his critique of empiricism, namely that it is less economical in explanatory terms than an innatist account. If concepts are innate ideas, then there is no need to postulate an underlying recognitional *capacity* for the generation of concepts, as empiricism needs to. All that a neonate has to do is to match the words of his mother tongue to ideas already held in the mind. There need not be anything mysterious about this; by attending and participating in everyday life, the neonate can relatively quickly succeed in making the necessary matchings.

But there is a graver difficulty, pointed to by Berkeley and Hume, which is that of showing how a singular idea could represent a general idea. Any impression or idea has some individual qualities. The idea of a triangle has to be, for example, equilateral, isosceles or scalene; it cannot be all of these things at the same time. If it is one of them then it cannot represent triangles in general. Abstractionism, in suggesting that general ideas are representatives of the general features of kinds, *through their resemblance properties*, is unable to show how something could be an image of a kind without at the same time being an image of some particular. It was in order to get around this difficulty that Hume developed an *associationist* account of concept formation.[10]

Associationism

Berkeley and Hume rejected the abstractionist account of concepts and their formation because they considered the notion of an abstract idea to be unintelligible.[11] Particular ideas, they held, *could* have a general application in the right circumstances. When I form the concept of a triangle, I form the idea of numerous particular triangles. One of these triangles, say an equilateral, is customarily associated with the word 'triangle' and for ordinary purposes will serve as the signification of that term. But by 'custom' (in Hume's peculiar sense of mental faculty), this triangle-idea is associated with other triangle-ideas which can be called up as and when necessary. So, for example, if it is asserted that all the sides of a triangle are equal in length, the customary association of the equilateral with the image of isosceles and scalene triangles will call these other ones up and move us to reject the proposition.[12]

Associationism avoids some of the difficulties of abstractionism and the apparent incoherence of the notion of a general idea. But the difficulties with it were pointed out by Wittgenstein and are to do with the impossibility of attaching a sense to the notion of 'the same idea'. If we grant that it is difficult to see how the same idea could exist in the minds of different people, could we not, nevertheless, admit that the same idea can persist in the mind of one person? So there would be problems about the discursive use of concepts, but not about their individual use. Once an individual use had been established, however, agreement in definition of the use of terms could suffice to make communication possible.

The difficulty with this proposal lies in the fact that if no clear sense can be attached to 'the same idea' in one person's mind, then it is not possible to form concepts as ideas.[13] Berkeley proposes that agreement in definitions can allow us to communicate without recourse to direct referral to ideas, but he also thinks that language can easily distort our thoughts.[14] But if we are unable to form concepts in the first place, this route to the discursive employment of concepts is not available. The difficulty of re-identifying 'the same idea' is precisely the difficulty suggested by Wittgenstein; if there is no criterion of right or wrong identification, then there is no coherent use of the phrase 'the same idea' either. If this is the case then custom cannot associate an idea with a word, even a private signification for the idea, hence the possibility of being able to handle concepts in thought will not be available. This remains the case even where thought takes place directly, without the intermediary of names for the ideas, since the question of the identity of the ideas posed the difficulty for accounting for a language naming the ideas in the first place. The source of the difficulty rests, then, in the possibility of providing meaningful criteria of identity for ideas/concepts. This, incidentally, is also true of the general ideas proposed by abstractionists.

Innatism: the Cartesian account of concept formation

Innatism in its strongest form holds that all concepts are present in the mind at birth. What we ordinarily call concept formation is the fitting of linguistic labels on to already held concepts.

> In fact, try to define a word like 'table' or 'book' or whatever, and you'll find that it's extremely difficult. There is, in fact – just

to give one example – a recent issue of a linguistics journal that has a long detailed article trying to give the meaning of the word 'climb'. And it is very complicated. But every child learns it perfectly right away. Now that can only mean one thing. Namely, human nature gives us the concept 'climb' for free. That is, the concept 'climb' is just part of the way in which we are able to interpret experience available to us before we even have the experience. That is probably true for most concepts that have words for them in language. This is the way we learn language. We simply learn the label that goes with the preexisting concept. So in other words, it is as if the child, prior to any experience, has a long list of concepts like 'climb', and then the child is looking at the world to figure out which sound goes with the concept. We know that the child figures it out with only a very small number of presentations of the sound.[15]

It is highly unlikely that a child could gain a perfect acquisition of the concept *climb* 'right away'. He might well learn a range of correct usages for the term 'climb' in a relatively short period of time, but it is unlikely that he will be able to grasp the full range of the concept for a long period, particularly when it is used in an analogically extended way in, for example, the idea of social climbing. Much of the difficulty relates to the fact that many concepts are best seen as *family resemblances*. They are not susceptible to a ready definition and are not used in accordance with definitions. Instead, they are arrays of overlapping similarities in usage whose identification and successful use is often dependent on context.[16] And there will be variations in the application of the concepts according to different languages and cultures. In one language, for example, it might be the case that only animals with limbs can climb, so that the ascent of a tree by a snake would require a different word to describe it. We would be inclined to say that there are cross-cultural and linguistic variations in concepts, but the innatist could not say that; he would have to say that the same concept had different words for different usages or that the ascent of snakes and the ascent of limbed creatures were simply different concepts.

The first response suggests an important concession to the view that concept formation is related to mastery of linguistic usage; the second response leaves a hostage to fortune in the shape of the known cross-cultural variation in the range of possible different concepts, If different usages reflect different concepts, then the innatist account risks the fragmentation of innate concepts according to different linguistic usages. But despite these difficulties, it is maintained that innatism has distinct advantages over empiricist accounts for other reasons.

One argument, due to Fodor, is that the only psychological theory of learning that has ever seriously been developed is that of learning by hypothesis formation and testing.[17] In order to learn the meaning of the word 'cat', a child would have to form hypotheses about what the word could correctly apply to and then test that hypothesis against the available data. An initial hypothesis might be that the word 'cat' applies to what adults would call 'animals', and so in due course the hypothesis would come to be modified, until it corresponded with the adult use of the word. However, in order to form these hypotheses about the meanings of words it is first necessary to possess the concept that one wishes to test. Hence concepts are innate, otherwise we would not be able to learn to use concept words. It is important to note, though, that this line of argument does not show that the concept *cat* is innate, only that some concept that serves as part of a hypothesis about cats is. This undermines Chomsky's claim in the passage above that such a concept is innate.

One major problem with this line of argument is that learning by hypothesis-testing is not the only way of learning. We can also learn through training and practice and through the application of attention and memory. Indeed, most people who had not reflected in a philosophical way about the matter would probably say that these were the ways in which people commonly learned. If concept formation can be explained through practice and memory applied to experience, then the innate possession of concepts no longer seems necessary.

There is a tension, therefore, in innatist claims about concept formation. On the one hand, if all concepts are innate, then the only hypotheses one could meaningfully form would be about the words that express those concepts. This leads to the difficulties mentioned earlier. On the other hand, if one *forms* concepts through the testing of hypotheses, then all one needs to possess is a set of conceptual archetypes (presumably encoded in the language of thought) capable of serving as hypotheses for the generation of further concepts. Once again, the claim that early learning can only take place through hypothesis formation and testing is simply not plausible.

Carruthers' modified empiricism

The difficulties with traditional empiricism relate to the doctrine of sense data, an imagist account of thinking, and the doctrine of innate mental faculties. If these lead to insuperable difficulties, are we forced to abandon the idea that conceptual structure is, in some way, based on experience and to embrace innatism in its entirety? One recent writer who does not think so is Peter Carruthers. He proposes a modified account of empiricism that strips away the sense datum doctrine and the imagist account of thought, and makes some concessions to innatism without accepting any pictorial theory of representation. In this way he hopes to make intelligible the idea that we acquire at least some of our concepts through experience.

He distinguishes between three senses in which it is possible to possess a concept.

1   *As the possession of a discriminatory capacity* Animals, who are evidently able to distinguish between different features of their environment, are able to and do possess concepts. They have such capacities both through instinct and through learning. There is also evidence that they can be conditioned to discriminate *under certain conditions* between certain kinds of things that it is commonly thought only humans can. In this sense, pigeons can be conditioned to peck only at pictures with humans on and, in a sense, will then be able to recognise humans and so possess the concept *human*. Some commentators seem to be unaware that there could be any difficulty in attributing the same kinds of recognitional capacity in animals as in humans and calling it *concept possession*. The fact that animals lack a language is not thought to be a problem provided they show their ability to recognise in some other way.[18]

2   *As the possession of beliefs and desires associated with a discriminatory capacity* In this sense, it is not thought sufficient that an animal possesses a recognitional capacity, but that it also demonstrates that it possesses certain beliefs and desires associated with that capacity. It would be possible, for example, to attribute to a dog the concept *being taken for a walk by owner*, if the dog was in fact able to discriminate between walk-associated and non-walk-associated features of its immediate environment. It might also be able to anticipate being taken for a walk by the presence of certain signs in its immediate environment; for example, its owner putting on a coat. The dog may well desire to go for a walk and manifest that desire in anticipatory behaviour. Through so doing, it also manifests a *belief* that it is going to be taken for a walk. It may also manifest this belief by, for example, picking up its lead in its mouth and bringing it to its owner. We might even explain the dog's action by saying that given its *desire* to go for a walk and its *belief* that it was going to be taken for a walk, it picked up the lead in its mouth and brought it to its owner. We do not have to ascribe consciously articulated thoughts to the dog or the ability to explain its actions. All we need to say is that the dog's actions can be explained on a desire + belief = intention/action model.[19]

3   *Being able to entertain conscious thoughts in which the concept occurs* In this sense, possession of the ability to use correctly the corresponding term of a natural language would be a sufficient condition for the possession of a concept.[20] One might argue that the requirement of entertaining conscious thoughts is too hard. One can certainly employ the concept in judgement without necessarily entertaining a conscious thought at the same time. More fundamentally perhaps, the

notion of *entertaining conscious thoughts* needs careful handling. To be conscious and to speak thoughtfully about something does not imply that one is having conscious thoughts, in the sense that there is some kind of accompaniment to one's thinking. One may say then that possession of a concept, in the sense in which humans may be said to possess concepts, depends on their ability to use language and to make discursive judgements in which the concepts are employed. In doing so they are not necessarily entertaining conscious thoughts in which the concepts occur. Carruthers seems to have missed a level at which it is possible to say that one can possess a concept. Possession of concepts in this linguistic sense is, then, a necessary condition for possession of concepts in the sense of having the ability to entertain conscious thoughts, an ability which can be characterised, following Geach as an analogous extension of our ability to make judgements linguistically.[21]

Carruthers is sceptical both about the claim that learning must take place through hypothesis-testing, and the claim that thinking takes place in a language of thought, both of which entail innate concepts. He inclines to the idea that some concepts are formed from *prototypes*. Initially, one learns *paradigms*. For example, I see a cat and remember what it is like. I then judge whether other things are sufficiently similar to the paradigm to be classified in the same way. I am aided in this process by correction and further exemplification, so that I do not over- or under-extend the concept. I then acquire other paradigms, like *tail*, *whiskers* and so on. A prototype is a weighted array of paradigms out of which various sufficient sets of paradigms can be constructed that will count as an instance of a concept.[22] For example, the concept *dog* will consist of a set consisting of: *barks*, *mammal*, *wags tail* and so on. Carruthers argues that complex concepts can be built up from prototypes by, for example, logical multiplication, so the concept *brown cow* can be arrived at by joining the concept *brown* to the concept *cow*. However, he thinks that the ability to form complex concepts is dependent on innate logical concepts such as *and*,[23] and that the ability to appraise non-deductive arguments is innate.

Prototype theory is a revised version of Hume and Berkeley's associationism. Paradigms are ideas (in this case, perceptions rather than sense data, and laid down in memory); they are concatenated associatively (barks, wags tail, has fur, etc.) and can serve in reasoning in the way that Humean ideas can. For example, if it is asserted that all dogs are less than 1 foot high, the paradigm of an alsatian can be called up to enable me to reject this proposition. Hume's proposal founders on the private language argument, but need the modern version do the same? If concept formation proceeds *ab initio* through the acquisition of paradigms, then the answer must be 'yes', for the theory is then one that is essentially of the same sort as that of Berkeley or Hume. If, on the other hand, it does not, then some further account of paradigm formation is needed in order to explain how the process gets going. The innate capacities for deductive and non-deductive inference that Carruthers postulates will not do this of them-selves, for they need empirical raw material to work on, and it is the availability of this raw material that is in question.

There are, then, a number of objections to Carruthers' modified empiri-cist account of concept formation. First, he neglects to provide two senses in which conceptual ability can be said to be acquired; as non-discursive agreement in judgement and as linguistic ability. Second, the postulation of an innate reasoning ability seems to be required more by prototype theory than by the intrinsic plausibility of such a proposal. Third, prototype theory is not sufficiently distinguishable from associationism to provide an alternative empiricist account of concept formation which meets the well-known difficulty advanced by Wittgenstein.

A different view of concept formation

Neither empiricism not innatism can account for the human ability to acquire and use concepts. What, then, is the alternative? A good place to start would be to remind ourselves of Carruthers' distinctions between senses of the term 'concept' and to see if there are any distinctions that he failed to make. Among these are, first of all, the idea of *agreement in judgement*, that is, the patterns of actions and reactions that show non-discursively what we are certain about: for example, that some things are relatively permanent, that our appearance is not constantly changing, or that we use the same terms for the same things.[24] Such patterns of judge-ment underlie our *specific* judgements. Second, the exercise of concepts as recognitional capacities connected with action presupposes, in its full rich-ness, their employment in language, without presupposing that they are exercised in a parallel mental medium of thought.

I will follow Geach in describing concepts as abilities exercised in acts of judgement.[25] More specifically they are abilities to follow rules for the use of words or other non-sentential expressions.[26] When someone acquires a concept, they have acquired, in the first instance, the ability to use the word or phrase that expresses that concept in an assertion or other speech act. This is likely to mean that they are able to use the word in an enormous variety of different contexts and in different sentences not uttered before to make (in the main), correct judgements. It does not mean that the rules for the use of concepts need to be determinate and laid down in a canonical form. It is sufficient that they be adhered to tacitly in the everyday usage of the linguistic community to which the speaker belongs. To say that possession of a concept is tantamount to possession of an ability might seem to *individualise* concepts. The danger would be that there are as many different concepts of, say, *red* as there are users of the term 'red'. This, as Geach points out, is not the case. Just as there is no contradiction in saying that being able to swim is an ability of individuals and saying that a group of individuals have the same ability, namely that of being able to swim, so there is no contradiction in saying that possession of a concept is a capacity of an individual and saying that different individuals possess the same concept.[27] The concept is individuated by a network of common use, unlike the mental images that Hume hoped would stand in for common concepts, which must be individuated to particular minds. This account has the immediate virtue of being able to explain the family resemblance nature of much of our conceptual structure; in mastering the network of uses that amounts to mastery of a concept like 'game', we master the similarities and differences between the uses of the term in different contexts.

Concepts are abilities exercised in assertion, commanding, promising and so on. In this sense they are linguistic abilities. But they are also abilities exercised in acts of *judgement* which need not be articulated. But these abilities are dependent on the use of language – as Geach puts it, they are *analogical extensions* of the exercise of our conceptual abilities in overt linguistic acts.[28] So concepts can be exercised in acts of mind, but these are neither temporally nor conceptually prior to their discursive exercise in communication with others, and subsequently private linguistic use. As has been argued, the exercise of concepts in soliloquy is not intelligible if it is taken to be the exercise of an ability *prior* to its use in language. The analogy with the exercise of concepts in speech is not just that the one is audible while the other is silent. Assertions, acts of promising, etc. not only can be dated, they can also be timed. Although not often done, it is possible to say that it took so many seconds to make a promise. Although one can say with some degree of precision *when* someone performs a silent act of judgement, it makes no sense to say *how long* that act of judgement took.

The role of experience

We want to be able to say that, in some non-trivial sense, concepts relate to experience and are largely formed through experiential learning. Three accounts of how this takes place, namely abstractionism, associationism and prototype theory, have been rejected. A more illuminating way of looking at the matter is to draw attention to the development of discriminatory abilities that are closely connected with motivation and action. Babies soon develop these and the process can be seen in animals as well. But in human learning, such abilities are the background against which language use develops. Above all, it is through the social and participatory experience of using language and following rules in which judgements, questions and so on are used in ordinary human transactions, that the acquisition of concepts takes place.

Concepts are not acquired in one go, as Chomsky suggests, but instead develop over time and are used for a while in an incomplete form. There is evidence to suggest that not only do children go through a period where they have only a partial understanding of concepts, but that they put a great deal of effort into extending and clarifying their conceptual competence. The limited knowledge that young children have can plausibly be described, at least in part, as the incomplete possession of a range of concepts.[29] But it also means that with the partial acquisition of a range of concepts, mistakes are possible. To take an example of Tizard and Hughes,[30] if a child has an incomplete grasp of the concept of money, realising that it is a medium of payment for goods and services rendered, it does not follow that the child will recognise that there is an associated practice of giving change, and may instead see the act of giving change as a kind of gift-giving on the part of the buyer.

However, this does not mean that the child has a different concept of money to that of the average adult, merely that a partial grasp of the concept of money has led to an incomplete understanding of the significance of certain acts of monetary exchange. The Chomskyan version of innatism has some difficulty with this, as the possession of concepts is thought to be an all-or-nothing affair. Some writers influenced by cognitivism have thought that children actually possess different concepts from those of adults. If one accepts Fodor's thesis that learning takes place through hypothesis-testing, this is not so implausible. Each child has a self-contained theory of what the world is like, with its own conceptual structure, which is gradually modified by experience until it resembles the one held by most adults. However, this has the following consequence: a child who understands the concept of birth to mean only live birth has a different concept to someone who understands that birth can occur through, say, hatching. They actually mean different things by the word 'birth'.[31] But this is misleading. All we need to say is that the child has a limited knowledge of how different animals are born and an increase in knowledge will develop the child's own possession of the concept of birth more fully. If children actually use different concepts from adults in a wide range of cases, then it is difficult to see how adult–child communication could be possible.

It is evident that there is a great deal of tension within cognitivism over the question as to whether or not concepts are innate and the contention that learning takes place through hypothesis-testing. If concepts are innate, then the only learning that can reasonably take place concerns the meanings of words in the mother tongue. But this is implausible as an account of what happens when a child forms the concept of *birth*. If the concept is innate, then it is difficult to see why the child does not possess it as a unity – why should a child not be able to recognise that live birth is a specific example of a more general case? To say that he has not properly acquired the meaning of the word 'birth' is not to say that a concept has been mislabelled, because the concept *birth* in this instance has not been mislabelled; 'birth' does apply to live birth, among other phenomena. Maintaining that it is a different concept muddies the waters still further – do children have *inappropriate* innate concepts, from which they gradually, through hypothesis-testing, form appropriate ones? The implausibility of such ideas has already been discussed in Chapter 7.

It is much easier and much more plausible to say that children acquire concepts through participation in human life and their growing use of language and that, in the initial stages, their concepts are partial, incomplete and, on occasion, mistaken in certain respects. The formation of concepts is a gradual process that takes place through *experience* understood in a philosophically non-problematic sense. What might plausibly be held to be *innate* are the capacities to participate in reactive behaviour, to follow rules, to learn to speak and to be motivated to extend one's conceptual repertoire.

This is not a *theory* of concept formation, but a set of reminders about how young humans acquire concepts. It will be inadequate as a set of reminders if it fails to take account of certain important phenomena. The most important of these will be looked at below.

Family resemblance concepts

Many concepts are neither acquired by using definitions nor do they depend on definitions for their use. Their meaning is to some extent context-dependent and consists of a series of overlapping common features, none of which covers the whole range of usages of the concept. Wittgenstein uses the term 'family resemblance' to describe these loosely associated and ramified concepts. Examples are *game*, *language* and *thinking*, and there are many others that are central to human life.[32] It could be objected that it is possible, with sufficient ingenuity, to provide definitions for many or all of these concepts. But this is to miss the point: they do not depend on definitions for their use and neither are they learned through definition. A definition is always vulnerable to a previously unnoticed, but quite acceptable use of a term and it is possible for someone to have a good understanding of the meaning of a family resemblance concept without either being able to formulate a definition or being acquainted with every usage, which may vary from context to context.

Theories that presuppose that there is something essential to any concept that we need to acquire before we can be said to understand it, have a difficulty with accounting for family resemblance concepts. Associationism postulates a determinate set of ideas held together by a common resemblance; abstractionism postulates a common general form; prototype theory a determinate set of paradigms; and innatism a determinate set of features. None of these is necessary for a family resemblance concept; they are acquired by learning the use of words such as 'game', 'thinking' and so on in different contexts.

It might be objected to this account that the alleged rules are not clearly definable, that they are a tangle of context-dependent norms from which no clear principles of application can be extracted. And, if this is so, then it is not clear how the rules could be taught to anyone. But this objection is not serious. The rules for the use of words are indeed often complex, context-dependent and not fully articulable. In other cases, however, they may be clear and defined. Although the rules for many of our words and concepts are vague in this way, it does not follow that they are not teachable. It may be difficult to teach some of them fully by certain methods, such as instruction and definition, but other approaches (like participation in activities in which the concepts are used by others who have a full command) are likely to be effective and they are then learned as part of learning one's native language. They can then by applied in an analogous way in silent acts of judgement and so on. Some concepts, on the other hand, may be more amenable to learning through the memoris-ation of definitions followed by practice in the use of words.

Why animals do not possess concepts in the full sense

When it is claimed that animals can form and use concepts, different levels of discriminatory ability are confused. Animals are capable of possessing reactions and discriminatory abilities that enable them not only to survive but also to form *beliefs* which, when described by us, would involve the use of concepts. Animal beliefs are, however, non-discursive and do not involve the exercise of concepts except in this very limited sense.

Natural kind concepts

According to Aristotle, some things are what they are in virtue of intrinsic natural properties. Plants and animals are among these *natural kinds*. Concepts of these are formed in the same way that any other concepts are formed, through the use of the concept words in a range of different contexts. Leaving aside the question as to whether or not there are intrinsic natural properties recognised by the use of such concepts, an everyday understanding of natural kind concepts does not pose a particular problem.[33]

Concepts employed in reasoning

Those who argue that concept formation takes place through the testing of hypotheses have to assume that there is an intellectual apparatus that allows this to take place. As we saw, Carruthers argues that deductive and non-deductive inference must be innate. In the latter case he argues that this involves possession of the concept of *inference to the best explanation*. The possession of this concept is innate, it is argued, because its prototype structure cannot be derived from experience, nor do children need to be trained in order to be able to use it.

Some of the marks of the concept *inference to the best explanation* are: that it is *simple, consistent, coheres well with surrounding beliefs, is broad in scope, and fruitful in generating new predictions.* Carruthers also claims that the concept of inference to the best explanation is *normative*. The virtues of this account of inference seem to be that:

1   It is sufficiently general to explain local variations in the ability to infer among different sections of the human species.
2   It can account for practical as well as theoretical reasoning ability.
3   It is a plausible mechanism to explain the evolutionary adaptivity of the human race.

There are, however, some difficulties. The first of these is that one could be in possession of an innate ability to infer to the best explanation without having the concept of *inference to the best explanation*. Indeed, this seems quite likely, since the concept has recently been introduced into philosophy as a technical term for certain kinds of inference. So it is not at all clear that the ability in question requires possession of a concept of it, any more than possession of the ability to walk requires possession of the concept of *locomotion*.

Second, the concept is *normative*, as Carruthers acknowledges. It implies that it itself is a standard against which actual explanations are to be measured. This seems to be difficult to reconcile with its innateness. To say that an explanation is the best available is to say that, measured against existing social practice, it is more effective in the contexts in which it is employed than any other explanation. Carruthers concedes that what is to count as a best explanation will depend on the context and set of issues in which that explanation is framed. If this is so, then the concept becomes relativised to the norms of explanation that exist in relation to different kinds of activity in different cultures. But once this is conceded, it is hard to see how such a variegated concept could be innate: for explanations are judged to be good or bad, convincing or unconvincing, appropriate or inappropriate, according to the rules prevailing for those activities in those cultures. These rules are themselves socially constituted; there is no such thing as a natural rule. If this is so, then the idea of an innate concept of *inference to the best explanation* is chimerical.

It might be replied that the rules to which *inference to the best explanation* appeals are like Wittgenstein's rules of cooking; that is, they are rules given by nature rather than by man. Thus, the rules for making a cake relate to the natural properties of the ingredients rather than to the arbitrary norms of a society which may set out, for example, when cakes may and when they may not be eaten. The problem with this riposte however, is that it is the *naturalness* of the norms that is in question. There does not seem to be a good reason why all our explanations are dictated by nature in the sense that rules of cooking can be said to be.[34] True, like rules of cooking, rules for inferring to the best explanation appear to be *teleological*, but this does not imply being natural in the relevant sense. When we infer, we use rules that we hope will give us the best available explanation for the phenomenon in question. But if what is to count as the best explanation is dependent on the context and culture in which the explanation is required, it is hard to see how it could only be subject to natural constraints. An explanation for why somebody misbehaved, for example, might refer to constraints and temptations which could only be properly understood in the context of that particular society. We might wish to look for an explanation in terms of physical dysfunction, but that might only be in particular cultural traditions where such explanations were regarded as acceptable ways of explaining human behaviour and even then, perhaps, only in certain circumstances. To conclude, the *normativity* of inference to the best explanation seems to rule it out as an innate concept.

Third, the concept of inference to the best explanation seems itself to be compositionally complex, and, if it is innate, presupposes the innateness of other concepts. Carruthers does not see this as a problem: 'the constituent notions are no easier to define in their turn; nor is it easy to see how they might be derived from experience'.[35] This seems odd. Concepts like *consistency* and *simplicity* seem to be learned concepts. We learn to use them in a variety of contexts. What is more, some at least are *qua* concepts and thus highly context-dependent in their applications. For example, a mathematical problem may be simple *qua* undergraduate mathematics but hopelessly complicated *qua* primary school mathematics. We learn about the *qua* nature of the concept of simplicity in relation to the various activities in which we engage as children. We then learn to extend it in the course of adult life. It is always possible to say without contradiction, 'He understands what simplicity is in relation to his everyday life but has no idea what it means in the context of physical science.'

Far from it being difficult to see how such concepts could be acquired through experience, as Carruthers maintains, it is difficult to see how they could be acquired otherwise. The traditional type of empiricist might well have difficulty with them, it is true, but this is because he wishes to tie the formation of concepts quite strictly to sensory experience in the form of impressions or sense data: this will not work very well, if at all, for concepts like *consistency*. But this is a problem for traditional empiricism rather than a triumph for the innatist hypothesis. An alternative explanation for the formation of the concept of *consistency* is that it is gained through participation in activities in which consistency matters, whether it be in argument, the holding of opinions, the adherence to friendships, standards of workmanship, and so on. Although there will be variations in what the concept amounts to in different contexts, there will be enough of a family resemblance between its different applications to allow us to talk of a single, though variegated concept. The way in which family resemblance concepts are typically built up is by learning the application of a term in a range of different contexts related to one another in various ways. This account will allow us to take account of the *qua* nature of the concept and of the fact that one's grasp of it is, to some extent, context-relative. The arguments for saying that the marks of the concept *inference to the best explanation* are innate are not convincing and appear to rely implicitly on the truth of the empiricist account of concept formation for concepts derived from experience. However, a better account is available; one that need not tempt us to see either the concept or the associated ability as innate.

Conclusion

Various forms of empiricist and innatist accounts of concept formation have been examined and found to be inadequate. The alternative is not to put forward a new theory of concept formation but to see it as bound up with the learning of language in the fullest sense. It is also bound up with the language-related abilities of speaking to oneself, entertaining thoughts, and forming judgements 'in the mind' without asserting them. To learn to make inferences is to learn to take part in a variety of language-based activities in which the giving of reasons for or against conclusions or actions plays an important role. The scope of such activities is constrained by very general facts of nature but such limits do not make our reasoning innate.

This is not to say that 'anything goes' as regards the concepts that we could possibly have. Our size and natural powers, our relation to the natural world, and very general features of nature and of our primitive reactive behaviour set limits on what concepts it would be intelligible for us to form, including inferential concepts. But it is misleading to say that these constraints cause us in some way (perhaps by natural selection) to possess concepts innately.

10

MEMORY AND LEARNING

When something has been learned then it has, in some sense, been retained for future use. Our ability to do this is *memory* and it is fundamental to learning. Gaining clarity about memory and its relationship to learning in contemporary societies is the principal theme of this chapter.

Aspects of memory

The phenomena of memory are extremely varied and affect all aspects of human life in such a way as to provide sense and continuity to virtually everything that we do. The following list of abilities that depend on memory is not exhaustive, but it covers the central areas of my concern:

1 the ability to fly an aeroplane, examine a witness, play a game of chess;
2 the recall of facts;
3 the recollection of personal experience.

Ability (3) above has usually been taken to be the paradigm of memory for philosophers (with (2) as a possible subsidiary). Personal recollection is thought to be of particular philosophical importance because personal identity is said to be bound up with the ability to recall past experiences as the experiences of a particular person. This kind of memory is also important to us in an everyday sense. The affective reactions of pleasure, longing, sadness, regret and contentment that we feel about aspects of our lives are closely tied in with the act of recollection and cannot readily be understood separately from them.[1] However important personal recollection is to philosophers on a theoretical level (and is to all of us on a personal level), over-concentration on it has tended to distort our concept of memory and has stopped us from fully appreciating its importance for human learning.

Accounts of memory

Representation

Some of the earliest accounts of memory such as that of Aristotle and Augustine stress the *representational* character of memory imagery and, in the case of Augustine, the conceptualisation of the memory as a kind of storehouse of representations.[2] In the act of memory, according to Augustine, these representations are retrieved and re-presented in immediate personal experience. In Locke, the ideas that are formed from initial experience are stored and become available again in acts of memory.[3] Hume's account attempts to show how the pastness of ideas is signified through their being etiolated versions of impressions. An etiolated (memory) image is to be distinguished from a product of the imagination by the fact that it is a copy of what is remembered, whereas a product of the imagination is a recombination of elements of other ideas.[4]

This is not the place in which to offer a thoroughgoing critique of the representational theory, but it will be clear from the preceding chapters that any representational account of the workings of the mind that assumes either that it is private in the empiricist sense or *ab initio* solitary in the modern cognitivists' sense, is going to be vulnerable to the criticisms already advanced in Chapters 4 and 6. In this chapter, one very influential version of the representational theory, the trace theory, will be subjected to detailed analysis and criticism.

Realism

The traditional rival to the representational theory of memory is the *realist* theory. Simply stated, it claims that in recall we have direct experience of the past, rather than a representational image of it; it should, therefore, avoid the pitfalls that we have already noticed in connection with the representational theory. According to this, memory claims are nothing more than claims to knowledge about the past. My claim to remember that p is a claim to remember that p has occurred or a claim to know that p when p is a proposition in the past tense. Memory is thus a particular case of knowledge. The realist theory appears to avoid relying on a particular phenomenology of imagery and concentrates on the distinctive character of memory claims, namely, their concern with the past. It also circumvents the problem, faced by the representational theory, of explaining how memory claims in general can be distinguished from correct memory claims on the one hand, and incorrect memory claims on the other. According to realism, the verification of memory will occur just like the verification of other claims, through cross-checking with other sources of knowledge.

However, realism, like representationalism, also maintains that remembering is a specific act engaged in by the person remembering. When something is remembered, then a specific act has taken place. But what act? Remembering is associated with diverse phenomena. Thus, when I remember that I gave an appalling lecture last week, I may have certain images of my stumbling performance: I may say to my colleagues, 'That was a dreadful performance that I gave last week' or I may break out in a hot flush. These are signs that I have remembered. But, as Malcolm points out, such signs can indicate both veridical and non-veridical acts of memory. Although I blush with embarrassment at the thought of the dreadful lecture delivered last week, I may actually be recalling a lecture given at the beginning of my career, a bad dream or even the experience of someone else whose lecture I had sat through. It is only in a certain context that a particular occurrence could be taken to be a sign of recall and in this example, the context requires further specification. There is no one act that constitutes veridical memory recall. Realism seems to be committed to there being such an act.[5]

Locke and Hume wished to give an account of memory that was context-free, but were unable to isolate the properties of imagery that would make it memory imagery rather than some other kind of imagery. Both in the case of imagery and in the case of external signs of remembering, *that* the signs are signs of remembering depends on the context in which they occur. There needs to be a connection between an utterance, a gesture or an image and *what is remembered*, and this can only occur within a broader context. Thus, a blush can be a sign of recall of a shameful *past* occurrence rather than the sign of a *present* embarrassing occurrence because the particular context makes it so. For example, I may be talking about a particular topic with colleagues and then remember the embarrassingly bad lecture that I gave on that topic. In this case, there is no *one* occurrence that we could say is necessary to my remembering the embarrassing lecture, although there are typical phenomena associated with memory claims, such as blushing, smiling, making a verbal recall claim or the presence of imagery. None of these is necessary or sufficient for the claim to be a memory claim. The point that context rather than the occurrence of a specific mental act is important in identifying a memory claim, is also important for the most influential version of the representational theory, as we shall see.

Memory and learning: the modern paradigm

The trace theory

The storehouse conception has already been mentioned as one of the most compelling conceptual pictures that we have of our powers of memory. It is not only ancient, but the conceptualisation of memory as *room* or *space* seems to work at a heuristic level as well. The representation of memory as room, building or even theatre has played a powerful role in history in the development of the memory ability of individuals, particularly in relation to propositional memory.[6] The storehouse conception is usually associated with a causal account of how memory works, known as the *trace theory*.

This account has been given a tremendous boost by the rise of computer technology and the way in which this technology has informed cognitivist accounts of mind. In the modern version of the storehouse, memory is encoded as traces in physical *places*, the most common example of which is the 'memory chip' of a computer. It has become natural to think of human memory ability as resting on the encoding of physical traces some-where in the brain. As Malcolm has shown, this account of memory has numerous flaws, some of which it holds in common with the representa-tional theory, some of which are its own in a special sense.[7] According to the trace theory, memory operates by the storage of traces or represen-tations of past events which can then be retrieved for inspection when required. It is not an account of the *physically necessary conditions* for memory to work. If it were no more than this, there would be no concep-tual difficulties with it. The biggest problems arise with its claims to encode *representations* of the past.

Items of perception are physically stored in the brain. If the storage process succeeds, then they are retained in memory; if it does not, then they are not. Even with this seemingly simple account, the storehouse analogy wears thin. Items of perception are not literally stored in the brain; this would be a *reductio ad absurdum* of the theory. What is retained is, in some sense, a representation of the original and it is this that is stored.[8] This does not bring us any nearer to understanding the physical storage aspect of memory, which trace theorists say is important. We say that someone has retained, for example, the words of a song he learned yes-terday, if he is now able to recite them; we do not make any further claims about neuro-storage.[9] A memory storage theorist is not claiming that one can do neurosurgery and actually see the representation in the brain tissue.

Even without this claim, the theory has departed from ordinary usage. We test memory claims by asking questions or putting a person through his paces. We would not recognise neurosurgery as a form of memory testing. The claim that a representational trace is located within the nervous system has to be a claim that there is a procedure that converts, say, an image perception into a trace, which can either be like a *groove* located somewhere in the brain or be a structural property of the brain. When a memory item is retained, there is a procedure that takes the trace and makes it a recognisable representation for the person remembering.

It is essential for the theory that the trace is at least *convertible* into a representation. The person who is memorising has to recognise the trace for what it is, namely a representation of a past perception. Some accounts of this suggest that, for example, a visual pattern is processed into abstract descriptions of patterns by a processor, which then places the description or abstract rule in a store, where it is retained for future use.[10] There is, however, Sutherland admits, no physiological evidence in favour of this account. Indeed, as Malcolm points out, it is difficult to see how there could be, for the claim that the brain makes use of symbols, rules and descriptions in the retention, storage and retrieval process is a nonsensical claim unless the terms 'symbol' etc. are analysed into accounts of physical processes and nothing more. Once this is done, however, all that we are left with is an account of the workings of the brain and not an account of how representations are retained, stored and retrieved, which was the original purpose of the trace theory.

We seem to be back with homuncular 'brain talk' and all its difficulties. A brain cannot use rules because rules can only be said to exist in a community of speakers and brains patently do not do that. If a child makes a mistake in memory we know what this would look like. I ask the child to recite a poem and he gets one word wrong. What about the child's brain? Does that make a mistake as well, so that the event of reciting the word was somehow an incorrect event in the brain? It should be evident that at this point the trace theorist is literally talking nonsense[11]. The confusion that is made in the trace theory is that of confounding the physically necessary conditions for remembering with a causally necessary account of remembering that conflates *retention* with *storage*. It is not necessary, and it is in fact mistaken, to expect that the account of the physically necessary conditions for retention will look like an account in terms of storage.

A natural reply would be to assert that we already have a workable and practical trace theory of memory in relation to computers, which do in fact retain represented information in physical form as a trace. The example of computers shows that memory can be preserved through electronic traces in materials like silicon, why should brain tissue not perform the same function? The answer lies in the fact that computers represent information to us according to *rules by which we interpret their electrical activity* (see Chapter 6). Humans know about the traces that exist in the computer's memory, because the computer memory has been explicitly designed to work in terms of physical traces that are representational for us. It simply does not follow that our own memories work, or could work, like this.

It is a consequence of the trace theory that what we 'really' mean when we say that someone has remembered something is that (a) a trace of an event has been deposited in the brain, either as a physical mark or as a structural feature of the brain; (b) this mark or feature is representationally isomorphic with the event of which the trace is a trace, and (c) the trace has been recovered and re-presented to us in consciousness. All that we can say of the first claim is that it is not known, although it is likely, that events have some effect on our neural system before we are able to remember them. Of the second, it has been argued that one cannot make sense of the idea of a *representation* outside a normative and social context and so that it makes no sense to talk of a representation within the brain. As for the third claim, it is simply not true that the criteria we apply for saying that someone has remembered something accord well with this part of the account of what it is to remember something. In order to see this, it will be helpful to use an example given by Malcolm.[12]

> Suppose that Jones planted a dogwood tree in his garden, and that when he finished the job he leaned the shovel against the trunk of another tree. Later his wife wants to do some transplanting, and she asks her three boys, who are standing there, 'Where did Daddy put the shovel?' The three boys (Tom, Dick, Jerry) had seen their father lean the shovel against that tree and they remembered that he had done so. This is surely an example of taking in and retaining information. In response to their mother's question, Tom replied, 'Daddy leaned it against the tree by the dogwood'; Dick pointed at that tree; Jerry ran to the tree and fetched the shovel for his mother.[13]

Malcolm's point is that it is impossible to specify the common effect of the neural trace in this example, even though all three sons remembered the same thing, that their father had leaned the shovel against the tree by the dogwood. Since the neural trace is supposed to play a central causal role in remembering as, in some sense, *representing* the event remembered, it is difficult to see what role it is playing in this particular example.

So far, I have not mentioned practical memory, which involves the retention of an acquired *ability*. According to the trace theory, an ability, such as that of riding a horse, will be retained through representational traces of the various activities involved. But it is evident that the ability to ride a horse does not rest on the ability to call up representational segments of different sub-parts of the ability. One might reply that, nevertheless, the ability is causally dependent on nonrepresentational neural traces. But this is to say no more than that neural traces are, in some sense, necessary conditions for the retention and exercise of the ability and this has never been in dispute. It would appear, then, that the representational theory has nothing interesting to say about human practical memory ability. That someone remembers how to ride a horse is shown by the exercise of the ability and nothing more, certainly not a mental act of recalling and recognising a representation.

The trace theory and learning

The trace theory has a profound impact on contemporary views of human learning and hence on educational practice. This can be seen in the following ways.

Learning is conceived of as a largely physical process, hence one that can be activated without effort or without reference to cultural factors.[14] The emphasis on a causal, physical process does not, in a logical sense, preclude other causally necessary factors in the operation of memory, but it does tend to play them down and thus makes it difficult to give them due recognition. The tendency is to see the ability to memorise as a given, rather as the memory capacity of a computer is a given which, provided the machine is functioning properly, normally operates at maximum capacity without training or encouragement. It is perfectly possible to combine a trace theory with further theories about jointly necessary conditions for memorising, but the physical or computational model of memory discourages that, precisely because, in the paradigm case, which is that of a computer, such further factors are irrelevant. *Practical memory* poses a particular difficulty for the trace theory in this regard since it is obvious that in the vast majority of cases, considerable training, practice and attention are necessary to master acquired human abilities, and encouragement and negative pressure are important factors in the training process (see below).

The mechanical model of memory fosters the idea that memory ability is invariant. Differences in ability to memorise can then be attributed to the *size* of storage capacity available to different individuals. Because this capacity is thought to be a physical given, the theory does not provide much motivation for educators to *improve* memory capacity, which is their preferred conceptualisation of memory ability.[15] Yet the improvement of memory in a range of different contexts may well be a most important educational objective.

This neglect of possible affective, motivational and cultural influences on memory makes the climate of opinion in memory research, generally speaking, hostile or indifferent to reflection on the ways in which the ability to memorise may be partly dependent on non-physical factors. Among these non-physical factors, the following are significant.

- *Attention:* people are more likely to memorise or to acquire a skill successfully if they pay attention to what they are learning about. Whether or not attention is paid is dependent on a number of factors, both within and outside the control of the learner, such as ambient noise, heat and comfort, but also social and cultural pressure and the willpower of the learner. No doubt there are also neurological constraints on the paying of attention as well, but it is misleading to describe these in computational terms.[16]

- *Encouragement:* Encouragement may come from a variety of factors, such as social reward, peer group approbation and parental approval. It works best when the learner wishes to succeed but is daunted by the difficulties that seem to lie in his way.

- *Negative pressure:* It is, of course, true that excessive pressure can damage concentration and successful memorising, but this does not distract from the truth that negative pressure, such as the fear of sanctions, often serves to whet the attention, and hence the ability to memorise, particularly when the subject matter is lacking in intrinsic interest for the learner.

- *Cultural/technological factors, such as literacy*: It is implicit in the three points made above that social factors may be important. They are important not merely in terms of the people with whom the learner is in immediate contact but also in terms of the society; moreover certain technological and cultural factors may affect the nature and importance of memory in that society. Most notable is literacy and, more recently, electronic and computer technology. Print and electronic media can substitute for memory by making information easily recoverable and hence they may diminish the need for people to commit information to memory. It is well documented that the careful cultivation of the memory was an established art and a branch of the discipline of rhetoric both in antiquity and in Europe into the Renaissance.[17] Even within the space of a lifetime, it is possible to note the decline in cultural value of certain kinds of memorising, such as the rote learning of poetry, spelling rules or 'times tables'. When such memory achievements are no longer valued or cultivated, they tend to fall into disuse. The tendency is reinforced, in the case of spelling and arithmetic, by technological developments such as spell-checkers and pocket calculators.

Implications of modernity for the role of memory in modern society

One notable feature of modernity is the compartmentalisation of human experience. As work and social roles become more specialised, it becomes increasingly unlikely that any one person will be able to undertake more than a small fraction of them. Because of this, it is also important that people understand something of the parts with which they will only be involved in a tangential way, in order that they are able to understand their own specialised place in the overall scheme of things.

A lot of the information that people have to remember in modern societies is, therefore, evacuated of affective resonance in two ways. First, it is not about their own personal histories or that of their particular local social group, such as family or community. Second, much of the information that it is socially desirable that they learn will have little or no personal impact on their lives. These largely unavoidable considerations, together with the volume of material that it seems desirable to learn, make the task of learning a challenge to establish an affective link between what is to be remembered and the memoriser. This challenge is largely unmet in modern educational systems and indeed what is disparagingly referred to as 'rote learning' has come to be regarded with suspicion and has, as a consequence, gone into decline. As we shall see in Chapter 12, proper acquaintance with a subject or a craft depends on a certain amount of basic knowledge and cannot be readily obtained except through instruction, training and memorisation. Since love of a subject cannot grow until some acquaintance has been reached, the affective link between teacher and pupil is of critical importance as a preliminary to the forging of an affective link between pupil and subject matter. But where a teacher no longer sees his role as that of trainer and instructor, that link falls into desuetude and can serve little purpose for the development either of memory or of acquaintance with the fundamentals of a subject.

The response of progressivism (the educational ideology derived from the Rousseauian outlook discussed in Chapter 3) has been to personalise educational experience to the extent that it is recommended that education be organised around the interests and outlooks of children themselves. In this way children will 'make their own' the experiences that they have in school and so will remember and learn better. There has been enough criticism of progressivism from other writers to make it unnecessary to pursue this in great depth in this chapter, but there is evidence enough to suggest that memorising in progressive-style classrooms is both haphazard and ineffective.[18] Some of the points made here are highly relevant to this failure. The affective link between a person and what is to be learned can, to some extent, be secured through making what is to be learned part of personal experience. However, without it being socially recognised as of value in a wider society, it is not likely to be recognised as important enough by an individual child to be learned effectively. The affective link, it might be said, needs some social glue. One must add to this the point that has been made elsewhere, that what a child is interested in does not necessarily coincide with a child's best interests. A child may well not recognise that what he is to learn is important both for him and for society.[19] This again reinforces the need for society to take a place in the link between a child and what has to be learned; the obvious place where this link can be made is through teachers, parents and relations.

We have seen that the link between memory, emotion and feeling has been weakened both by the conditions of modernity and by the influence of cognitivism. Progressivism does, in some sense, recognise the role of emotion and feeling in memory and learning but is poorly placed to remedy the problem, because the solution, which is to put the whole burden for learning on the young child, is quite inadequate to, and in some ways exacerbates, the problem. It is in any case necessary to challenge the idea that impersonal memory ability can develop satisfactorily without recourse to feeling and emotion. Among the relevant emotions is that of love. Love for what one has to, or wishes to, learn not only aids learning but brings into view a striving for excellence or perfection that applies not only to practical knowledge, and to the assimilation of literature or historical knowledge but also to any other kinds of factual knowledge that are valuable or culturally recognised. Indeed, the mistake may lie in thinking that any successful large-scale mastery of information and skill can take place without the engagement of feeling and emotion. This point was well understood by the memory artists of antiquity and the Renaissance. For example, the memory theatre of Giulio Camillo, which represents an attempt at giving an encyclopaedic account of human knowledge, uses the planets and the emotions associated with them as an organising principle for the knowledge that can be obtained in the theatre.

> The basic images in the Theatre are those of the planetary gods. The affective or emotional appeal of a good memory image – according to the rules – is present in such images, expressive of the tranquillity of Jupiter, the anger of Mars, the melancholy of Saturn, the love of Venus. Here again the Theatre starts with causes, the planetary causes of the various affects, and the differing emotional currents running through the seven-fold divisions of the Theatre from their planetary sources perform that office of stirring the memory emotionally which was recommended in the classical art, but perform this organically in relation to causes.[20]

All the different kinds of memory are important to learning because if reactions, information or ability that have been taught are not retained, then their benefits have been largely lost. The use of memory and the prestige that goes with having a good memory are in decline. Because mechanistic and representational models of memory are now so influential, the affective side of memory has come to be neglected as well. How then should the cultivation of a good memory be reinstated as a significant instrumental objective of education?

First of all, its value needs to be recognised. It is in many instances better to know something directly than to possess the skills for finding it out (which have themselves to be learned and learned well if they are to be of any use). 'Learning to learn' may be an attractive phrase but the practical difficulties involved in re-learning what collective human experience has already acquired are greatly underestimated by those who have a facile belief in 'learning skills'.

Second, its place in teaching and learning needs to be explicitly recognised. The idea that rote learning is a bad thing has come about through its identification with passivity and lack of autonomy. It needs to be recognised that if knowledge is a good and if rote learning, training, practice or any other form of memorisation is the most effective way of acquiring it, then it should be used in preference to other forms of learning. In any event, memory is not passive; certainly the *effective* use of memory requires the mastery of technique and the training of attention, rather than passive absorption of sense data on the empiricist model.

Third, given the first two points, it needs to be recognised that memory has to engage with the feelings and the emotions if it is to be fully effective. This means that it should acquire prestige and receive encouragement (or disapproval if its value is not recognised). This process has to start somewhere and the best place is within the education system.

Fourth, if the claims of the proponents of generic learning skills are faulty (see Chapter 12), then learning depends on the mastery of factual information before evaluation and argumentation can properly take place within a subject. The effective deployment of memory is, then, a necessity, rather than a luxury if critical skills are to be properly developed.

11

ATTENDING, THINKING AND LEARNING

Introduction

The aim of this chapter is to show how *attending* and *thinking* affect the way we learn and why they are important. Thoughtfulness and attention tend to promote learning. This is more than an empirical truth, it is a conceptual point because if thoughtfulness and attention *never* promoted learning, our concept of learning would itself be drastically altered, having become separated in everyday life and talk from the connections that it has always enjoyed. So the statement that thoughtfulness and attention tend to promote learning is more than an obvious truth, it is a remark about the grammar of 'learning'. Despite this, the connections between attention, thoughtfulness and learning are a relatively neglected feature of academic writing about learning.

This is no accident. None of the theories of learning so far discussed is capable of dealing with the concepts of thinking and attending in a very satisfactory way. Cartesianism and cognitivism wish to construe them as internal events in the mind or brain, and, unable to give a good account in this way, tend to neglect them. Behaviourism can only accommodate them if they can be specified as particular, overt behaviours – an extremely difficult task. Developmentalism of the Piagetian variety shares the problems of cognitivism, while the romantic tradition of Rousseau and his followers cannot comprehend the social and cultural context in which thinking and attending have their life. The time is ripe, therefore, to take a fresh look at these concepts and to show their critical importance for learning. At the conclusion of the chapter, implications for more formal learning situations such as schools will be discussed.

Thinking and attending

Attending and thinking are closely related. Neither are processes, although both are aspects of activities that include the *entertaining of thoughts*. It is tempting to say that to think is to pay serious attention to what one is doing.[1] While it is true that most thinking involves taking what one is doing seriously, and therefore it is indisputable that there is an important conceptual connection between seriousness and thought, it is also wrong to identify thinking as the serious aspect of what one is doing, since one can do something seriously without thinking about it (e.g. standing to attention) and one can think about something in a nonserious way.[2] Attending, although it need not involve the entertaining of thoughts, does appear to involve taking what one is doing with at least some degree of seriousness.[3] If learning cannot always take place without some awareness of the significance of what is being learned, then it is plausible to suggest that much learning takes place when the material is treated seriously because it is understood to be of some considerable significance.

The importance of attention

If attention is an important aspect of reflection in action, it is also an important aspect of learning in general. It is possible to learn some things without attending to them, but I believe that there is something more than just a statistical or inductive link between the attention devoted to learning and the success of the learner. Part of what we mean by learning (in the task sense) is paying attention to what is to be learned. Were attending and learning to be divorced in practice, they would be divorced conceptually as well, as the innumerable links in our everyday talk about learning which tie together attention, effort, motivation, interest and learning would also be severed. *Attention* is a central concept in our understanding of what learning is, hence any accounts of learning that are constructed on a faulty account of attention, or which do not take it seriously, will encounter dire problems.

There are, broadly speaking, three commonly accepted ways of approaching the question of attention.

- The first is to regard attention as an internal process. This could be called the *Cartesian* approach; it seeks to describe attention as an internal focusing on the matter in hand.
- The second approach is the *cognitivist* one. Attention is seen as a reflection of the ability of the brain to process information.
- The third approach is *behavioural*. This sees attention as a certain sort of behaviour and nothing more.

None of these accounts does justice to the complexity of the concept and each is seriously misleading in a different way. They will each be described and discussed in turn. Next, a positive account of attention will be offered and its importance in relation to learning will be assessed.

The Cartesian account of attention

In order to understand the Cartesian account, we need to review what Descartes said about the nature of consciousness. Consciousness or thought is the essential property of mind. Descartes does not commit himself to the thesis that one can only attend to one idea at a time, for he wishes to be able to say that in thought one can, for example, compare ideas and that in order to do this, it must be possible to have more than one idea before the mind. But this is to have one thought containing more than one idea. He does, however, see thinking, attending and concentrating as purely mental activities. For example, during the Second Meditation he considers the possibility that a malignant deceiver has misled him about all that it is possible to deceive him about. Descartes then asks whether or not he has the least part of the characteristics that belong to the essence of body. 'I concentrate, I think, I consider; nothing comes to mind.'[4]

Attention, then, seems to consist in thinking about what is before one's mind with a certain intensity. All possible mental content that is not related to the primary matter under consideration is evacuated from consciousness. Attention, then, is thought in a pure and concentrated form which is focused on the contents of one's mind. There are persuasive aspects of this account; we do associate attention with the focusing of our thoughts. We also accept that one cannot pay full attention to more than one thing simultaneously (although some forms of semi-concurrent attention-paying are possible: for example, when one attends to two matters in alternation). There are, however, difficulties with the account.

First, Descartes and his followers seem to be committed to the following proposition:

Attention is the focusing of one's thoughts on one idea or comparison of ideas.[5]

How could one know this? At the stage in the *Meditations* where he argues for this point, he has not yet established his essential non-corporeality, so to that extent he has not made an argument, rather he has made an assertion about the nature of attention. Since, however, a claim about the nature of attention is not essential to the development of his argument that his essence is to be non-corporeal, it is possible to allow Descartes to infer retrospectively what the nature of attention is from his inference that he is a being whose essence is thinking.[6] Attention is a mental phenomenon and therefore not one to be examined through looking at corporeal characteristics.

Normally speaking, one's thoughts are often about X or Y where these are not other thoughts but matters outside the mind of the thinker. Thus, in having the thought that 'the sun is hot', I am thinking that a particular astronomical body has a physical quality. If I am attending to the sun in the sense that I am seriously having thoughts about it, then the focus of my attention is not something in me, but something in the world.

This, however, is where the difficulty arises. For if paying attention involves focusing on one's thoughts, then paying attention to one's thought that the sun is hot is not to focus on the sun, but one's idea, concept or thought of the sun. But we can certainly distinguish between paying attention to the sun and to our thoughts of the sun. If, for example, my idea of the sun is of a molten bronze disc a few hundred metres in diameter, then my idea of the sun and the sun differ greatly, not merely in one being mental and the other physical, but in what *I* would be inclined to think and say about the sun and what other, better informed, people would be inclined to think and say about it.

It seems, then, that an account of attention that explains it as a focusing on one's thoughts is not adequate to explain what it is to focus on something that is not a thought. This, however, is precisely what we do in a wide variety of everyday cases of attention. Not only do we pay attention to processes, events and particulars that do not occur in our own minds, but we also pay attention to our own activities, like driving a car or shaping a pot.

These considerations help to account for why I can be mistaken in thinking that I am attending to something. If I think that I am attending to the sun when I am attending to a particular idea of the sun, then I have made such a mistake. So I could judge that I was attending to X but be mistaken when I was doing nothing more than focusing on my thought of X.[7]

The fact that we attend to a wide variety of features of our activity and experience suggests that an account of attention that concentrates solely on the introspective fixing on one's thoughts is seriously deficient. This in turn suggests that an alternative to a purely mentalistic account of attention will have to be found. These difficulties with the Cartesian account of attention are connected with the fact that, like so many other mental concepts, *attending* is attributed to corporeal creatures (people) and cannot be fully accounted for in terms of internal mental life.

Cognitivism and attention

Probably the most influential account of attention at the present time is that based on cognitivism. As in so many cases, the analogy with computers is drawn very strongly and, in this case, the notion of *processing*, the manipulation of electronic pulses within the computer, is thought to be the key to explaining attention in human beings. The processing account of attention starts from an unexceptionable observation, namely that our capacity for paying attention is limited.[8] However, this observation is then reinterpreted to mean that our *capacity for processing information* is limited. It is not clear whether it is information-processing capacity or *conscious* information-processing capacity that is limited. The distinction matters, because it is a commonplace observation that people are capable of carrying out a limited number of actions simultaneously. It is also a commonplace, as we have seen, that we can only fully attend to one thing at a time, in the sense of focusing our mind on it. Since we can only fully attend to one thing at a time, it seems to follow that attending requires such a lot of processing capacity that our brains could only ever concentrate on one thing at a time.

Putting it this way makes it seem as if it is only a contingent matter, owing to limitations in neural circuitry and processing power, that we are fully able to concentrate on only one thing at a time. Were we to have larger, better brains, we could concentrate on a number of matters at once. If this is an account of the nature of attention, then it is seriously mis-leading, for it is not a contingent fact that someone can pay full attention to one matter at a time. In paying full attention, one is devoting oneself exclusively: this is what we mean by 'giving something our undivided attention'. This suggests that to define attention as the use of extra pro-cessing power is mistaken, as it implies that one could pay full attention to more than one thing simultaneously (as opposed to doing more than one thing simultaneously) if only one had the brainpower, and this seems to be nonsensical. If extra processing power is a necessary condition for explaining how we are able to pay better attention to one thing or partial attention to more than one thing, then it is a hypothesis. On the other hand, if extra power is a sufficient condition for this to happen, it is false because it cannot account for the fact that to pay attention is often to have experiences with a certain quality.

But attention, like thinking, is an *aspectual* rather than an episodic or dispositional quality; it is that aspect of doing something that involves making it the exclusive object of one's care. If paying attention were the putting into action of very large amounts of neural circuitry, then it need not be making an activity the exclusive object of one's care, except as a contingent matter. If a computer is powerful enough, it can carry out more than one operation at a time. There is no analogy with human attention, which is to do with the *way* in which we do things, not with the number of things that we do. For us to say that we are giving something our undivided attention is to say that we are taking it extremely seriously or are caring about it to the exclusion of all else.

Describing thinking in terms of electronic processing is a temptation, because it seems to offer the prospect of a 'scientific' account of one of the concepts psychologists find puzzling. One starts by saying that all action involves processing. But it is difficult to see how the same act should require different levels of processing if the computer model is to be taken seriously. According to the account, acting while paying attention involves more processing than does acting without attention. Since all acts involve processing, and processing is what leads to or *is* action, it follows that acting and attending to acting are either two different activities or the same action under a distinctive aspect. But as we have seen, the processing account cannot make sense of the aspectual feature of attention, which is accounted for by the way in which one cares about something or takes it seriously, and there is no general account of what this looks like, independent of context or activity. All it could mean in the computer case is that it was being done better because more resources were being devoted to it.

If, on the other hand, paying attention is a separate action to the activity which it accompanies, then again it fails to capture the aspectual nature of attention, making it episodic instead. And if it is episodic, we might expect the act of paying attention to go on even if there were nothing to attend to. It would be possible to say that someone paid attention to his driving and then continued to pay attention, even after he had parked the car, only not to anything in particular. But this is nonsensical; the fact that attention is always paid to something or other suggests not that it is a separate activity, but that it is an aspect of an activity. One might reply to this that there are activities that are dependent on other activities if they are to take place. For example, there can be no backroom paper settlements in a bond dealer's office unless a transaction has taken place on the selling floor. But this is not a useful model for attention, for the idea is that attending to something is not a *consequence* of doing it, but is either its precursor or its accompaniment.

Another damaging feature of the cognitivist account is that it cannot explain what Descartes and the empiricists considered to be an essential feature of attention, namely the focusing of awareness. There are some cases, and focusing on one's thoughts is one of these, where someone who pays attention is conscious of what they are attending to. No one, however, is inclined to attribute awareness to a computer because of the size of its RAM or the speed of its CPU. Since the cognitivist cannot even account for those features of attention that Descartes and others thought were central, it is even more inadequate.

Behaviour and attention

Is it possible then to give a satisfactory account of attention purely in behavioural terms? After all, it has been observed that one of the problems with both of the accounts examined above is that they ignored the fact that it is corporeal people who pay attention, work with care and so on. We pay attention to our thoughts, but this is a part of paying attention. Most of the time we attend to what is outside our mind and the Cartesian account is inadequate to describe this. The cognitive processing account is even more inadequate, since it can account neither for awareness nor for the outward direction of attention.

Once one starts to look at examples of what it is to attend to something, then a unitary account looks implausible. Even such a phenomenon as directing one's attention to a colour is highly variegated. Wittgenstein gives a number of examples:

> 'Is this blue the same as the blue over there? Do you see any difference?'
> You are mixing paint and you say 'It's hard to get the blue of this sky.'
> 'It's turning fine, you can already see the blue sky again.'
> 'Look what different effects these two blues have.'
> 'Do you see the blue book over there? Bring it here.'
> 'This blue signal-light means . . .'
> 'What's this blue called? – Is it "indigo"?'
> You sometimes attend to the colour by putting your hand up to keep the outline from view; or by not looking at the outline of the thing; sometimes by staring at the object and trying to remember where you saw that colour before.
> You attend to the shape, sometimes by tracing it, sometimes by screwing up your eyes so as not to see the colour clearly, and in many other ways. I want to say: This is the sort of thing that happens *while* one 'directs one's attention to this or that'. But it isn't these things by themselves that make us say someone is attending to the shape, the colour and so on. Just as a move in chess doesn't consist simply in thoughts and feelings as one makes the move: but in the circumstances that we call 'playing a game of chess', solving a chess problem', and so on.[9]

Just because the phenomenon of attention is so variegated, Wittgenstein suggests, we ascribe a spiritual accompaniment to the phenomena which is what attention 'really' is. This is not to deny that certain characteristic experiences may accompany the different forms of attention, but these are not what attention is. Attending is, in many cases, nothing more than the way in which someone shows the seriousness of their concern with what they are doing and this is manifested in what they say, their body movements, the way in which they work with materials, and the context of their activity.

On the personal level, *interest* and *motivation* play a large part in ascribing attention in an activity. We can often use the terms so as to mean more or less that attention is being paid to the activity in question. We say that so and so is showing an interest in fishing when we observe that he is fishing in an absorbed way on a particular occasion. Interest and motivation are as much dispositional as episodic and it would not be wise to link their grammars too closely. There are, though, links with attention on the one hand and these concepts on the other, in that ascriptions of interest or motivation are often among the criteria we use for saying that someone is paying attention; they help to put his actions under a particular aspect. We use aspects of someone's past, character and predilections to make a judgement about an aspect of their current behaviour. In such cases, we are not making a judgement about the character of their activity based solely on what we are now able to observe, but on what we know about the person as well. In fact, even our judgement that someone is now attending to this activity is often based on our knowledge of how they go about things. Because I know James, I am inclined to think that his habit of staring out of the window is a sign of absorption in what he is doing; it is a preliminary to effective work. Were someone else to do this, I would be inclined to say that they were merely daydreaming. The posture adopted towards an activity to which one is committed may be one of a range which we would think are 'natural' expressions of attention-paying.

The physical environment is important: noise, heat, cold and uncomfortable furniture can all distract us, even if we are interested in, and absorbed in, a particular activity. Events outside our immediate range of concern can engage our attention, even against our will. Discomfort may incline or oblige us to attend to the source of the discomfort, rather than to the matter in hand. When this happens, we often find ourselves forced to switch our attention and we 'lose the thread' of what we are doing. This is simply a reflection of a point made earlier, that people find it difficult, if not impossible, to pay close attention to more than one thing at a time. Paying attention to something does not necessarily mean *having thoughts about the activity in hand*, it may involve checking, measuring, trying again, comparing, not to mention other activities that have a clearly behavioural dimension. In other words, being distracted need not mean *losing conscious awareness* of what one is doing, in the sense of having thoughts about the undertaken activity being disrupted.

So it is misleading to say that when we are distracted we switch our sole focus of consciousness over to another activity, for it is misleading to say that, in all cases, paying attention *is* having focused thoughts of this kind. There is an alternative explanation, namely that we are only able to 'process' so much 'input' from outside and that when input reaches a certain level of intensity, we are obliged to switch our processing capacity to the new input that is impinging upon us.[10] This, however, is not so much an explanation as a way of redescribing a well-known feature of human natural history in 'scientific' terms. We have already noted the confusion in the processing model of attention and it casts no further light on the concept of distraction. This is not to say that distraction is not important. It is arguable that far too little attention has been paid in recent years to the sources of distraction and how they affect attention and learning.

Attention and learning

Learning is most effective when a learner is able to and does pay attention to whatever it is that he is learning. This is not to say much more than that learning tends to be effective when undivided attention is given to the learning task in hand, whether it be of facts or skills. This statement is almost, but not quite, a tautology, drawing our gaze to an important aspect of human natural history. Yet the implications of taking it at all seriously would mean great changes in the work practices of many institutions, but most notably in primary schools.

One has to learn to be effective at paying attention; it is not just an ability that develops, although it does seem to be the case that as a child gets older the ability to attend grows as well. Learning to concentrate and to pay attention can be cultivated through the serious pursuit of those activities whose mastery requires that attention be paid. In other words, one does not learn to pay attention *as such*, but through taking what one is learning seriously. Children may have limited powers of paying attention when they are young, and may not be able to sustain attention for as long as adults can, but this does not entail that their powers of doing so cannot be cultivated, not through generic 'attention developing' activities, but through various kinds of learning: factual, practical and affective.[11] As Gramsci remarks:

> In education one is dealing with children in whom one has to inculcate certain habits of diligence, precision, poise (even physical poise), ability to concentrate on specific subjects, which cannot be acquired without the mechanical repetition of disciplined and methodical acts.[12]

Many primary schools have adopted practices that are more suited to the Rousseauian model of learning, which was examined and criticised in Chapter 3. In the Rousseauian scheme of things, the child's autonomy and self-directedness is paramount. Rousseau's Émile, whatever the theoretical shortcomings of his tutor's approach, did at least have the time, space and opportunities to concentrate, that are denied to thirty or so 5-year-olds following an Émile-like programme of autonomous learning. In such a situation, the development of powers of attention and concentration becomes a struggle against circumstances that constantly work against such a possibility. Constant conversation distracts attention from the task in hand. Constant movement is both an opportunity for distraction on the part of the child and itself a direct distraction when lots of other children are moving. Finally, there is the distraction of multiple curricular activities taking place in the same teaching area, which again serve to unfocus the concentration on a single matter. The fact that many activities are thought worthwhile pursuing at the same time implies also that none of the activities currently being pursued is any more worthwhile than any other. This reflects badly on the prestige of what the child is doing and this poor reflection is made worse by the fact that the teacher himself has to concentrate on many activities at once, which, in practice, means that he is concentrating on one at a time for short bursts of time. It is by now well enough documented that classrooms like this are less effective than classrooms where there is relative quiet, calm and concentration upon a single matter in hand.[13]

The importance of proper attention for learning and for attending to what one is doing cannot be underestimated. Training and the cultivation of memory can best take place when there is little or no distraction. Focusing on the learning of one activity at a time indicates that the teacher is taking that activity seriously and is asking that the learner also take it seriously. Taking what one is doing seriously is a large part of what is meant when one says that someone is thinking about something, is reflecting on it, or is paying attention to it. These observations are not blinding flashes of insight; they are remarks in the 'folk psychology' of human learning, which have become obscured through a mixture of romantic and pseudo-scientific theorising.

Attention is important in another respect. If someone is to love what they are learning, then they will need to attend to it; that is, they will need to take it seriously, devote themselves to it exclusively (at least for periods of time), strive to achieve excellence, and stick with it in times of adversity.[14] Attention is a condition of love. To love someone or something is, among other things, to pay a particular kind of attention. Those who cannot attend properly cannot take a subject or an activity seriously, devote themselves, strive to achieve excellence, or stand by it in adverse circumstances. If education is about the development of love of a subject or activity, then attention must be central to learning.[15] Making it central to learning involves treating what is to be learned as something serious and worthy of devotion.

12

LATER LEARNING

Introduction

So far I have been largely concerned with early learning. It is now time to look beyond infancy. One of my particular concerns is to explore the extent to which it makes sense to say that someone becomes a more independent learner as they mature. Many claims have been made for the idea that one can 'learn to learn' or that it is possible to teach people general 'thinking skills' which they can then go on to apply in a wide range of contexts. These ideas have, arguably, two roots: first in the Rousseauian dislike of authority; second in the representational model of the mind found in cognitivism and some forms of developmentalism.

One of the themes of this book has been the importance of *training*, taking place in a human context of affective, reactive and social behaviour, which is necessarily connected with some notion of authority. Training is important in early learning, but it continues to be important throughout childhood and into adulthood. But as people grow up, their understanding, skills and knowledge mature and they become more independent. A consequence is that independent learning becomes more possible as children are able to make use of what they already know. In this sense the growing independence of children as learners is not a particularly controversial idea.

Much that is learned, then, builds on previous knowledge. Much that is learned cannot be learned until other matters have been learned first. This is particularly apparent in, for example, mathematics, where it is not possible to learn how to carry out calculations containing more than one different kind of operation until one has first learned to perform the operations individually. Previously acquired knowledge often has a *heuristic* function. When teaching is done through the use of metaphor or analogy, for example, then the point of the metaphor or analogy must itself be understood. Knowledge of atomic structure does not logically depend on knowledge of the structure of the solar system, but the former can be elucidated by analogy with the latter. It is, however, a requirement of logic that if I am to explain atomic structure by means of this metaphor, then my pupils must understand the structure of the solar system.

This example illustrates another important feature of learning, that it often occurs as a result of teaching. Teachers work in different ways – we have already noted the importance of an affective bond between teacher and learner – but the teacher's knowledge and his ability to deploy it in ways that are illuminating to the pupil are also of critical importance. Among these skills is the use of analogy, metaphor and example, and their use becomes possible because of the perspicuous view that the teacher has of his own knowledge, together with a knowledge of which examples, analogies and metaphors are likely to help pupils. The ability of teachers is, therefore, of critical importance in enabling effective learning to take place.[1] But this is more than just the ability to *enable* learning to take place, it is also the ability to train, instruct and to give an exposition. If learning is to take place through the deployment of an illuminating analogy, for example, then the teacher has to deploy that analogy in appropriate ways.

Knowledge and ability are intentional concepts; one knows that p or one is able to do p. Since this is the case, knowledge and ability are, by nature, specific to some degree. Someone can be very able, but they are so in virtue of being able at one or more specific activities; it makes no sense to say that someone is able *tout court* or even able at being able. Neither is there any such thing as general knowledge apart from knowledge of many specific things. There are all kinds of relations between different aspects of knowledge, some of a heuristic, others of a logical nature, but the existence of these relationships does not alter the fact that knowledge and ability are specific.

One important way in which these relationships are recognised is through the grouping of knowledge into subjects or groups of abilities. It has been fashionable for quite a period of time to complain that subject boundaries are artificial, and it is true that they do, from time to time, change. But the structure of subjects and the relationships between them reflect real differences between different subject matters in respect of social priorities, modes of acquaintance, central concepts, criteria for truth determination, and methods of enquiry. Some writers have claimed that there are also differences in the underlying logical structure of different subject areas.[2] However far one wishes to take this general thesis, it is clear that there are significant differences between some subjects and others, even though knowledge and skill from one subject may be used in another. One need only point to the differences between history and mathematics, for example, to appreciate this point.

Generally speaking, the greater the degree to which there are differences between subject matters and to which there is a differentiated structuring of knowledge within a subject area, the smaller the possibility there will be that one skill or restricted set of skills will be adequate to learn effectively across the range of subject matters. The point goes for subject matter as skill as well as knowledge. If all metal engineering requires skill at operating a lathe, then this is a skill that is presupposed in various different metal engineering activities, but not in a different sort of practical activity like cooking. Just as it is implausible to suggest that one can acquire a single capacity to learn practical activities, so it is implausible to suggest that one can acquire a single capacity for acquiring propositional knowledge.

Writers like Ryle, who have drawn attention to practical knowledge, have been criticised for their lack of emphasis on propositional knowledge in practical activities.[3] The point is that in order to learn a skill, one often needs to know something about the structure and properties of what one is working with. This knowledge can take many different forms, ranging from the systematic technical knowledge of the motor mechanic, to the diffuse folk knowledge of a country craftsman.[4] The latter kind is particularly difficult to pick up without a prolonged period of participation in the relevant activity and even then it is likely to remain diffuse, not the property of any one particular individual.

The differentiated and hierarchical structure of knowledge and ability are the accumulated product of centuries of human endeavour, in the course of which what has previously been learned forms the basis for what is subsequently learned. The logical structure of a subject does not necessarily correspond to its chronological development (physics, for example), but the logical structure may develop over time as central concepts change. The important point for learning is that knowledge is structured, that the structure is there to organise the subject matter and, to some extent, indicates the most effective way of learning that subject. This is particularly true of academic and technical subjects, less true of folk knowledge such as that of rural crafts, and not true at all in certain areas such as our folk psychological knowledge of ourselves and other people.[5] But even these types of knowledge require something more than pure personal discovery: they require respect for authority and wisdom, and a willingness to participate in activities on their own terms.

These considerations suggest that much of our knowledge is dependent on previous learning, our own and others. If this is so, then some sequences of learning are likely to be more effective than others, particularly for structured knowledge and ability. These sequences will be the ones that best reflect the structure of the subject and allow for general principles to be taught first, followed by more specific material. The same principles will apply to practical learning. There is no reason to think that children will know what these effective routes are; if they did, they would already have some grasp of the logical structure of the subject matter, which, *ex hypothesi*, they do not. Since they do not, they will need to be guided in the sequence of their learning by those who do have some idea of how the logical structure of a subject can best be disclosed so as to make learning most effective. The recognition of authority in some sense is a condition of being able to go on in this way; it is through being told what is the correct sequence in which to learn something that one is likely to learn most effectively. It is not surprising that 'learning to learn' is attractive to Rousseauian educators, as it appears to circumvent this requirement.

This discussion suggests the importance of teaching in learning and, furthermore, teaching that involves some degree of training, instruction and exposition. There is no doubt as well, that there are some fundamental contrasts between various different subjects in terms of modes of apprehension and kinds of verification: the contrast between mathematics and logic on the one hand, and empirical sciences like physics and biology on the other, has received plenty of attention from mainstream philosophers and philosophers of education. Likewise, the contrast between morality and religion on the one hand and the aforementioned subjects on the other has been much discussed. In addition, there is much debate as to whether or not the epistemology of social inquiry is radically different from that of the various natural sciences.

These discussions seem to imply that in both logical and epistemological terms there could be fundamental differences between different subjects and different groups of subjects. Paul Hirst has put forward a theory that human knowledge is, in principle and in practice, divisible into different *forms*, each with their own modes of verification, central concepts and structures of inference.[6] This last matter is perhaps the most controversial, both in what it claims and in the implications that it has for the thesis that one can learn a capacity to learn. For, if there is such a capacity, it will allow someone to *infer* from what is known to what is not yet known. Central concepts and modes of verification and apprehension may be unavoidably different in different subjects, but surely modes of inference must remain the same?

If modes of inference are the same across subjects, then it is natural to suppose that once these have been acquired, learning can readily take place through their application across a range of subjects. In the next section I shall seek to show that while it is not possible to show that inference is subject-specific, neither is it possible to demonstrate that a 'learning to learn' inferential skill could ever be usefully employed in most subject areas that require some degree of propositional knowledge.

Toulmin's account of the varieties of reasoning

Toulmin starts by explaining that he wishes to study reason and argument as part of human natural history. He thinks that such an approach will lead to a rather different view of logic to that usually expounded in logic textbooks. It will be, nevertheless, one that does more justice as a description of our reasoning processes than the picture offered by formal logicians. Toulmin represents the structure of everyday argument as follows. When we express an opinion, we are invariably required to produce a reason for it and we typically appeal to a piece of information as the source of our being able to express an opinion. Our conclusion (represented as C) is backed up by information (represented as D (for data)). Schematically, the situation can be represented as follows:

Figure 1

It is now natural to ask why D lends support to C. Toulmin argues that there can be no general answer to this question, but many answers, dependent on the *field* (or subject matter) in which the argument is offered. He calls the field-dependent principles for moving from D to C *warrants*. A warrant is a licence to move from premise to conclusion; it is a rule-like proposition rather than a factual one. For example, if *Petersen is not a Catholic* is the conclusion C of an argument and *Petersen is a Swede* is the premise D of the argument, it would be natural for someone unacquainted with the relationship between Sweden and Catholicism to ask why Petersen being a Swede was in any way relevant to his not being a Catholic. The inference might well look like a *non sequitur* to anyone who was not knowledgeable about the religious affiliations of Swedes, but to one who was, there might be no difficulty about accepting the argument. If questioned about the soundness of the transition from D to C, he could reply that the *warrant* for his inference was a further statement (this time hypothetical) to the effect that

Anyone who is a Swede is not a Catholic.

The structure of the argument will now look like this:

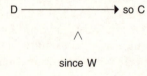

Figure 2

This constitutes the warrant W of the argument and need not be appealed to by those conversant with the field in which the argument was offered. The warrant for an inference is more than just a hypothetical statement; it has the practical character of a rule that allows one to proceed from premise to conclusion. One's *entitlement* to use a warrant may, however, be challenged and, on occasions such as this, a response will probably be called for. In such a case, the speaker will usually be expected to produce a *backing* for the warrant and this will be in the form of an empirical statement such as, in our example:

No observed Swede has ever been found to be a Catholic.

The structure of the argument will now look like this:

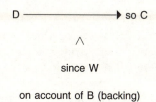

Figure 3

The backing may, however, be cited in place of the warrant.

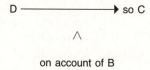

Figure 4

So there are two possible patterns of inference. The backing need not be the same statement as the warrant, it may also be *categorical* rather than hypothetical. On the other hand, it serves as a statement rather than a licence, thus becoming another premise in the argument. Since backings for warrants are field-dependent, Toulmin thinks that it follows that warrants themselves are field-dependent, since they are usable only on the basis that the field-dependent backings of the warrants are true and can be used to justify the warrants. He also denies that arguments of the form displayed in Figure 2 are usually analytic, even though they would be conventionally classified as such by logicians. It follows, therefore, that much argumentation that logicians would regard as *analytic* and *field-independent* is neither on Toulmin's account of the nature of arguments. It would further follow that generic learning skills based on field-independent analytic logic do not and could not exist.

There is no space here to criticise Toulmin's proposals in detail and I have done so elsewhere.[7] There are four major problems with them which

141

make it implausible that they could be used to mount a robust defence of field-dependent inference and, by implication, field-dependent learning.

- First, his account of analyticity is too restrictive, applicable only to inferences for which the backing statements authorising them contain the information contained in the conclusion itself, either implicitly or explicitly. Tautologies for Toulmin are statements in which the conclusion is already stated in the premises.[8]
- Second, his verificationist account of tautologousness breaks down for what he calls 'quasi syllogisms'.[9]
- Third, the soundness of arguments is based on the truth of backing statements. Toulmin seems to run together empirical proof and soundness and appears to place an erroneous reliance on verification as a criterion for soundness when it should be a requirement for empirical proof.
- Fourth, there are many examples of field-independent deductive reasoning that Toulmin does not consider, even though they are neither analytical nor tautological on his account.[10]

Finally, his account of field-dependent inference rests on an underlying, field-independent logic expressible in the inference form *modus ponendo ponens*. If a D statement is true and a warrant W holds, then the conclusion S follows. Given that D is true and W holds, then C is true. A similar point can be made for arguments with backing statements. So Toulmin has not replaced reasoning as it is described at a very abstract level by logicians, but he has complicated and confused our way of looking at argumentation. This is not a price worth paying for the defence of field-dependent reasoning when, as I shall show, such reasoning can be explained in terms compatible with more conventional accounts of field-independent reasoning. In what follows I shall show that Toulmin's insights about the field-dependent nature of much of our everyday reasoning can be preserved and that criticisms of the idea of generic thinking skills are still, therefore, very potent.

An account of field-dependent reasoning

Why is much of our subject-specific reasoning field-dependent even if we decide to cling to the field-independent logic of formal logicians? The argument from

You are going to hell.

to

So, good or bad, you are going to hell anyway.

seems to rely on just one premise. The conclusion seems to contain more information than is available in the premise, yet it could be classed as a tautologous argument that relies on the meanings of logical words within it. It can be shown that this argument, in strictly logical terms at least, relies on steps that nobody bothers to make when carrying out the inference in an everyday context.[11]

Even a simple piece of field-independent reasoning illustrates that we reason *enthymemically*, that is, we do not articulate all the premises and steps that are strictly necessary to complete an argument. We should be able to, if we are called upon to do so, in order to demonstrate exactly what argument we are relying on, or to demonstrate the factual statements that we are relying on as suppressed premises. However, when these common premises are well understood by all the participants in a conversation, this becomes unnecessary.

This helps to show why it is that a proper account of reasoning *within* fields need not entail an affiliation with a radically revised view of logic. Most everyday reasoning is enthymemic because otherwise it would be extremely cumbersome and most of the steps taken in any argument would be otiose, since they would be rehearsals of steps that are mutually known already. In the case of face-to-face communication, it is possible to clarify any obscurities during the conversation. Whenever reasoning from premises to conclusions takes place within the context of a particular subject, with its own core of accepted propositions, it takes place against a background of the assumptions of these statements as unstated premises in arguments, both inductive and deductive. This is so because those knowledgeable in a field have no need to articulate common knowledge and assumptions, and would find it very cumbersome to do so. Naturally sometimes these unstated premises may be reviewed and, in this case, the backing statements will be brought in, this time as premises to arguments whose conclusions are the warrants that issue from them.

This suggests that Toulmin's account of warrants needs to be revised. It is possible to say of all the kinds of arguments that he describes, that they usually rely on unstated assumptions that do not need to be articulated. In contexts where they are not articulated there is no harm in calling them law-like, provided one does not make this observation the basis for a systematic revision of logic. When they need to be invoked their assertorial status may be made abundantly clear in those cases where the underlying pattern of inference has to be articulated in terms closer to those of context-free logic. In other contexts, they may simply be appealed to as law-like statements for those unacquainted with the subject matter. This means that people who have originally accepted them as matters of fact have now been *trained* to use them in a law-like way.

Doesn't this, after all, entail a revision of logic in the way suggested by Toulmin? Not if one refuses to make the distinctions between empirical statements and rule-like statements into something hard and fast in all contexts.

> But if someone were to say 'So logic too is an empirical science' he would be wrong. Yet this is right: the same proposition may get treated at one time as something to test by experience, at another as a rule of testing.[12]

In a similar vein, the same proposition may get treated at one time as a premise and at another as an inferential rule, depending on context.[13] Toulmin's account of backing statements obscures this simple point. The backing statement is primarily a support for the warrant when it is treated as a *major premise* in an argument, rather than as a *local rule of inference*; it is not a further support for the original argument. It may indeed replace the warrant on a particular occasion, then it serves to make the argument a different one, not to support the original argument in a different way.[14] This is not to say that backing statements are not important, but the way in which Toulmin introduces them obscures their true role, instead making them the underpinning of field-dependent forms of argumentation through their verificatory role, rather than the factual supports for major premises when these arguments rely on non-local rules of inference.

Anyone who wishes seriously to engage in argument within a particular field or subject needs to know and understand the importance of the statements that serve as enthymemic premises or local warrants. Any serious engagement with a subject or a practice involves a pupil in getting acquainted with that subject's central propositions. So one of the prime requisites for effective thinking within a subject is that of taking it seriously enough to engage with its central claims, those that serve as premises for more detailed arguments within it, or in some contexts, as local inferential rules. Moreover, it is also necessary for someone who wishes to engage in debate within a field to have a good idea about how statements that serve as implicit premises or warrants relate both to each other and to the less obvious statements that may actually be articulated within an argument. Argument within a field is, then, practically impossible without the re-quisite background knowledge and cannot be conducted without a prior acquaintance with that background knowledge. All this is a consistent with Toulmin's arguments; the radical revisions that he proposes to logic are not, however, necessary to sustain those claims. I do not wish to claim, however, that logic as it is described by logicians is, by itself, adequate to account for the evaluative and justificatory reasoning that is required in the practice of any serious discipline or activity. It cannot account for the localised use of propositions as warrants in certain contexts; formal logic is an essentially context-free and somewhat limited description of our reasoning; it is not a radically mistaken account.

Neither can logic be enough to characterise all that there is to be said about reasoning within activities whose evaluative vocabulary contains, as Gaita points out, such notions that might be considered 'merely' affective, like *common sense, sentimentality, shallowness* or *depth*, but which constitute a vital part of understanding what is important and worth attending to in a discipline or activity.[15] But these considerations point to the need for a deep engagement with and respect for what one is learning, which are requirements of the possibility of aiming for excellence within the discipline. Gaita's point could be stated as follows. Learning the 'local logic' of the discipline is not enough to master it, one needs to have the kind of response to it that can only come from active participation and the consequent development of respect. But it is through participation that one comes to learn both the local inferential structure and a respect for the discipline or activity. Participation within the practice on its own terms is, therefore, a precondition both of learning its internal logic and of coming to respect it.

Conclusion

Later learning is sometimes characterised in terms of movement from context-bound to context-free thinking. There is a sense in which this is correct. At some point in a child's acquisition of language, the use of quantifiers and expressions for tense allows him to talk about matters not immediately present in space and time. But this point occurs at an early stage in life and, although all the implications of spatio-temporal scales will not be understood for a while, if only because they require a great deal of further knowledge of history, geography and measuring systems, context-free thinking is not the culmination of intellectual development but, in a certain sense, its commencement.

One of the main features of later learning is the close engagement with the particularity of disciplines and activities. Some of these subjects may concern themselves with matters far beyond the immediate context, but to master them requires acquaintance with detailed knowledge and very specific techniques. To some extent, earlier learning is more generic in kind than later learning, but one needs to be careful about how this is described. The acquisition of literacy, numeracy and certain relatively generic practical skills is important for further progress. So is the ability to be able to discipline oneself, to pay attention and to practise recall memory.[16] None of these generic forms of knowledge and ability constitutes any kind of 'general thinking skill' with which it is possible to 'learn to learn'. Rather they are useful forms of knowledge and skill which it may be possible to use in a range of disciplines *provided that the particular values and form of life of that discipline receive the respect that is their due*; that is, a respect that is capable of growing into love.

In many ways, later learning is densely contextual: one learns very particular detailed factual knowledge; one learns about the particular properties of the materials with which one works; one gains an acquaintance with the social practices associated with the activity in which one is engaging; and so on. But the habits one acquires in becoming say, a good mathematician, do not necessarily translate readily into those required of a good philosopher. Nor does the skill of an engineer necessarily translate into that of a gardener or a bookbinder. Sometimes the ways of working in a particular discipline and the kind of respect that it requires prepare someone badly for a different kind of activity. It often requires a great deal of humility to realise that one's excellence at one subject may actually be a barrier to competence at another; even greater humility to realise that this may, to some extent, be a personal matter, not just dissonance between two different subjects.

That this can be a problem *within* 'forms of knowledge' can be illustrated by the remarks of Stephen Jay Gould on a comment by L. Alvarez, the physicist. 'I don't like to say bad things about paleontologists, but they're really not very good scientists. They're more like stamp collectors.'[17] Gould goes on to comment:

> The common epithet linking historical explanation with stamp collecting represents the classic arrogance of a field that does not understand the historian's attention to comparison among detailed particulars, all different. This taxonomic activity is not equivalent to licking hinges and placing bits of colored paper in preassigned places in a book. The historical scientist focuses on detailed particulars – one funny thing after another – because their coordination and comparison permit us, by consilience of induction, to explain the past with as much confidence (if the evidence is good) as Luie Alvarez could ever muster for his asteroid by chemical measurement.[18]

Hirst's original thesis was mistaken in certain ways: in its focus on the kinds of knowledge beloved of traditional liberal education to the exclusion of anything else; in its positivistic emphasis on verification as a knowledge criterion; and in its flirtation with the idea that different subjects had different underlying forms of logic. As Hirst now accepts, knowledge and practice are not readily separable. All practices are informed by knowledge, while most areas of learning (*all* if they are still being pursued) are practices with their own values, habits and modes of investigation. Different forms of knowledge are, in an important sense, different forms of practice; moreover appreciation of the practice, as much as the knowledge within it, may be the beginning of wisdom.

Wisdom is not something that can be passively acquired, it must be achieved through living life in a certain way, with receptiveness, humility and an enduring capacity to love what one is engaged with. All of these qualities require attention to particulars, not an assumption that one can learn to learn and then just master a subject more or less solely on the basis of already acquired skills. This is also an observation about the moral qualities required for learning.

13

LEARNING ABOUT RELIGION

Introduction

This chapter will apply the approach to learning developed in previous chapters to a particular issue, namely the place of religious education in a mainly secular society. It has been argued that learning takes place through participation in and commitment to particular forms of life. It seems to follow that learning about religion should best occur through children's participation in religious forms of life. Many, however, would object on the grounds that they did not wish their children to become religious believers or at least to be *indoctrinated* into religious belief. It is widely claimed that children can learn what religion is without first becoming committed to any particular religion. I shall argue that it is unlikely that this could be so. The secular religious educator is presented with a dilemma. Should he make children religious believers and so violate his own principles and, perhaps, those of parents, or should he teach children about religion and run the risk that they will remain ignorant of why it is important for many people or even develop a contempt for its apparent irrationality?

This is not just an abstract problem for educators, but one that affects the conduct of public education systems in different ways. The problem is particularly acute in the UK, which developed a public education system in large part built up initially by the churches at a time when the temper of society was mainly Christian. In the late twentieth century, the temper of society has changed drastically. The problem for policy-makers concerns the currently contested character of religious experience, the perceived controversiality of religious beliefs by some and their indubitability by others, and the overall difficulty of making sense of religious experience for children in a largely secular world where relatively few adults take established religions all that seriously. A large and obvious exception to this generalisation is the presence of ethnic groups with a strong attachment to their religious beliefs. Their presence adds to the complexity of the situation that I describe and contributes to the choices that I propose at the end of this chapter.

Teachers run the risk of being branded as indoctrinators if they teach religious beliefs as if they were true, or as a superficial kind of value tourist-courier if they treat them as the beliefs of others. In addition, they have to meet the conflicting expectations of parents in respect of their children's religious education. In the UK, the 1944 Education Act made the teaching of a non-denominational but confessional form of Christianity obligatory for state schools. This requirement is implicit within the act, but can be inferred from its requirement that religious *instruction* should be given in every county school and that each day should begin with an act of worship.[1] The Education Reform Act of 1988, on the other hand, makes the requirement implicit that religious education should reflect the predominantly Christian outlook of the UK, but in a *non-confessional* way. This can be seen in the change of terminology from that of religious instruction to religious education and in the model syllabuses issued by the statutory curriculum body, which provides for education at all ages in a variety of the major religions.[2] In the curriculum document it is stated as an aim of religious education that, among other things, it should help pupils to 'acquire and develop knowledge and understanding of Christianity and the other principal religions represented in Great Britain'.[3] The ambiguity of the 1944 Act might be excused on the grounds that, at that time it was universally assumed that religious education would be confessional, but the 1988 Act, drafted in more secular times, could be seen to be deliberately ambiguous in order to avoid having to take up a position on an issue that teachers were bound to find difficult. Teachers were, in effect, being given a 'nod and a wink' to teach religion non-confessionally in non-church schools without any guidance as to the difficulties that this might pose.[4]

There are fundamental difficulties with the project of providing a non-confessional *ab initio* religious education to non-believers. These difficulties can be brought to light by considering the nature of religious practices and the kind of educational endeavour that would be necessary to enable children to understand them. Difficulties arise whether religion is interpreted as an assertorial practice (concerned with truth-claims) or as an expressive practice unconcerned with truth. The relationship between these two interpretations of religious experience will be outlined and the implications of each for educational practice considered.

Religion and truth

It is commonly, although not universally accepted that religion claims to provide insight into and knowledge and understanding of a transcendent reality which is the sphere of the divine or of an immanent presence of

149

the divine in the everyday world.[5] Philosophers have often felt troubled about how one can account for religious knowledge, given accounts of knowledge in areas that do not involve acquaintance with a transcendent or immanent divine presence. One conventionally accepted account of knowledge is that it consists of justified true belief. This account has been disputed over the centuries, but I shall take it that some form of account like this will work for a wide enough range of cases to support the discussion.[6] To say that *A knows that p* is to say that:

1   A believes that p;
2   p is true;
3   A is justified in believing p to be true.

In most cases, a necessary condition for saying that A is justified in believing that p is that p is *justifiable*, that is, it belongs to a system of inspection and assessment that allows the determination of the truth of p *independently* of whether or not anyone asserts p.

This account does not, by itself, commit one to the view that a claim that A knows that p entails that p is true for all time. That commitment is picked up when 'p is true' is taken to mean that p is in some kind of relationship to a sempiternal or a transcendent reality. The account given in the *Tractatus Logico-Philosophicus* aligns propositions with sempiternal (timeless) states of affairs. A weak form of correspondence theory can be derived from Aristotle's claim that for a proposition to be true, it must be true *of* something.[7] Since this something is, in the view of many religions, an eternal and transcendent reality, many of the major propositions of religious belief, at least in the Islamic and Judaeo-Christian traditions, are about eternal or sempiternal entities whose central attributes do not change. If propositions about religion are claims to truth, they are claims, at least in part, concerning transcendent beings, their properties, and relationships with each other and the rest of the world. Since such propositions cannot be verified by the means adopted in other practices, any account of truth which bases itself on the procedures adopted in non-religious contexts will be ill equipped to deal with the phenomenon of truth claims in religious contexts. One response is to deny that religious propositions, despite appearances, are at all concerned with truth. Another response, implicit in the treatment adopted in this chapter, is that there is no one way of characterising the concept of truth as it occurs in different practices or forms of life; it needs to be studied in the contexts in which it is used and may not necessarily lead to a uniform, extra-contextual account. And in this case it seems clear enough that many religions presuppose the existence of some kind of religious reality about which claims can be truly made. Such an account would differ significantly from an account of truth in scientific contexts, for example, where the possibility of the independent checking of truth claims through well-established procedures would be held by most to be an essential feature of the ascription of truth or falsity to a scientific proposition. In such a context it is not enough that a scientist is able to justify his claim for the proposition to be accepted as true, but that the scientific community can validate whether or not that justification is sufficient to account the proposition as true.

Any system of belief involves some degree of commitment. If I claim to know that p on the account given above, then I am justified in believing that p and I could, if called upon give an account of why I believe p, citing appropriate evidence and argument. To the extent that I am prepared to do that, I am committed to the truth of p, that is, I am not aware of any reasonable counter-evidence. But I am also committed to the system of assessment and inspection within which the truth claim concerning p is evaluated. This commitment is a necessary condition of knowing *any* p-type proposition, for it is only through the use, with others, of the evaluative procedures that lead me to believe, know, doubt or reject p and other propositions like it, that I can make or deny claims of this sort. I am, therefore, committed to a form of life in which these practices occur. In the case of science, this takes the form of being committed to procedures that allow for the evaluation of propositions irrespective of whether authoritative individuals hold them to be true or not, at least in certain circumstances. In everyday life, *authority* plays a significant role in determining belief, but there is also plenty of scope for arriving at belief through the assessment of evidence and argument, the more so as one grows more knowledgeable, skilled and independent.

In one respect religion is no different. Induction into religious belief takes place through inculcation into those forms of life in which the practices of religious assertion, validation and denial are located. They have an important characteristic, however, that makes them different from those of science: they make very great use of accredited authorities in asserting truths, validating some and rejecting other propositions. Such authorities might be canonical texts such as the Koran or the Bible, officials such as priests, or charismatic figures like prophets. There are two important features of religious authority that distinguish religion from other forms of life. First, religious authority, whether traditional or charismatic, depends to a large degree on the surroundings in which it is introduced: the use of ritual, ceremony and personally affecting experiences like participation in forms of worship, prayer or confession evoke the emotions of awe, wonder, joy and humility, which are characteristic of religious experience and which form a psychologically vital basis for the recognition and acceptance of religious forms of authority. In a sense primary reactions to religious experience are the result of training to take part in religious activities and to react to them in appropriate ways. Second, because the truths of religion rest on authority (ultimately one or two authorities deemed to be infallible), it is difficult, if not impossible, to reject any particular propositions without denying the authoritative status of their author. A denial of the authoritative status of the author leads quickly to doubt of the other propositions of which he is the author. There is little or no role for independent justification of religious propositions: they tend to stand or fall together as a particular way of looking at the world. This is because the structure of religious inference is one that depends on the truth of singular authoritative assertions. When this authority is undermined, so also are the propositions that rest on it. This helps to explain the differences in commitment between religious and some other forms of life. Religious commitment tends to be to a near-totality of propositions and is secured through a strongly affective element, which does not usually exist to anything like the same degree in relation to other forms of life. This affective element tends to be a psychologically necessary condition for the recognition of religious authority.

Those who feel uncomfortable about the status of religious propositions as claims to truth may feel more at home with an account of religious experience that takes account of its expressive character demonstrated through ritual, ceremony and prayer, but takes utterances that arise in these contexts not as assertions or quasi-assertions as their surface grammar might suggest, but as non-assertorial performatives such as expressions of hope, exhortations to worship or injunctions to good behaviour. In such an account, religion is a form of life that is expressive rather than assertorial, but different from and deeper than other forms of expressive behaviour such as music and dance (although it may make extensive use of these) through a concern with morality, human mortality and the timeless aspects of human life (itself an aspect of what Carr has called the spiritual).[8] Thus, to take an example of D.Z. Phillips, the statement 'Christ has risen', when uttered in an appropriate religious context, should not be taken as an assertion about the movement of an individual from one place to another (transcendent) place, but as an invitation to exalt a particular religious figure.[9] Whatever one thinks of the correctness or otherwise of this interpretation of religious experience, Phillips's insight into the primacy of the expressive in religious experience is extremely important. An account of religion that does not note this fails to do justice to the significance of religion in human life. But an acceptance of the importance of the expressive in understanding religious experience does not logically commit one to the 'fideist' account of religion sometimes attributed to Phillips.[10]

Religion and education

The aim of an educational activity in a particular subject matter is to engender knowledge, skill and understanding so that its central concepts, its distinctive truth tests (where appropriate) and methodology of investigation (where appropriate) will be grasped.[11] In addition, where appropriate, central abilities should be mastered, affective responses developed, and the significance of the subject in human life understood. These are ambitious aims, but to ask for anything less over an extended period of education is to risk superficiality. For most educators, the preferred way of doing this is to develop learning through a practical engagement with the subject matter. Thus, a pupil learning about science will learn central facts about the discipline, but he will also, at some stage, be expected to master concepts, tests and methodology in a practical way through engagement in scientific investigation at an appropriate level. Even the study of science at a relatively superficial level should aim to introduce pupils in a practical way to the idea of an independent test for a prediction. There are enough non-arcane opportunities in the everyday world for this to be possible through the availability of materials, liquids, plants, animals and the atmosphere in the immediate environment for some progress to be made even in the primary school. In the case of a very different subject matter, namely morality, there are unavoidable situations where a practical engagement is required within the exigencies of life at home and school. Although discussion and vicarious experience through literature are important aspects of moral education, few would dispute that these have little value if divorced from practical engagement. It is through practical engagement with moral situations, together with discussion and reflection on those experiences, that one comes to appreciate morality and moral truths.

Where does this leave religious education? There are two broad possibilities. The first is that religion is an assertorial practice with a strongly expressive aspect, as was argued in the previous section. The second is that it is a species of expressive practice without a significant assertorial element. In the first case, the cognitive aims of understanding central concepts, methodology and truth tests will apparently be important. On the general educational arguments advanced so far, some form of practical engagement with religious practices through participation in those practices seems to be required at some stage. But this is to accept that the primary form of religious education is a *confessional* one, since to engage in the practices is, on the argument of the previous section, to engage in those affectively loaded experiences that lead to the acceptance of religious authorities *as* authorities and hence as sources of religious truths. One important difference between a scientific education and a religious one is that pupils educated in science appreciate that many scientific propositions are independently justifiable, while pupils educated in religion appreciate that few religious ones are. But the appreciation of these differences is part of what it is to be scientifically or religiously educated. Through engagement in religious practices, then, pupils come to understand central religious concepts, distinctive truth tests and methodologies of investigation, in so far as these are relevant to religion. In addition, certain specific abilities, affective responses and an understanding of the significance of religion both in itself and in relation to other subjects are engendered.[12]

While a parent who wished to engender religious belief in her child would welcome such a religious education, the secularly minded parent and educator would not, because they would regard the subject matter of religion as inherently controversial and the practices of inculcating religious belief as indoctrinatory. Those who take this view face a dilemma. How can one religiously educate in anything other than a superficial sense without indoctrinating? One could take the view, advocated at one time by Paul Hirst, that religion is not, properly speaking, a form of knowledge and so ought not to be taught as such, although it may be taught in a non-confessional way as an account of beliefs of a particular kind.[13] On Hirst's later view, that education involves initiation into practices that are likely to engender critical rationality, induction into religious practices involves a practical engagement with religion in such a way as to promote critical reflection on it.[14] The problem with this view should by now be apparent: the practice of religion involves submission to religious authority, that is, *obedience* of an unconditional nature and this is hardly likely to engender any critical reflection on the practice itself, but, rather, commitment to it and its truth claims.

Phillips attempted to answer Hirst's earlier, negative recommendation by arguing that religious education can elucidate the nature of religious beliefs by showing how they work for religious believers.[15] This would involve explaining the stories and holy texts, showing how ritual is related to belief, what are the central tenets, and how these relate to the morality and culture of believers. Phillips's account does not, however, address the problem just raised, which also arises for his own preferred account of the nature of religious experience, namely how does one do this without engendering religious belief? Phillips was, at the time of writing *contra* Hirst, less willing to agree to the assertorial nature of some religious practices that has been defended in this chapter. On his own account, however, religious experience develops through story telling, ritual and ceremony.[16]

On the assertorial account suggested in the previous section, it would seem that a practical engagement with these characteristically religious activities would, for the reasons mentioned above, lead to at least the strong possibility of pupils accepting religious truths. One reply to this might be that *elucidation* need not involve participation and so the possibility of indoctrination does not arise. (*Non ab initio* religious education is not affected by these arguments. It is the case of *ab initio* that I am arguing is problematic.) However, this makes religious education different from other forms of education in that a practical engagement with the subject matter is to be deliberately eschewed. Given that participation is thought to be a necessary condition of achieving educational depth, it is, to say the least, puzzling to see how educational depth could be achieved in religion through abstinence from techniques deemed to be indispensable in other subjects. The puzzlement might be increased on reflecting that religion, with its affective and expressive aspects, looks like just the kind of study that would benefit from practical engagement, just as movement, dance and music do.

If this is the case, then elucidation, unless it involves participation in some sense, will not be and could not be sufficient to introduce someone to the nature and significance of religion, for elucidation without participation would not be sufficient to allow a child to appreciate why someone might come to believe a religious proposition to be true through coming to understand and accept the nature of religious authority. Elucidation may well work for someone who has already had some form of primary religious experience, but it will not be enough by itself as an introduction to religion. Participation in worship, ceremonies and prayer, as well as instruction in religious knowledge, would seem to achieve what elucidation cannot, except perhaps in a much less satisfactory way, namely an appreciation of why religious authority matters to people. Other forms of authority with which a child is acquainted work in a different way; in appreciating religious authority a child may come to appreciate his relationship with other forms of authority familiar to him, but he will have no ready frame of reference for religious authority without some familiarity with religious practices. Participation may lead to an acceptance of that authority or it may not, but given that one of the principal aims of inducting children into religious experience is to get them to develop firm religious beliefs, the possibility is always present. It might be argued that *spiritual education* could take place through participation without religious indoctrination. Carr has argued that spirituality can be developed through distinctively spiritual virtues whose practice gives meaning to spiritual content.[17] A participative form of education would seem to work admirably here, but although there is a strong connection between spirituality and religious belief, they are not the same, and spiritual education cannot be a substitute for religious education.

If religious practices are non-assertorial but expressive, as Phillips appeared to believe at one time, would the elucidatory approach work any better than a participative approach? It would seem, on the face of it, that if religion is non-assertorial then there can be no danger of indoctrination since there are no propositions to indoctrinate. However, some parents, even if they believed that religion was non-assertorial, might still find the idea of their own child participating in religious practices distasteful for aesthetic or spiritual reasons and would thus favour an elucidatory approach.

To examine the elucidatory approach further, it is necessary to look at other expressive subjects such as music and dance and to ask whether or

155

not an elucidatory approach is the most appropriate one for them. The analogy with dance and music does not favour the elucidatory approach. For if a musical education is to lead to an appreciation of what is difficult and important about music, its satisfactions and frustrations, and a sense of love and respect that comes through struggle with something difficult, then it seems self-evident that practical engagement, as far as this is possible, is a necessary feature of a decent musical education. One may argue that it is possible to teach someone to appreciate music through listening to it and learning about different forms of music, different compositional techniques, the capacities of instruments and so on, but one could hardly maintain that this was a *more* satisfactory form of musical education than one that involved singing, playing or composing. However, the secular religious educator would be committed to non-participation in the expressive musical, poetical and ceremonial activities of the religion in their context, so that even the musical, poetical or dance aspects of the religious practice would be learned about in a less than satisfactory way. Alternatively they could be taught participatively as forms of music or dance, but to do this would be to miss the fact that they are not just dance or music but *religious* dance or music. At best they might be seen to have a spiritual significance through such a form of 'secular participation'. But most religious educators maintain that not only is the elucidatory approach not a *pis aller* but that it is *more desirable* than a participative approach. If the analogy above has any force, this cannot be the case. The only justification for teaching religion in a non-participatory way is that, if it were not, large numbers of people would object, either because they believed that religious doctrine was false or controversial, or because they felt that it was aesthetically or spiritually distasteful.

We could conclude that elucidatory, non-confessional religious education was a second-rate form of education, but nevertheless hold pragmatically that this was the best that could be achieved in a secular climate, and that anyway it was better than nothing. However, if a child fails to appreciate the importance of religion in the lives of many people we must ask what exactly *does* he get from the experience of being taught about religion? For if religion is seen to be unimportant despite the fact that some think it important, there is a danger that the child is likely to think that not only are those people in the grip of false beliefs, but that they indulge, for no apparent reason, but with the utmost seriousness, in practices that systematically lead them to develop unshakeable beliefs in manifest falsehoods. The danger is, in short, that elucidatory religious education given to children in a society of a secular temper might lead them to see religion not as a human phenomenon of profound significance (whether or not one subscribes to its central tenets), but as a form of irrational and delusive behaviour.[18]

Conclusion

If the arguments above are sound, then attempts to promote learning about religion from a secular stance are deeply confused. The form of non-confessional religious education currently offered in the UK is worse than useless. It cannot tell non-believers what is important and distinctive about religion to its practitioners, and it runs the risk of making their practices seem delusive if assertorial, or merely aesthetic or spiritual if non-assertorial. Either way, it runs the severe risk of systematically misleading pupils about the nature of the subject matter taught and this cannot be an outcome of any satisfactory educational practice. There seem to be two coherent alternatives. One is to abandon religious education in non-church schools for children whose parents do not wish them to have it. The other is to provide confessional religious education of an appropriate kind for those whose parents desire it. In this way, those who wish their children to learn something about religion will have their wishes satisfied while those who wish their children to have nothing to do with it will have theirs satisfied. Those non-religious parents who think that their children can learn something important about religion through a confessional religious education should opt for the latter alternative and hope that their children will eventually 'grow out' of it while still retaining a sense of what it is and why it is important to many people.

14

MORAL LEARNING

Introduction

In order to understand moral education, it is necessary to recapitulate some of the factors that are important in learning.

1   Humans are *social animals*: living in society is a requirement of their own well-being. It is not, however, *sufficient* because people need to live together in ways that promote flourishing; they need, arguably, to pursue a conception of the good for human life. In post-Enlightenment societies it is a commonplace to say that the achievement of autonomy is necessary for individual well-being and self-respect. Some advocates of autonomy do not see it being tied to any particular conception of the common good; these are strong autonomists. Weak autonomists think that autonomy is compatible with at least a minimal conception of the common good, if this is seen as a finite disjunctive set of aims and values that a society regards as promoting a viable conception of human flourishing.[1] In this chapter it will be assumed that the achievement of individual autonomy in the weak sense will be one of the main aims of moral education.[2]

2   Human life is *rule-governed* and there are general principles, laws, codes of conduct and advisory codes that regulate human action.

3   Human engagement with the world is largely a *practical* one, related to purposes within a social framework. Our perception of the social world and our dealings with other people are a condition of the formation of moral judgement, which involves the identification of morally relevant properties in situations and the identification of the morally relevant principles that apply to them.

4   People seek, and are expected to seek, their own good within a social framework so that moral education has to do with the development of *autonomy*[3] and independent action as well as with the development of perception and understanding of rules. In the sense that it is to do with the development of autonomy and action, moral education is also

158

to do with the development of good *character*; those traits that enable someone to act independently and responsibly in ways that are recognised to be conducive to their own well-being and that of the rest of society. This involves commitment to principles, rules and codes but also the development of attitudes and dispositions and a training of both perception and the will. Commitment, attitude, disposition, perception and volition are all essential features of what are commonly called the virtues, such as courage, patience, trustworthiness, compassion, and so on.

5 Each morally relevant situation has its own *particular characteristics* which, in many if not most cases, implies that right action cannot simply be 'read off' from a cursory glance at the main features of the situation.

6 Morality involves *reflection* and *judgement* as well as action, not only on the actions of other people, but, at least as important, on one's own behaviour.

Moral education is complex and can occur more or less successfully. In most known societies moral education takes place under the auspices of a religious outlook which provides the cognitive and affective framework for it. Contrary to what is often believed, religion does not just provide a set of commands and sanctions that channel action in socially approved ways that take no account of the complex particularity of social life. A religious moral education may result in a person who acts solely in response to commands, sanctions and, possibly, the hope of reward, but it would arguably not be a very successful form of moral education. A religious moral education that resulted in people who followed the rules rather than practised the virtues would be regarded in the Judaeo-Christian tradition at least as something of a failure. However, the argument of this chapter does not presuppose the necessity of a religious background to morality, neither does it presuppose the superiority of moral education divested of a religious background.

Conditioning, training and instruction

Humans are born neither with a sense of right and wrong, nor a knowledge of the moral beliefs of the society into which they are born. It will be argued that moral training is fundamental to moral learning and that a failure to appreciate the importance of training will lead to a misunderstanding of the nature of moral learning. It has already been remarked that early learning is based on human animal reactions and the ability of babies and toddlers to recognise and act on those reactions. Children learn very early on in their lives that some of their actions excite pleasure while others provoke resentment. They learn by provoking reactions and recognising, through those reactions, that what they do has an influence on the social as well as the natural world. Being dependent on the succour of others, those reactions matter to the child. Through coming to understand the nature of the responses that they elicit and through trying to anticipate the nature of those responses, they learn to take responsibility for their actions. They recognise that, through the exercise of their will, alternative courses of action are possible. This is a gradual process, and we recognise that children do not have complete responsibility for their actions for quite some time. In the meantime, while they are learning about the reactive behaviour of others and about their own behaviour and how to control it, we could say that they inhabit a border area between being responsible for their actions and not being responsible. Thus P.F. Strawson writes that parents and others concerned with the upbringing of young children, 'are dealing with creatures who are potentially and increasingly capable both of holding, and of being objects of, the full range of human and moral attitudes, but are not yet truly capable of either'.[4] A process of *conditioning* children to behave in certain ways gradually becomes a process of *training* them to recognise and to act on the reactive attitudes both of themselves and of others, before they seriously come to be considered as being fully responsible for their actions and as being able to recognise the differences between good and evil. For Aristotle and those who have followed him, the inculcation of habit at an early stage is an essential feature of moral learning.

> [B]ut the virtues we get by first exercising them, as also happens in the case of the arts as well. For the things that we have to learn before we can do them, we learn by *doing* them, e.g. men become builders by building and lyre players by playing the lyre; so do we become just by doing just acts, temperate by doing temperate acts, brave by doing brave acts. . . . It makes no small difference, then, whether we form habits of one kind or another from our very youth; it makes a great deal of difference or rather all the difference.[5]

Children's perceptions of the reactive attitudes of others and of their own reactive attitudes towards others leads to the development of the concept of harm and benefit to others and themselves. Through the growth of these and associated concepts, they begin to understand how the concepts of good and evil operate within human life. They may thus come to associate good with the promotion of human flourishing and harm with the opposite.

A number of points can be made about this account of early moral learning. First, it is incomplete. But as we saw in the previous chapter, the early growth of religious experience comes through the training of reactions, so in a sense, there are important similarities between a religious and a non-religious form of moral learning.

Second, although moral growth has been described in terms of conditioning followed by training, the contrast between the two is of the greatest importance. While conditioning seeks to elicit certain reactions and nothing more, training involves the development of judgement on the part of the young child. Moral training involves the child learning to recognise and to seek to influence the reactive attitudes of others, while at the same time learning to recognise and control his own. As he does this, he develops dispositions and attitudes that are themselves the subject of moral evaluation, as we attach moral importance to the development of character. These dispositions and attitudes have a cultural and social, as well as a purely moral dimension, and their development is to a large extent contingent on the prestige and importance that the cultivation of such traits has in the culture.

Third, it is important to recognise that the process described in the previous paragraph could be seen, to some extent, as an idealisation of early human moral upbringing. Although very young children cannot avoid coming across the reactive attitudes of others, how they are trained to respond to them, or even *that* they are trained to respond to them, is by no means determined. Not only is it possible, and indeed likely, that there will be variations in moral training across different societies, but there is also the possibility that the training provided within a society may not be such as to promote an adequate enough recognition of the human well-being and harm that we would say was necessary for the promotion of human flourishing. Indeed, the training may not take place at all or at best incompletely, and a child may acquire values, character traits, behaviour patterns and attitudes that may set him at odds with the values held by much of the rest of society. As Auden writes:

> A ragged urchin, aimless and alone,
> Loitered about that vacancy, a bird
> Flew up to safety from his well-aimed stone:
> That girls are raped, that two boys knife a third,
> Were axioms to him, who'd never heard
> Of any world where promises were kept,
> Or one could weep because another wept.[6]

An important aspect of moral training involves the development of character in such a way that virtues are recognised and practised. However, virtues vary to some extent between different societies. With this reservation in mind, the concept of virtue answers to the requirements that an account of moral learning must (a) illuminate a young human's transition from dependence to some form of responsibility, (b) give an account of the lengthy and varied nature of the growth of moral understanding and (c) show how the moral growth of an individual is set in a social context of moral values and moral order.

When children are able to understand speech, they can also understand the verbal embodiment of reactive attitudes in the form of codes of conduct, such as that it is wrong to hurt other people or to be inconsiderate. These codes provide guides to behaviour which are sanctioned through approval and disapproval. Children also learn the more fundamental principles of morality in their own societies through becoming acquainted with the Mosaic Law or its equivalent, for example. Finally, children become acquainted with regulative principles of conduct such as the categorical imperative and its close relation, the golden rule or the Aristotelian rule of the mean, which offer them guidance which neither codes nor moral principles can on their own. Although it has traditionally been said that such principles are laws of nature, discoverable by the use of reason alone, even those, like Hobbes, who take that view, do not regard their recognition as a matter of course but recommend instruction in them and the principles derivable from them.

> And for the Law which *Moses* gave to the people of *Israel* at the renewing of the Covenant, he biddeth them to teach it to their Children, by discoursing of it both at home and upon the way; at going to bed, and at rising from bed; and to write it upon the posts, and dores of their houses; and to assemble the people, man, woman, and child, to heare it read.[7]

Training and instruction allow for the development of the identification of the moral features of situations, that is, those features that contribute, and those that do not contribute, to well-being as it is seen in their society.[8] They also contribute to (a) the development of attitudes to situations and people, habits or dispositions of behaviour and action and (b) the ability not just to control unruly passions, but to channel desire and affection, as well as dislike and repugnance, into characteristic modes of action that contribute to the well-being of the individual as well as his society.

We are now in a good position to consider the shortcomings of Rousseau's account of upbringing. In the account outlined above, moral education, as something complex and delicate, can succeed more or less well or it can fail. Its success requires a balance of conditioning, training, instruction, practice, action and reflection. Many need to be involved, hence the saying 'It takes a village to raise a child'. Rousseau, in his desire to evacuate the normative from childhood and to confine it to the formation and practice of a polity of rational adults, is left with conditioning in a largely asocial world as the sole means of bringing up children. He excludes training and instruction; action is largely controlled by the tutor, and reflection takes place only on the limited range of moral experience to which Émile has been introduced. If the account offered above is anything like accurate, then Rousseauian moral education is likely to fail spectacularly in most cases.

Beyond moral training

Moral training is vital in enabling children to anticipate and respond appropriately to the reactive behaviour of others and to recognise and respond to the harm done by their own actions. However, training can only take children so far; very soon, they need to reflect if their moral understanding is to progress. They need, principally, to reflect on and discuss moral behaviour and the proper interpretation of moral values if their moral understanding is to gain in depth.

Morality is rule-governed in the sense that learning to practise the virtues involves, at least in part, codes of behaviour on the one hand, and regulative principles that are applied to the interpretation of morally relevant situations on the other. As children become more capable of moral action and reflection, they will move from learning correct ways of behaving to the justification, evaluation and interpretation of the rules that they use. This kind of reflection is not purely cognitive; early moral behaviour tends to be primarily emotional in its reactive aspect and to consist of trained responses in its active aspect.[9] But in order to be able to deal with variety, nuance and complexity, moral action needs to move towards reflection at quite an early stage.

The question, 'Why did I do that?' may take one kind of answer in relation to a *trained* response, like 'because that is what I had been brought up to do in those circumstances' or 'this is what you should do in these circumstances'. But trained responses are not always adequate to deal with the complexity and ambiguity of many morally relevant situations. However, there are many situations where it may be necessary to interpret or investigate further. For example, one may wish to ask: 'Is this one kind of situation or another?' This is not to deny the importance of moral perception, but it is to point out that *immediate* perception cannot always yield all that is relevant to a case, or that there are sometimes genuine puzzles about categorisation that require further thought. One may need to seek further information or another point of view or, again, one may need to relate the present occurrence to one's own past experience. One may also wish to ask if one's response was the right or most appropriate one to the circumstances (the response needs to be evaluated). There is a little bit of give in every rule (even a signpost may need to be interpreted) and this is the case with moral rules, particularly where differing requirements of morality may appear to conflict with one another. Finally, one may be called upon to justify an action or a judgement; one may be asked,

'Why did you act like that?' or 'Why did you react so strongly?' These questions cannot always be satisfactorily answered in the way outlined at the beginning of this paragraph.

Training, therefore, needs to be complemented with forms of *education* that allow an appropriate response to the varied forms of moral experience. Reactive judgement and behaviour need to be complemented with reflection and discussion; they also need to be connected with considerations of the place of moral conduct in the light of the culture and values of a community as a whole. Of growing importance in this ongoing *moral education* will be an appreciation of the particular in moral situations. This does not mean that principles do not matter or that they are necessarily overwhelmed by the intricate particularity of morally relevant situations, but that the application of codes of conduct has to be interpreted in the light of the peculiar demands of the situation with which the moral agent is faced. This is not usually, or is hardly ever, a *calculative* requirement, as utilitarians might say, but it often is a requirement to pay attention to the consequences[10] of one's actions in terms of the good or evil that may follow from them. Alternatively it may be a demand that one be honest about oneself and one's own motives in acting, and it is a requirement that one attempts, where necessary, to see the situation from the point of view (both in terms of character and in terms of interest) of other parties who are or may be affected. In this last respect, it involves the application of a regulative principle that should be learned as part of the moral instruction that accompanies training, namely the 'golden rule', that one should not do unto others what one would not wish done to oneself.[11]

It is now possible to see the analogy between morality and apprenticeship to a craft.[12] Learning a craft involves training and instruction, but cannot be exclusively described in those terms. It involves the extension of repertoires to cover new, puzzling and more complex situations and tasks. It involves situating action in a broader social context than the workshop and making use of the individual and social wisdom embodied in fellow practitioners of the craft. There is also an element of self-realisation in the development of craftsmanship. The analogy should not, however, be taken too far. Morality is far more concerned both with our relations with our fellow human beings and with our own self-realisation than is craftsmanship. The aesthetic element in craftsmanship is also stronger than it is in morality. Morality should not be seen as either *technique* or *expertise*. Morality, more than the practice of any craft, concerns itself with the development of the individual human character. Like a craft skill, however, character should develop through the practice of virtues initially under the tutelage of those who value their development.

Membership of a community is an inescapable requirement for moral learning. The importance of parents and family in the recognition and shaping of reactive behaviour has already been mentioned. As a child grows and becomes an active member of a wider community, the members of that community also assume importance in his moral education. Of particular importance are teachers during the years of schooling and workmates and companions in the early years of employment and homemaking. School and workplace, as well as family, form the practical context in which moral learning takes place in a variety of situations of increasing complexity and moral depth. It is therefore of great importance that teachers are both moral exemplars and that they possess the practical moral wisdom to promote the moral learning of children.[13] It is, however, important to recognise that, after a certain age, this pedagogic role does not entail that teachers need to be (even if they could be) some kind of moral expert because individual people have to decide what *they* should do in certain circumstances. They can be advised what to do; if they are always *instructed* in what to do, then they lose the autonomy that is characteristic of mature moral action.

The point also applies to evaluation and justification of moral action, not just of oneself but of other people. This inescapably involves the consideration of particular examples seen through the points of view of different individuals with different experiences of life. The reactions that one has to events with a moral dimension are inevitably charged with an affective dimension. But we also have to make judgements, to justify and evaluate within this affective context. This means that our emotional responses to moral situations in which both ourselves and others are involved also have a cognitive aspect. We need to become confident enough in our emotional responses to moral situations to be able to form views and arguments on the basis of them. We learn to employ an evaluative vocabulary that is necessary to moral thinking (although as Gaita implies, by no means exclusive to it), which involves such notions as *sentimentality, coldness, shallowness* and *depth*.[14]

Similar points have been cogently made by Evan Simpson.[15] He emphasises the importance of attention to particulars, the cognitive dimension of affective response, and the importance of conversation in the development of a moral sensibility. However, he neglects the period of moral training that must precede the development of a deeper moral sensibility. Moral training involves acting according to moral injunctions which then become principles adopted as one's own. Alone it cannot carry a young person on to the interpretation, evaluation and justification that are often required in more mature moral deliberation. But if it has not been diligently attended to, then none of the rest is of any great value. Only someone who has gone some way towards practising the virtues or who appreciates the importance of moral principles concerned with respect for life, fidelity and honesty can ponder upon their meaning in complex situations encountered in the course of everyday life. To build a moral education on the basis of civilised conversation about the particularity of moral situations perceived through a cultivated affective/cognitive response is to misunderstand priorities. This is not a psychological point about the stages of moral development, it is a grammatical point about what it makes sense to say about the order of moral education. The interpretation of principles and the examination of character require the acquisition, appreciation and understanding of principles and the formation of character (at least to some extent) before they can take place. Simpson is quite right to criticise moral developmentalists for tending to see moral development as a primarily cognitive realisation of ever more abstract principles of moral rationality.[16] This does not affect the logical requirement that developed moral action and reflection require a basis of trained action and perception if they are to engage with anything substantial.

Moral developmentalism

Much modern thinking about moral education lies in the developmental tradition described and criticised in Chapter 7. The account offered in this chapter, although it describes moral education as proceeding through a series of stages, each of which is necessary if the next is to take place successfully, is not a developmental theory in the sense introduced in that chapter. The ordering is primarily a grammatical one and progression is not automatic but dependent on social as well as individual effort.

The best known of the moral developmentalists, Piaget and Kohlberg, see moral development as proceeding from 'egocentricity' through a regard for social approval, through rule-bound conceptions to contractual and, finally, universal rational autonomy conceptions of morality.[17] These writers have been criticised for not regarding the stages as genuine moral alternatives, but as stages on the path to moral maturity. Simpson, in particular, has pointed out the dangers for rational political debate about alternative arrangements for society if it is held that some forms of political organisation are the result of nothing more than relative moral immaturity.[18] Such developmental schemata are largely Kantian in their inspiration, to the extent that the empirical data on which they purport to be based have, arguably, been refracted through the lens of a Kantian perspective to yield the stages of progression to which those writers adhered in the first place. There are problems with taking the responses of children to moral questions at face value; indeed, the perceptions and the motives of the children being questioned by adults need to be very carefully taken account of before any conclusions can be drawn. More damaging is the normative order imposed on the different kinds of response. What could allow one to order moral responses on an ascending scale of egocentricity, heteronomy and autonomy, other than a belief in the value of autonomy relative to the other two? The fact that there may be genuine moral alternatives along the way is ignored.[19]

Even more serious is the assumption that moral growth is related to an affectively and motivationally detached view of moral action as the universalisable act of a rational will. Moral growth is described as progression towards a Kantian ideal. But in this picture, the development of character and regard for the virtues is ignored. In fact the Kantian picture, with its emphasis on duty as opposed to inclination, lies in danger of detaching morality from the social, motivational and affective aspects of life from which it grows, with potentially dire consequences for the way in which the young regard morality.

The response of Kohlberg to those who stress the importance of a regard for the virtues in moral education, is to dismiss such calls as advocacy for a 'bag-of-virtues' account of morality, whereby children are taught nothing more than to act unreflectively on a series of injunctions not to steal, lie or cheat.[20] In the light of the discussions in earlier parts of this chapter, this criticism can be seen for the caricature that it is. For someone concerned with the growth of character and a regard for the virtues, unquestioning obedience to a set of moral principles encountered in a fairly limited range of circumstances is a necessary step, but no more than a step, along a path that takes in the growing complexity of moral experience. This goes together with a growth in the complexity of human character in the light of response to and reflection on a range of moral situations in which young people are increasingly expected to show independence of judgement. In the nature of moral learning, the growth of experience and the development of character are bound up with each other. Moral training in the sense described is the beginning, not the end, of the development of a regard for and the practice of, the virtues.

Moral education and human flourishing

In order to develop further a modified defence of the development of character and the practice of virtue as a basis for the understanding of moral learning, I want to discuss some criticisms of the work of MacIntyre made by Raimond Gaita.[21] A *reductionist* account of the virtues would claim that they exist in order to promote human well-being, happiness or flourishing. MacIntyre sets out to provide a non-reductionist account of the virtues, but, argues Gaita, because he seeks to provide an account of *why* we need the virtues, he ends up giving a reductionist account none the less. Gaita takes pains to acknowledge that there must be a connection between human needs and morality if morality is to be serious.[22] But it does not follow that an account of moral beliefs and practices has to be completely explicable in terms of universal human needs. In order to understand why the practice of virtue is important, we need to see that there is an inescapable connection between virtuous conduct and the fulfilment of human need. It does not follow that the significance of the practice of the virtues can be exhaustively explained by showing how they contribute to the fulfilment of those needs.

While acknowledging the force of these points, moral education as a form of character development can be defended. It does not follow from what Gaita has written that the virtues should be practised solely for their own sake, in Stoic fashion. Children should be taught to be good not solely because it will help them to be respected and to get on in life, nor just because that is how one should be. The practice of virtue is connected with human harm and well-being, but, both for oneself and for others, the well-being is a by-product, not in every case a necessary by-product, of the exercise of virtues. Children need to want to act virtuously even when it may not be in their immediately perceived interests to do so; but they also need to know and to understand the harm that can be caused through failure to do what is right. For example, harm may be caused mainly to themselves through the neglect of self-regarding virtues like courage and industriousness, and harm that may be done mainly to others through neglect of other-regarding virtues such as dependability and charity. Having been habituated to act courageously and compassionately and having come to value those traits in others, they none the less need to understand that acting in that way is not a futile exercise but one that, in the long run, and if practised collectively, contributes to social and individual well-being.

This entails that they come to appreciate that humans are social beings whose happiness depends on the well-being of the society in which they live. The well-being of the society, in turn, depends on the nature of its values and how well they are preserved by past, current and future generations. Thus, although it may make little or no sense to say that someone who is chronically and terminally ill has the possibility of flourishing, it does make good sense to say that the awareness that we have of the importance of our values and of the place that they have in our lives depends on our attending to the needs of fellow human beings unconditionally, and without consideration that we are doing so because we wish to promote these values. That is, we can come to understand that such character traits can be valued for themselves even though we are well aware of their wider ramifications.

These remarks should make it clear that moral education is a complex and difficult matter, which has no obvious point of completion. This is one reason why the foundations need to be right, before a child can be brought to appreciate the significance of his actions in the context of the community and culture in which he lives. There is a danger that a child's appreciation of morality may not even get off to the right start without the right kind of training and instruction. There is also the danger that it may remain stalled in a particular and limited conception, perhaps confined to the prudential observance of codes for prudential reasons. In such a case one might say that someone in such a situation has learned something about morality but that his moral education lacks depth and does not prepare him well for wise and considered action in circumstances of moral complexity.

Conclusion

The earliest forms of moral experience lie in a child's perception of his ability to cause pleasure or resentment to those around him and his reactions to those perceptions. However, moral conditioning gives way to moral training, where the aim is to encourage confident actions and reactions that increasingly embody elements of judgement and reflection. During this time, a child is acquiring individual character traits that have an inescapably moral dimension. In this sense he is beginning to develop character through the development of attitude, habit, action and reflection in ways that, if things go well, are both to his long-term benefit and to that of the society in which he lives. It should be emphasised that this is a social process; although the child has to reflect as an individual on the consequences of his actions, his ability to do so depends on responses and on the support of those around him, particularly those wiser and more experienced than himself.

It is most important that there is an affective dimension to this training; we would hope that a child would try to become virtuous because he wants to, not merely out of duty or even against all his inclinations. The Kantian conception of moral action solely according to the dictates of duty has some dangers for moral learning because it severs the connection between moral action and inclination in a quite radical way, detaching morality from the wider sphere of human action and concern in which it should be placed.[23] But in addition, there is a cognitive dimension to moral learning: it is important that children see situations as morally relevant and that they also, as they grow up, learn to see that the morally relevant features of a situation may look different from a point of view other than their own. In this respect they need to be able to appreciate the significance of principles such as the golden rule but also to appreciate that its application from a vicarious point of view may not be always simple. This, again, should lead to complexity and nuance in moral judgement, but in the context of a rule-governed framework. An important aid to the growth of this complexity lies in the availability of opportunities for vicarious experience through study of literature, biography and history, and for reflection on the significance of one's own actions and those of others. Finally, the acquisition of moral wisdom can only come about through great experience of life, through the development of qualities of character and through a habit of moral reflection.

All societies take their morality seriously and few, if any, completely neglect the training and education of their young in matters of morality.

To the extent that they are concerned with more than mere obedience to codes, they attend to the development of individual character through the practice of attitudes, dispositions and actions that are valued both for themselves and for their contribution to the well-being of their society. To this extent, a description of morality in terms, at least partially, of the cultivation of virtue is meta-ethical. It is an account of what we would expect in any society that takes morality seriously. It does not follow that because there is disagreement amongst philosophers about the nature of morality that a society is thereby confused about the character of its own moral beliefs.

Different societies tend to emphasise different virtues; some place more emphasis on moral codes than others; others emphasise the importance of autonomy, and so on. It is difficult for a meta-ethical theory to capture this variety and complexity in any given society and it is, therefore, easy to conclude that the confusion must also exist 'on the ground'. This would, however, be misleading. Societies may get confused about how to bring up their young, particularly in periods of transition: for example, from a Christian to a largely secular society or to a society in which different moral and religious systems co-exist. Such confusion may lead to serious damage, as this chapter has argued. But it does not follow from this very important observation that we live in a society and an epoch where we are confused about the very nature of morality or that we lack a common language in which to discuss the subject. Where confusion arises, the way out is often to be found in politics in its most general sense, namely through agreements to differ on certain matters of value, agreements to implement common values that all can agree on, and through the construction of common arrangements for negotiation and compromise about how a common moral understanding can be achieved.[24]

However, where any conception of the common good is thought to be problematic by moral educators, even in the sense of the pursuit of weak, as opposed to strong, autonomy (in the sense in which these concepts were introduced at the beginning of the chapter), then the kind of framework adopted for moral education suggested in this chapter comes under attack, because, in order to promote strong autonomy, consensual moral norms need to be rendered problematic, or at least conditional. This can hardly be done while they are at the same time said to be non-negotiable for children. There are good reasons for thinking that strong autonomy and weak autonomy are incompatible, if not contradictory, aims for education; also that the adoption of strong autonomy threatens the kind of moral educational framework developed in this chapter.[25] In order to clarify this issue, at the very least, political consensus needs to be developed about which values are thought to be possible objects of moral choice; a rejection of any attempt to reach agreement about that makes the possibility of consensual agreement highly unlikely. The pursuit of strong autonomy as an educational aim is, then, fraught with very serious difficulties for any project seeking to arrive at a consensus about which moral values it is acceptable to choose and hence for an education system to develop. But the answer to that problem is simple: strong autonomy is not an acceptable educational or moral aim in a society that wishes to take morality seriously. This does not entail, of course, that no society should ever review the values and aims that it considers worthwhile for citizens to pursue.

Another related way in which confusion might arise is through adoption of the Rousseauian conception of normativity, which rejects the overt imposition of norms on beings who are not yet fully rational and free and therefore evacuates normativity and overt moral formation from child-rearing practices. The confusions inherent in that idea have been examined in Chapter 3. Both of these confusions, however, are endemic to socially liberal societies and their unravelling must take place in the sphere of politics. They do not, in themselves, lead to the destruction of the possibility of moral education; that would happen only if they came to occupy such an important part of everyday beliefs that they threatened the existence of the current moral framework. Were that to happen, the MacIntyrean nightmare of a breakdown in moral discourse would become a serious possibility.

15

LEARNING TO MAKE AND TO APPRECIATE

The arts and other aspects of life

The aims of this chapter are: to emphasise the rule-governed nature of artistic and aesthetic activity; to acknowledge the central concerns of the arts with human life; to argue for a reintegration of aesthetic and artistic education into vocational education on the one hand and moral education on the other; and, finally, to emphasise the importance of both making and appreciating as central features of aesthetic and artistic learning and education.

The artistic and aesthetic aspects of life are nowadays considered to a large extent as a distinct sphere of activity from the economy, science and technology, religion and morality.[1] The sundering of different aspects of life is a condition of modernity rather than an abiding feature of human existence; it does not always seem to have been the case that the arts have been considered as a largely distinct sphere. There are in particular well-established connections between art and religion, art and morality, and art and craft and technology. The idea that art and aesthetics are a largely separate aspect of life is a relatively new one.

A number of factors have brought about the severing of art from other human concerns: the decline of religion; the increasing influence of subjectivism within the arts and morality; and an increasing economic division of labour, including mass production techniques, which has tended to diminish, although not to eliminate, the role of the craftsman. As the arts have tended to become detached from other areas of activity, so the influence of subjectivism within the arts themselves has grown. As they have become freed from external norms, they have become governed by norms that are more or less internal to artistic activities. In addition, the rise of anti-authoritarianism, which we have seen to be a powerful force in educational thinking, has contributed to a certain rejection of even internal norms governing the production of art.

This is not to say that there are no constraints on artistic production: economic demands and the hankerings of some artists for a return to an older normative structure preclude a complete move into subjectivism. But the prevailing movement has posed particular difficulties for art education and learning generally, since it is no longer clear to many what the aims of arts education are. This chapter seeks to understand what is involved in artistic learning as it has been more traditionally conceived, and what it might look like in modern conditions if it were to be taken seriously again as part of the experience of all children and young people.

Making and appreciating

There are two aspects of learning in art: making and appreciating. Very often the same people are involved in both; it would be difficult to see how one could be a skilful painter or writer if one could not, to some extent, appreciate the work of others. It is natural to think that artistic learning depends on being able to learn from the work of others. The contrary does not seem to be so obviously the case; one can appreciate without being able to make. Although making may well enhance appreciation, given the specialisation and skill involved, it would be surprising if a division of labour did not arise in any society when it comes to the making of worthwhile objects of artistic appreciation. This is not to say that children cannot experiment with artistic creation at an elementary level, but it does not follow that they should all be expected to learn to make worthwhile objects of artistic scrutiny and appreciation that would bear comparison with the work of skilled adults.[2] Learning to make and learning to appreciate are distinct but closely connected activities which, to a certain extent, need to be considered separately.

What are the forms of learning that go with each kind of artistic activity? If the realm of the artistic extends beyond high culture and includes the appreciation of cultural products that may occur at work, in a domestic setting or as part of religious and political ritual, then it is quite proper and natural to think of it as embracing nearly all aspects of human life. Learning to appreciate will, then, be a part of learning from the earliest stages. This is perhaps obvious in the case of language. Very young children are introduced to story and verse from their earliest years and come to sing and recite, if not to compose, as part of the participative actitivities through which they learn their mother tongue.[3]

The observation extends further than language; children are introduced to music as well as to story and poetry through imitation and participation. The connection between language and music is intimate, particularly through verse, poetry and song. Learning to speak involves acquiring the ability to use pitch, intonation, rhythm and rhyme and a more developed and self-conscious attention to these skills is required for singing. In most societies, these connections are made, in a more or less explicit manner, from the earliest stages of education.

But singing and verse-making are also connected with expressive activities like dance and, once again, a child is likely to come across dance, not as an activity spatially and temporally distinct from verse and song, but bound up with them in a single activity or set of activities. These activities are likely, in many societies, to be part of some larger event with a particular cultural significance, such as religious festivals. We can see then, that learning both to appreciate and to take part in artistic activities may quite properly occur at the earliest stages. They are learned through participation, training and instruction, rather than through any process of discovery.

But these are only a small part of the spectrum of artistic activities. All societies require techniques and skills that are necessary for the production of artefacts for everyday life. These artefacts, because they form a part of everday life, assume a decorative as well as a functional role. They are made to please us as well as to serve us because pleasure in the small matters of life is considered to be an important ingredient of the good life in many, if not most, societies. In such societies, the distinction between the two roles is hardly remarked on; a useful object that did not please its user would be diminished in its usefulness. A sharp distinction between the two is perhaps clearer to contemporary Western man than it is to the people of other epochs and places. It would, perhaps, be more helpful to say that, for most societies, what we call the artistic is a dimension of things that cannot be separated from them, any more than the surface of a table can be separated from the table. To suppose that, in many societies, one can separate utility and beauty, is to commit a similar error.[4]

Learning about the artistic in young childhood often involves learning to participate in activities of which the artistic is but an aspect. Early appreciation of objects of artistic awareness comes through learned reactive behaviour. Children learn from the reactions of others to works of art and artefacts, the kinds of things that are appreciated and particularly valued in their own culture. They are *trained* to appreciate through being *shown* and *taught* about the different aspects of objects of artistic awareness from the point of view of adults. Early appreciation of art is not, therefore, grounded in subjectivity (a judgement not based on any socially accepted norms), although children may be encouraged by adults to develop personal reactions to works of art, to express likes and dislikes, to comment on features of works of art, and to relate their significance to their own lives. But children are only able to do this when they have gained an acquaintance with objects of artistic and cultural significance. Whatever they may develop in the way of individual taste will be against a background of the artistic traditions of the societies in which they live.

Learning and genre

So far the discussion has emphasised the social nature of the appreciation of art. Implicit in this emphasis is the recognition that social life is rule-governed. It is natural to suppose, given its importance, that artistic activity generally, including the activity of making works of art, is also rule-governed. If this is so, then we can only make and appreciate works of art successfully if we understand the rules or conventions that govern their construction and the norms that govern judgements as to their quality.

This is not a popular line to take in art education; subjectivism has a very powerful hold both within the art and the educational worlds and its proponents tend to be resistant to any idea that there are objective criteria for judging the merits of works of art. There are various reasons for this point of view; the influence of the empiricist tradition of regarding judgement as private and incorrigible is certainly one of them. Another is the view that art is expressive of feeling or emotion rather than of reason and hence that it is almost a category mistake to say that one can judge a work of art.[5] It is not difficult to show that subjectivism is incoherent, but refutations do not seem to carry too much weight with its adherents precisely because they are subjectivists. If subjectivism were true, then all expressions of artistic appreciation would be equally valid and there would be no room for a discursive practice of art, since only competing voices would be heard, rather than any form of mutual understanding. Subjectivism cannot even maintain a distinction between art and any other kind of activity whatsoever, since judgements about what constitutes art are both subjective and incorrigible. It follows that the idea that one could learn anything about art or that one could educate children in the arts does not make sense; if subjective judgements are incorrigible, it is inconceivable that one could make them better.

The difficulties that are experienced by art education parallel those of religious education. Truth in art is different from truth in science and different again from the religious truth, although there are important connections between all three and also strong and relatively unexplored connections between truth in art and in morality. As with morality and religion, the significance of artistic statements and judgements as to their truth or falsity needs to be understood in terms of the community who uses them and to whom they make practical sense. They are not to be compared with a paradigmatic notion of truth such as is found in science or in textbooks of philosophical logic and therefore found to be wanting on those criteria. It is important to notice that I am not claiming that works of art are themselves true or false in the scientific sense, although there are senses of 'true' and 'false' for which it makes sense to claim that some works of art are, for example, truthful and unsentimental or false and meretricious without being depictions, in a straightforward sense, of reality.[6] This issue will be discussed below.

If the subjectivist claim is incoherent, what is the substance of the claim that one can make judgements about the value of ways in which art is made or appreciated and hence normative statements about how we can learn how to do these things? One answer is that there are rules that govern the production of artwork and further rules that allow us to judge the quality of that work. Such an account might just work for some forms of highly stylised and conventional forms of art but is difficult to maintain in the face of some quite obvious examples. Very often we value works of art not just because of their individuality, but because they appear to break the rules of a medium or a genre, or at least radically to reinterpret them. Examples of this abound in the modernist canon, from Joyce's *Ulysses* to Wagner's 'Tristan' and Picasso's *Guernica*.

In fact, a straightforward, conventionalist account of art involves a somewhat simple-minded account of rule-following. As we have noted before, not only must it be possible for rules to be taught and for people to be corrected, but rules must also be capable of *interpretation* and the following of those rules must be capable of *evaluation*. In many cases, the rules are themselves subject to evaluation.[7] These practices are internal to rule-following and they assume particular importance in the production and appreciation of art, where the artist's own interpretation of a genre and the audience's evaluation of his own interpretation play a critical role in the practice of art-making and appreciating. This feature of art, although it goes some way towards explaining the individual qualities of works of art and of our evaluative reaction towards them, leaves us a long way short of subjectivism, where interpretation and evaluation, if they take place at all, are incorrigible processes. On the account offered here, interpretation and evaluation are themselves social practices and take place in a discursive mode as part of a community of artists and patrons of the arts. This is not to say that such a sense of community may be lost, just as I argued it could be in religion and morality, but what we have then is the effective death of that sphere of life or at least its partial dissolution, rather than a reconstitution of the practice under new rules.

As we saw in Chapter 9, Wittgenstein distinguished between the rules of grammar and the rules of cooking.[8] This distinction is commonly taken to be between rules that are quite arbitrary in their nature (such as rules of grammar) and rules that are more like teleological principles that take account of laws of nature.[9] Although the principles by which works of art are made and judged are conventional to a certain extent, far more so than rules of cooking (although one should not underestimate the artistic or aesthetic dimensions of cookery), many of the arts have to take account of the natural properties of the materials in which they exist, such as paint, metal, stone and wood. In this sense, learning how to make works of art is, at least partially, coming to terms with given features of nature which will, to some extent, condition the nature of the work of art. In this important respect, learning to make works of art is like learning to make other things of a more obviously utilitarian nature, like buildings, bridges and tools. If one does not understand through experience or instruction what are the possibilities and the limits of the materials with which one is working, then it is not possible to produce something worthwhile or even to produce anything at all.

This implies that artistic production is a rule-governed activity, albeit one with a certain distinctiveness connected with the emphasis placed on *interpretation* of what is made on the one hand, and *recognition* of the natural constraints of the materials worked with on the other. It follows then, that children who are learning about art by drawing, painting or carving, for example, need to follow both the conventional and the teleological rules governing these activities. In particular, they need to be trained in certain techniques and to be corrected if they get them wrong. Only later will they be able to interpret and evaluate those rules with any degree of confidence, although they will need to know at an early stage that they should try to develop an individual voice in what they do.

Children's art work, whether it be painting, sculpture, music or literature, cannot be creative. It *can* be original, interesting or a highly competent essay in a genre. But until a genre has been successfully mastered, it is not possible to be creative within it. This is not just an empirical, but a loosely conceptual point: given the normal cognitive capacities of human beings, we cannot reinterpret a genre in a practical sense unless we are first able to interpret it by working within it. This is true even of the greatest creative geniuses like Mozart, whose preparation for the production of master works takes thousands of hours of lower-order work or practice and years of being an apprentice and journeyman before achieving 'master' status.[10] If, therefore, it is an educational aim to raise children who are capable of becoming creative artists at some stage in their lives, they need to be introduced to genres and taught how to work within them.[11] For example, they need to be introduced to poetic forms; to understand that stories have settings, plots and characters; that there are different kinds of painting with their own conventions and modes of composition, and so on. They need to be trained and instructed in the practice of those conventions and only then should they be free to explore the full possibilities, as well as the limitations, of a genre.

It might be objected that this is a normative account of art education which would ignore and stultify the creative process within individuals which is necessary if creative art is to be produced. To this it can be replied that if the idea of a creative process is the idea of something that is private and unconstrained by any convention, then it is a vacuous notion. In this sense, any unobserved mental activity can be a creative process, but that is scarcely an interesting claim. On the other hand, if we judge that a creative process has occurred because a creative work of art has resulted from it, then we are claiming that the process, however inscrutable it might be (and talk of process is a little odd in this context) takes account of genre conventions. If the process of creation did take account of them then, normally, it would have been shaped by a training that acquainted the artist with them and enabled him to use them.

It is no doubt true that there is something mysterious and inexplicable about the creation of works of art.[12] But it does not follow that the creation of works of art can be utterly subjective and unconstrained by previous experience and education or training. In the sense that artistic endeavour depends on intuition, then it also depends on prior learning in order to develop the powers of perception, the mastery of genre, and the trained imagination that make good art possible. David Best quotes Ben Shahn who says: 'Intuition is actually the result of prolonged tuition.'[13] If this is true, then the subjectivist tradition in art education needs to be rethought in a similar way to that in which ideas about other kinds of learning need to be rethought, with much less emphasis on inner processes and a much greater emphasis on natural reactions, instruction and training.

This point holds for appreciating as well as making art. It is possible, as Best argues, to have an aesthetic appreciation of a work of art without at the same time understanding it *as a work of art*. We can appreciate beauty, dignity or mystery in a painting or a piece of music much as we can admire these things in a landscape, even though we may be unable to appreciate them as works of art because we are not familiar with the cultural tradition and the genre conventions that inform them. This applies as much to works of art in our own culture as it does to works of art produced in other cultures. Children do not become acquainted with all aspects of their culture simply by living among the people whose culture it is; they need to be taught about and trained to notice and appreciate aspects of their culture which might never have come to their notice or aroused their interest without the guidance of a teacher or parent. When that acquaintance becomes a *practical* one, achieved through trying one's hand at some of the genres, then the ability to appreciate a work of art *as art* is likely to be enhanced through some experience of the complexity of working with particular materials and the conventions of a particular genre. Education in the appreciation of art is, then, if done properly, as much a practical as a theoretical activity.

Art, aesthetics and vocational education

It was stated earlier that a clear-cut separation between the arts and other activities is to an extent artificial and a consequence of a fairly radical division of areas of activity within modern societies; moreover, this division is not inevitable but a product of powerful currents of thought in modern life. One area which has tended to occupy a Cinderella role in psychological and educational thinking about learning has been vocational education. This has tended to be associated with training, which has in turn been associated with *conditioning* under the influence of behaviourist theory.[14]

These associations have helped to consolidate a cultural prejudice against vocationally oriented forms of learning and consequently have led to a neglect both of the nature and of the value of vocational education and training. This is particularly relevant to art and aesthetic education as there is a close connection, which is not always recognised, between them and vocational education. The separation made between the artistic and other aspects of life is, to some extent, artificial and the product of our own particular culture. Useful objects such as tools, crockery and cutlery, not to mention bridges and buildings, inevitably have an aesthetic dimension to them. Whether their makers intend it or not, a vase, a knife or a bridge can excite a reaction of appreciation or aversion. Useful artefacts are always potential objects of appreciation. Vocational education may concentrate on their utility and may completely ignore aesthetic or artistic considerations. This does not mean, however, that an object made for a utilitarian purpose will thereby cease to be a potential object of aesthetic appreciation. It will continue to be so, if only by default, because people will react to it in terms of its beauty or lack of it, as well as its usefulness. Most people would agree that if something were to be the subject of an aesthetic judgement, then it would be preferable for it to be regarded as beautiful rather than ugly. This entails that the aesthetic dimension ought to be a central part of vocational education. This is more likely to be the case when the public, to whom useful objects are sold, is sensitive to aesthetic value.

The relative neglect of the artistic/aesthetic dimension in the production of objects of utility is regrettable and unnecessary. There is a tendency to see vocational learning as a lower-order, rule-governed activity, on the one hand, and learning to make artworks as subjective expression on the other: consequently; the affinities between the two are frequently overlooked. But this difficulty arises through seeing each through distorting lenses. It is as inaccurate to describe the production of useful objects solely in terms of low-level, routine manufacturing activity, as it is to describe the production of works of art solely as unconstrained subjective expression.

A craftsman or a technician striving for excellence out of love for what he is doing, needs to be able to judge and to adjust his plans, to have an awareness of the purposes for which he is making, and a sense of how it will fit into the situation for which it is designed. If he is committed to his work, he will aspire to produce something that can be appreciated by those who use it. He needs to do this as well as having as his aim the production of something useful which is fit for the primary purpose for which it is designed. An artist or craftsman ought to be able to exploit the strengths and understand the limitations of the materials with which he is working; furthermore he ought to understand and be able to exploit the conventions of the genre in which he works. He also needs to have an understanding of where the artefact he is making is going to fit and its significance, in human terms, in that place. In other words, he ought to make something beautiful as well as useful.

Although these descriptions of the work of a technician, craftsman or artist are normative rather than descriptive, they are put here to bring out the fact that the affinities between vocational and aesthetic/artistic education are not fully enough exploited in either form of education, to the detriment of both.

Best's reluctance to consider the artistic aspect of vocational education and his wish to assign only aesthetic, rather than artistic, significance to objects of utility, tends to reinforce the sharp separation between vocational and other forms of education which this chapter has been questioning.[15] For it is quite possible for artefacts, as well as natural phenomena, to have aesthetic value accidentally. It is then too easy to attribute their aesthetic value to accident rather than to design, particularly if vocational education does not encourage attention to the aesthetic dimension of artefacts and ignores their potential for having an artistic dimension.

Art and knowledge

To what extent is it possible to learn from the arts? One answer is that it is perfectly possible to learn *about* the arts, but difficult, if not impossible, to learn *from* them. I shall argue that the arts yield knowledge in both senses and it is only by thinking of knowledge in a very narrow sense that one can be blind to the fact that the arts can yield knowledge in the second sense.

One can learn about the arts in three main ways. First, one can learn about the history of art, about works that were produced, the techniques used to produce them, the cultural milieu in which they were produced, and so on. Second, one can learn how to produce works of art and, along the way, the rules for the production of art. Finally one can learn to appreciate works of art as a form of either personal or discursive enjoyment. These things are all a very proper and necessary part of an arts education, but are they all that can be learned from the arts or are there further insights to be gained *through* the experience of art?

The subjectivist tradition suggests that the only learning that one can have through the arts is about one's own feelings, whether these are generated through making or through appreciation. One does not have to be a subjectivist though, to be sceptical about the idea that knowledge of truths about the world can be gained from the arts. Hirst's characterisation of the arts as a distinctive form of knowledge is odd, since he emphasised that by forms of knowledge he means forms of *propositional* knowledge which express truths about the world.[16] In this sense of knowledge, the arts rarely if ever yield it. On the contrary, if they were taken to yield knowledge in this sense, then their nature would be seriously mistaken. In one way, Plato's doubtfulness about the arts rests on mistakenly taking artworks as representations in the sense that a description of an event might be, and then measuring their worth against the yardstick of what an accurate depicting representation is like. This is to try and set the arts up as something that they are not and do not set out to be.[17] This is not to say that the arts cannot convey falsehood as well as truth in another way, however, and that is the concern of this section.

If the arts do not represent in such a way that they give us something like true empirical propositions, in what sense can they be said to give us knowledge? It is probably more accurate to say that they are capable of yielding knowledge in the sense of *understanding*. They are capable of altering our view of life so that we come to see aspects of it in a different light and this, in turn, alters the way in which we act and react to other human beings. Artistic representations should not be taken to be real but to show up aspects of reality that might be difficult to bring to people's attention in any other way. They are not a pretence but a form of representation that tries to show important features of human life truthfully (with care and sincerity) and without distortion.[18]

The kind of truth that the arts are capable of conveying is the truth that we mean when we talk about truthfulness, sincerity or honesty. They can allow us to see an aspect of a situation of which we were aware but whose significance or importance we had not fully appreciated. This need not just mean that they can give us certain feelings (although they may well do that), but that they can also give us new understanding. To say this is to imply more than just that we have been given a subjective experience, for that may have no further consequences in our lives. It implies that the way we see the world has been changed and perhaps that the way in which we behave has changed as well.

For example, I may know that adultery is a destructive act both to its perpetrators and to those who are affected by their actions. However, it may be through reading *Anna Karenina* that I come to appreciate the way in which adultery affects the human soul and why it has the destructive effects that it has. The immediacy and force of this message might have been difficult to convey in any other way, even through the experience of adulterous passion. While the arts can express truthfulness, insight and sincerity, they may also express the contrary: falseness and sentimentality, shallowness and dishonesty.

It was this aspect of the arts, together with, in the Greek context, their expression of a moral code of which Plato disapproved, that made him suspicious of their value, although he appears to have thought that this was an inevitable consequence of their representational character. There is an important distinction between good art and bad art which is not just about technique and execution, but also about its moral and human dimension. Art education is then, a species of or a part of moral education, in that an engagement with the arts can heighten our awareness of human experience through the provision of vicarious moral experience. It can also fail to do so, which is why the subject matter of arts education is of no small importance and why it is often fiercely contested. Choice of the content of the arts curriculum is, then, partly a moral choice, in the sense that teachers have to form a view as to what is truthful and what is fallacious and to have the capacity and commitment to guide their pupils to recognise the truthfulness (or lack of it) in the works of art that they bring to their attention. This may well involve them in uncomfortable choices and debates, but where these take place there is at least an implicit recognition of what is at stake in education for the arts, including literature.

The modern Western world tends to think of the arts in terms either of technique or of subjective experience, and therefore it is difficult to see how conversations about the arts can take place even amongst people who have a reasonable acquaintance with music, painting or literature. They are reduced either to describing their feelings or to commenting (if they are competent to do so) on the technique by which a work of art was realised. But the fact that such a situation exists suggests that the notion of art education has been impoverished, both on the practical and the receptive side, and that it has become disconnected with other important aspects of life such as occupation, religion and morality.

16

CONCLUSION

Five themes but no grand theories

What conclusions can be drawn from these studies of various aspects of learning? Nothing like a theory about how learning takes place has appeared, for there is nothing in the studies to suggest that we are anywhere near, or could be anywhere near, such a theory. Grand empirical theory-building, as is attempted by cognitivism and developmentalism, rests upon sandy foundations which, as we saw in Chapters 6 and 7, cannot carry any theoretical or empirical weight. So one theme that has emerged is the uselessness of grand theories of learning, especially when they are underpinned, as they invariably are, by faulty epistemological premises. This is not to say that local theories may not emerge about particular aspects of learning that are based on evidence and that are sensitive to the cultural context in which learning takes place.

The above-stated theme about the inapplicability of theory is a negative one, but there are more positive themes which should guide anyone with an empirical interest in learning. What is more, some at least of these themes run through several fields of learning.

1   First, there is the necessarily *social* nature of learning, which is a consequence of the social nature of human life. The discussion of the private language argument in Chapter 4 was an important step in establishing that point and in undermining the pretensions of both cognitivism, behaviourism and some versions of developmentalism.
2   Then there is the *affective* nature of learning, which is closely bound up with the social nature of rule-following and the importance of reactive behaviour and our responses to it, in our ability to engage in rule-following activities. We saw in Chapters 5, 8, 10, 13, 14 and 15 how this was important in training, language learning, acquiring memory skills and learning to participate in morality, religion and art.
3   There is also the importance of *motivation* in learning which is not to be understood, as developmentalists since Rousseau have maintained, as a purely internal force, but as something that is personal but is also in constant interaction with society, with its values, priorities and

183

needs, which all have an effect on the self-esteem of individuals and what they aspire to learn about.

4   Of major importance is the *love* of what is to be learned. Only love of what is to be learned can explain how even a great talent can achieve excellence in a chosen field. Plato talks of divine inspiration but this does not contradict the point made here; the poet's ability is made manifest through his love of the deity who inspired him. In more secular language, such love comes to someone through the individual inspiration of interest, which is partly subject to the importance that society or a part of society attaches to an activity or a body of knowledge. The requirements of love make us do things of which others would not have dreamed us capable, and in this way we may become excellent at some of them. But the requirements of love are set, at least in part, by the requirements and expectations of society.

5   If love is a requirement of excellence, *respect* is a requirement of effectiveness. If one does not respect what one is to learn, or recognise the efforts that have gone into its creation and development, then success is unlikely. But it is part of the dogma of cognitivism and much of developmental theory that learning takes place through the checking of knowledge that one has already, in some sense, acquired. All that needs to be done is fine-tuning. The cultivation of such an idea is hardly likely to lead to any degree of humility on the part of a learner or a teacher. When it is combined with the suspicion of any form of society that is not predicated on a very strict idea of freedom and equality, such as we find in Rousseau, then the results are likely to be very disappointing.

The importance of human diversity

Learning takes place in cultures that differ very widely in their general natures, both in the importance which they attach to different activities and bodies of knowledge and in their attitudes to learning. In addition, the individuality of human beings is the result of an amalgam of biological endowment and social intercourse, to the extent that the two cannot be meaningfully disentangled. Add to this the sheer diversity of activities that could be considered worthwhile in any society, especially in a complex society such as ours, and the possibilities for the development of individuality within a social context are enormous. The development of individuality is not the same thing as the development of *individualism* (which appears to be closely associated with an absence of constraint or self-discipline); rather it consists of the development of distinct sets of abilities, interests and passions which both reflect and reflect back on society.

A society that does not take human individuality seriously is in danger of impoverishing itself. Theories of learning that do not take individuality seriously will contribute to that impoverishment. Most of them are unable to give a plausible account of individuality. In fact, through the adoption of various mechanistic models of mind they make it well-nigh impossible to discern what such individuality could amount to. Rousseau perhaps comes nearest to succeeding in accounting for individuality, but his contempt for existing society does not let him allow Émile to develop as a genuinely social individual with a meaningful place in the world.

Learning and education

Human diversity then is to be applauded and recognised, not regarded with suspicion. If that is the case, then the education that is offered to young people needs to recognise that as well. There is a clear implication that education needs to cater for different abilities and interests, whether in the form of different curricula, different schools or through other institutions such as apprenticeship. This need not mean that diversity has to be built into the system from the outset. All cultures can only proceed on the basis of a set of common understandings and some common skills. The uninterrupted growth of individualism has already tended to disrupt this common cultural capital in the developed Western societies, particularly the Anglo-Saxon ones. Individuality develops out of some form of independence which has to be gained; it does not arrive as part of a neonate's baggage.

Common reactions, skills, cultural knowledge and understanding may best be cultivated through training and instruction at the earliest stages, together with judiciously chosen opportunities for developing both sociability and independence as a child grows older. The implication is that there should be a common core of education to develop such a cultural bond, to allow diversity to develop in such a way that society is strengthened rather than fragmented by it and in a way that is satisfying to the individual as well. If this book has in any way contributed to the further realisation of such a possibility, it will have achieved its main aim.

NOTES

1 INTRODUCTION: RECONSIDERING LEARNING

1 L. Wittgenstein, *Philosophical Investigations*, Oxford, Blackwell, 1953, p. 232.

2 For a recent example see Peter Carruthers, *Human Knowledge and Human Nature*, Oxford, Oxford University Press, 1992. For a book with similar tendencies see Fred D'Agostino, *Chomsky's System of Ideas*, Oxford, Clarendon, 1986.

3 René Descartes, *Philosophical Writings*, selected, translated and edited by G.E.M. Anscombe and P.T. Geach, London, Nelson, 1966. See, for example, *Discourse on Method*, Part 5. See also, I. Kant, *Critique of Practical Reason*, 'The Antinomy of Practical Reason', pp. 117–118 in edition translated by L.W. Beck, Indianapolis, Bobbs-Merrill, 1956. First published 1788.

4 For more on this see Charles Taylor, *The Explanation of Behaviour*, London, Routledge, 1964.

5 The picture is further complicated by the tendency of some psychologists to amalgamate physicalist accounts derived from behaviourism on the one hand and cognitivism on the other to give a combined account of the laws of bodily and neural activity. See D. Lieberman, *Learning*, California, Wadsworth, 1990, Chapters 9 and 10.

6 See, for example, Noam Chomsky, *Language and Problems of Knowledge*, Cambridge, Mass., MIT Press, 1988, pp. 154–155.

7 This aspect of Wittgenstein's thinking can most readily be found in *On Certainty*, Oxford, Blackwell, 1969.

8 L. Wittgenstein, *Zettel*, Oxford, Blackwell, 1967, para. 608.

9 A point that has been made by, for example, C.A. MacMillan in *Women, Reason and Nature*, London, Macmillan, 1982.

10 I put it this way because, although Wittgenstein sets out his case in the *Philosophical Investigations* in terms of private *languages*, he is prepared to countenance something like a private language in other writings. This does not imply either inconsistency or a change in view on his part. He did admit the possibility of language as mechanism (which could be private) but not the possibility of language as norm (which could not). The passages on private language are directed against the latter possibility.

11 This is not to claim that animals cannot remember; but they cannot make memory claims.

12 The only other thinker to recognise this before Wittgenstein's work became well known was L.S. Vygotsky, a psychologist heavily influenced by Marxism. The social character of human behaviour (including the use of language) was

always recognised by Marx and it is perhaps of interest that the Marxist econo-
mist Piero Sraffa emphasised the importance of the social aspect of language in
a conversation that was to change Wittgenstein's early views about language as
they were expressed in the *Tractatus Logico-Philosophicus*. However, neither
Marx nor Vygotsky ever drew out the normative nature of human social existence that is so fundamental to our understanding of it. Indeed, it could be
maintained that Marx's general philosophical approach would have prevented
him from ever doing so.

13 'We observe that all nations, barbarous as well as civilised, though separately
founded because remote from each other in time and space, keep these three
human customs: all have some religion, all contract solemn marriages, all bury
their dead. And in no nation, however savage and crude, are any human actions
performed with more elaborate ceremonies and more sacred solemnity that the
rites of religion, marriage and burial', Giambattista Vico, *The New Science*. First
published 1725, quoted from Cornell University Press edition, 1968, p. 97. See
also, P. Winch, 'Understanding a Primitive Society', in *Ethics and Action*,
London, Routledge, 1972.

14 For a fuller treatment of these issues see C. Winch, *Quality and Education*,
Oxford, Blackwell, 1996.

15 J.J. Rousseau, *Émile ou l'éducation*, first published in 1762. English edition
translated by Barbara Foxley, published London, Dent, 1911, pp. 228–278.
Available in French, Paris, Éditions Flammarion, 1966.

16 I have in mind both Rousseau's covert teaching-by-conditioning and scientistic
attempts to shape learning through conditioning procedures, particularly evident
within the behaviourist tradition.

2 THE CARTESIAN AND EMPIRICIST HERITAGE OF LEARNING THEORIES

1 See, for example, G.P. Baker and K.J. Morris, *Descartes' Dualism*, London,
Routledge, 1996.

2 Ibid., pp. 60–69.

3 Locke, on the other hand, recognises relational judgements. J. Locke, *An Essay
Concerning Human Understanding*, London, Dent, 1961, Volume I, Book II,
Chapter XXV, pp. 266–270.

4 It does not follow from the premise that Descartes is a being whose essence is
thinking that he is a being distinct from his body. This move is criticised in,
for example, A. Kenny, *Descartes*, New York, Random House, 1969, pp. 79–80.
John Cottingham, *Descartes*, Oxford, Blackwell, 1986, pp. 111–118, also
advances criticisms of this thesis and gives details of objections from Descartes'
contemporaries such as Gassendi.

5 René Descartes, *Philosophical Writings*, translated by G.E.M. Anscombe and
P.T. Geach, London, Nelson, 1954, pp. 64, 77.

6 Ibid., p. 78.

7 Ibid., pp. 78–79; Descartes also refers to 'generic concepts' such as body in
general (ibid., p. 72).

8 Elsewhere this second kind of idea is described as factitious rather than innate
as it arises from the exercise of certain abilities (*Œuvres de Descartes*, Charles
Adam and Paul Tannery (eds.), Paris, Cerf [1897], 1913, Volume III, p. 303,
quoted in Kenny, op. cit., pp. 101–102. Henceforth abbreviated as AT).

9 Some of these items could be part of the experience of a sentient being, such
as experiences of heat and cold. Non-sapients could not form certain kinds of

judgements, e.g. 'It seems to me that it is cold'. If this interpretation is correct, then it is not just a *res cogitans* that could have ideas. See Baker and Morris for a discussion of the distinction between sentience and sapience.

10 Cf. Baker and Morris, op. cit., pp. 179–180, for Descartes' concept of welfare.
11 Ibid., pp. 130–134 for a discussion of this matter.
12 A capacity is here understood as the underlying faculty of being able to acquire an ability. For example, a neonate has a capacity for language acquisition. When it has learned a language it has the ability to use that language.
13 See Kenny's discussion of ATIII, p. 424 and ATVIII, p. 357 in op. cit., pp. 101–103.
14 Plato, *Meno* in B. Jowett, *The Dialogues of Plato*, London, Sphere Books, 1970.
15 This way of putting things, however, poses difficulties for both Descartes and Locke, who seem to think that ideas are required to be present in consciousness for them to exist.
16 Kenny, op. cit., p. 103.
17 At ATVII, p. 67 the suggestion is made that ideas not currently being thought of can be brought forth 'from the treasure house of my mind'. See J. Cottingham, op. cit., pp. 145–146.
18 ATVIII, p. 358; ATIII, p. 417 cited in Kenny, op. cit.
19 ATVII, p. 161. See also *Rules for the Direction of the Mind*, Rule XII (Geach and Anscombe edition), pp. 168–169.
20 This follows from their being images of an image or trace in the brain. See Kenny, op. cit., p. 108.
21 It may not be as platitudinous as all that, however, because some modern Cartesians believe that those concepts which, it is generally thought, we *acquire*, are in fact held innately. See Noam Chomsky, *Language and Problems of Knowledge*, Cambridge, Mass., MIT Press, 1988; J. Fodor, *The Language of Thought*, Cambridge Mass., MIT Press, 1975. These theories will be dealt with more thoroughly in Chapter 9.
22 P.T. Geach, *Mental Acts*, London, Routledge, 1957.
23 Locke, op. cit., Volume I, Book II, Chapter VII, p. 101.
24 Ibid., Book I, Chapter II, p. 16.
25 Ibid., Volume I, Book I, Chapter II, p. 11.
26 *Rules for the Direction of the Mind*, Rule XII, p. 168 of Geach and Anscombe edition.
27 Locke, op. cit., Volume I, Book II, Chapter X, p. 118. See also Don Locke, *Memory*, London, Macmillan, 1971, p. 4.
28 Cf. Baker and Morris, op. cit., pp. 29–30; 161–162.
29 J. Locke, op. cit., p. 15.
30 Ibid., p. 20.
31 G. Ryle, *The Concept of Mind*, London, Hutchinson, 1949, Chapters 2, 5. It is arguable that Ryle is too sweeping and that it would be more accurate to say that knowledge and belief are *largely* dispositional rather than episodic.
32 The most notable exponent of this way of thinking in twentieth-century philosophy is, perhaps, J. Fodor, see op. cit.
33. L. Wittgenstein, *Philosophical Investigations*, Oxford, Blackwell, 1953.

3 THE ROMANTIC VIEW OF LEARNING: ROUSSEAU'S *ÉMILE*

1 For a relatively benign overview of *Émile* from the point of view of a traditional liberal educator, see R.S. Peters, 'The Paradoxes in Rousseau's Émile' in R.S. Peters, *Essays on Educators*, London, Allen & Unwin, 1981. For a recent

account of the influence of Rousseau on other progressive educational thinkers, see J. Darling, *Child-Centred Education and Its Critics*, London, Chapman, 1994, Chapters 2, 3. All quotations from *Émile* are taken from J.J. Rousseau, *Émile ou l'éducation*, first published in 1762. For convenience, citations and quotations are taken from the English translation by Barbara Foxley, London, Dent, 1911.

2 Cf. N. Dent, 'The Basic Principle of Émile's Education', *Journal of Philosophy of Education*, 22, 2, 1988a, pp. 139–150.

3 Cf. J. Darling, 'Rousseau as Progressive Instrumentalist', *Journal of Philosophy of Education*, 27, 1, 1993, pp. 27–38.

4 Rousseau does not appear to subscribe to a systematic doctrine of innate ideas. But he does appear to believe that the sentiment of justice is innate (op. cit., p. 32). He also appears to believe that certain capacities are innate, although manifested within a social context (ibid., p. 340).

5 Rousseau does, of course, see the need for some kind of normative order, but only one that is based upon the free association of equals. But the question posed here is, 'What are the conditions that would allow the free association of individuals to arise?' and answering that question presupposes the prior existence of a normative order.

6 For more on this, see J. Darling, 'Understanding and Religion in Rousseau's *Émile*', *British Journal of Educational Studies*, 33, 1, 1985, pp. 20–34.

7 J. Locke, op. cit., Book II, Chapter 1, p. 78. First published 1690. Fifth edition London, Dent, 1961.

8 Rousseau, op. cit., p. 165.

9 Ibid., pp. 218–219.

10 Ibid., pp. 246–247.

11 Ibid., pp. 165–166.

12 See, for example, L. Wittgenstein, *Remarks on Philosophical Psychology*, Volume 1, Oxford, Blackwell, 1980.

13 Rousseau, op. cit., p. 166.

14 Rousseau, *Discourse on Inequality*, London, Dent, 1913, pp. 174–179.

15 N. Dent, *Rousseau*, Oxford, Blackwell, 1988b, makes out a powerful case for inclining to this view. The interpretation of 'natural' in this section owes a great deal to Dent's discussion.

16 Dent, 1988b, op. cit., pp. 14–18; 74–78 for a detailed discussion.

17 Rousseau, op. cit., p. 33; see also p. 36.

18 Ibid., p. 32. Contrast Wittgenstein's remark in *Culture and Value*; 'Anyone who listens to a child's crying and understands what he hears will know that it harbours dormant psychic forces, terrible forces different from anything commonly assumed. Profound rage, pain and lust for destruction.' Translated by Peter Winch, Oxford, Blackwell, 1980, p. 2e.

19 Ibid., p. 33. Here Rousseau appears also to sanction the existence of an innate sense of justice in humans.

20 Ibid., p. 32.

21 G.P. Baker and P.M.S. Hacker, *Wittgenstein: Rules, Grammar and Necessity*, Oxford, Blackwell, 1985, pp. 45–47.

22 It has quite correctly been pointed out that the tutor aims for total control over his pupil, but this control is concealed and manipulative, relying for its effect on Émile's lack of awareness of how he is learning (see E. Rosenow, 'Rousseau's *Émile*, an anti-utopia', *British Journal of Educational Studies*, XXVIII, 3, 1980, pp. 212–224). Both Peters (op. cit.) and Rosenow are, however,

wrong in thinking that this control constitutes authority; it is, rather, the covert employment of superior power.

23 In describing what Rousseau means by these terms, I am greatly indebted to the account developed in Dent (1988b), op. cit.

24 Rousseau, op. cit., pp. 173–175.

25 Ibid., pp. 175–176.

26 Cf. *L'Iliade, Poème de Force* cited in P. Winch, *The Just Balance*, Cambridge, Cambridge University Press, 1989, p. 105.

27 Rousseau, op. cit., p. 130.

28 Ibid., p. 253 footnote.

29 Ibid., p. 221.

30 Ibid., pp. 53–54.

31 Ibid., pp. 109–111.

32 Ibid., pp. 131–134.

33 See P.F. Strawson, 'Freedom and Resentment', in P.F. Strawson, *Freedom and Resentment and Other Essays*, London, Methuen, 1974.

34 See Rosenow, op. cit., Also C. Winch, 'Education Needs Training', *Oxford Review of Education*, 21, 3, 1995, pp. 315–326, for a fuller account of how this works in *Émile*.

35 Cf. K. Sylva and I. Lunt, *Child Development*, Oxford, Blackwell, 1982, for some examples.

36 For a fuller account of Rousseau on religious education, see Darling, 1985, op. cit.

37 Rousseau, op. cit., p. 220.

38 For the elements of such an account, see P. Geach, *Mental Acts*, London, Routledge, 1957.

4 LEARNING IN A NORMATIVE CONTEXT

1 See Rousseau, *Émile*, Book V, trans. B. Foxley, London, Dent, 1911, pp. 321–444.

2 See M.A.K. Halliday, *Learning How to Mean*, London, Arnold, 1978.

3 Cf. P.F. Strawson, 'Freedom and Resentment', in P.F. Strawson, *Freedom and Resentment and Other Essays*, London, Methuen, 1974.

4 This contrast is of considerable importance and will be further dealt with in this and the subsequent chapter.

5 Cf. G.P. Baker and P.M.S. Hacker, *Wittgenstein: Rules, Grammar and Necessity*, Oxford, Blackwell, 1985, p. 161.

6 Ibid., p. 161.

7 Cf. G.P. Baker and P.M.S. Hacker (1985), op. cit., pp. 45–47 for further discussion.

8 K. Perera, *Children's Reading and Writing*, Oxford, Blackwell, 1984, Chapter 3, pp. 88–158; P. Menyuk, *Language Development: Knowledge and Use*, London, Scott Foresman, 1988, Chapters 6–9.

9 Menyuk, op. cit., pp. 61–62.

10 See, for example, B. Tizard and M. Hughes, *Young Children Learning*, London, Fontana, 1984.

11 For an application of such ideas in an economic context, see F. List, *The National System of Political Economy*, New Jersey, Augustus Kelley, 1991, Chapter XVII. First published 1841.

12 See M. Hollis, *The Philosophy of Social Science*, Cambridge, Cambridge University Press, 1994, pp. 152–153.

13 For a sensitive development of this insight, see H. Stretton and L. Orchard, *Public Goods, Public Enterprise and Public Choice*, London, Macmillan, 1993.

14 'Love is not a feeling. Love is put to the test, pain not', L. Wittgenstein, *Zettel*, Oxford, Blackwell, 1969, para. 504, p. 89.

15 Cf. G. Jessup, 'Implications for Individuals: The Autonomous Learner' in G. Jessup (ed.) *Outcomes: NVQs and the Emerging Model of Education and Training*, Brighton, Falmer, 1991, pp. 115–117.

16 See, for example, R. Kirk, 'Rationality without Language', *Mind*, V. 76, 1967, pp. 369–386.

17 C. Verheggen, 'Wittgenstein and "Solitary" Languages', *Philosophical Investigations*, 18, 4, 1995, pp. 329–347.

18 Wittgenstein, 1953, op. cit., para. 32.

19 Wittgenstein, 1953, op. cit., para. 1–3.
Cf. T.S. Champlin, 'Solitary Rule-Following', *Philosophy*, 67, 1992, pp. 285–306, 298.

20 The practice here means the rule-following together with its circumambient normative activities.

21 See Wittgenstein, 1953, op. cit., para. 208: 'The gesture that means "go on like this", or "and so on" has a function comparable to that of pointing to an object or place.'

22 See, for example, L. Wittgenstein, *Philosophical Grammar*, Oxford, Blackwell, 1974, p. 188. For similar and related remarks, see Wittgenstein, *Blue and Brown Books*, Oxford, Blackwell, 1958, pp. 12, 97; Wittgenstein, *Philosophical Investigations*, Oxford, Blackwell, 1953, para. 495.

5 LEARNING, TRAINING AND BEHAVIOURISM

1 L. Wittgenstein, *Zettel*, Oxford, Blackwell, 1967, para. 419.

2 P. Abbs, 'Training Spells the Death of Education', *The Guardian*, 5 January 1987. R.F. Dearden is much more cautious but nevertheless thinks that training can subvert education. R.F. Dearden, 'Education and Training', *Westminster Studies in Education*, 7, 1984, pp. 57–66, esp. p. 64.

3 For this distinction, see R.S. Peters, 'Authority', in A. Quinton (ed.) *Political Philosophy*, Oxford, Oxford University Press, 1967.

4 Terry Hyland, 'Competence, Knowledge and Education', *Journal of Philosophy of Education*, 27, 1, 1993, pp. 57–68.

5 For the case of moral education, see T. Kazepides, 'On the Prerequisites of Moral Education: A Wittgesteinian Perspective', *Journal of Philosophy of Education*, 25, 2, 1991, pp. 259–272.

6 Abbs, op. cit.

7 More cautiously, R.F. Dearden (op. cit, p. 64) seems to think that training largely precludes understanding.

8 D. Lieberman, *Learning*, California, Wadsworth, 1990, p. 34.

9 For a critique of the idea of a data language, see C. Taylor, *The Explanation of Behaviour*, London, Routledge, 1964.

10 N. Malcolm, 'Thoughtless Brutes', in *Thought and Knowledge*, Ithaca and London, Cornell University Press, 1977.

11 Dearden, op. cit., p. 64.

12 Exactly why this is so will become clearer later in this section.

13 J.J. Rousseau, *Émile ou l'éducation*, Paris, Editions Flammarion, 1966, p. 122. Passage translated by C.A. and C. Winch; Foxley translation, p. 64.

14 Plato, *Meno*, in B. Jowett, *The Dialogues of Plato*, London, Sphere Books, 1970.

15 Rousseau, *Émile*, op. cit., pp. 232–235 (Editions Flammarion); pp. 143–144 in Foxley edition.

16 Ibid., p. 113 in Flammarion edition; p. 106 in Foxley edition.

17 P. Winch, 'Authority', in A. Quinton (ed.) *Political Philosophy*, Oxford, Oxford University Press, 1967.

18 See, for example, M. Galton, B. Simon and P. Croll, *Inside the Primary Classroom*, London, Routledge, 1980; P. Mortimore, P. Sammons, L. Stoll, D. Lewis and R. Ecob, *School Matters*, Wells, Open Books, 1987; R. Alexander, *Policy and Practice in the Primary School*, London, Routledge, 1992.

19 Mortimore *et al.*, op. cit.; Alexander, op. cit.; B. Tizard, P. Blatchford, J. Burke, C. Farquhar and I. Plewis, *Young Children at School in the Inner City*, Hove, Lawrence Erlbaum, 1988; P. Bryant and L. Bradley, *Children's Reading Problems*, Oxford, Blackwell, 1985.

20 S. Prais, 'Mathematical Attainments: Comparisons of Japanese and English Schooling' in B. Moon, J. Isaac and J. Powney (eds) *Judging Standards and Effectiveness in Education*, London, Hodder and Stoughton, 1990.

21 For this distinction see R.S. Peters, op. cit.

22 M.A.K. Halliday, *Learning How to Mean*, London, Arnold, 1978.

23 T. Kazepides, 'On the Prerequisites of Moral Education: a Wittgensteinian Perspective', *Journal of Philosophy of Education*, 25, 2, 1991, pp. 259–272; D. Best, *The Rationality of Feeling. Understanding the Arts in Education*, Brighton, Falmer, 1993.

24 R.A. Rescorla and A.R. Wagner, 'A Theory of Pavlovian Conditioning: Variations in the Effectivenes of Reinforcement and Non-reinforcement' in A.H. Black and W.F. Prokasy (eds) *Classical Conditoning II: Current Research and Theory*, New York, Appleton Century-Crofts, 1972.

25 Lieberman, op. cit., p. 134.

26 Ibid.

27 Cf. Lieberman, op. cit., p. 445.

6 REPRESENTATION AND LEARNING

1 J.J. Rousseau, *Émile ou l'éducation*, trans. B. Foxley, London, Dent, 1911; N. Chomsky, *Language and Problems of Knowledge*, Cambridge, Mass., MIT Press, 1988.

2 See, for example, Carl Rogers, *The Carl Rogers Reader*, edited by H. Kirschenbaum and V. Land Henderson, London, Constable, 1990, esp. pp. 304–322.

3 Cf. William I. Matson and Adam Leite, 'Socrates' Critique of Cognitivism', *Philosophy*, 66, 256, 1991, pp. 145–168.

4 It is important to realise that in most cognitivist theory such mental activity takes place beyond the level of consciousness. There are disputes within cognitivist theory as to whether or not the materials operated on constitute a form of *tacit knowledge* (see F. D'Agostino, *Chomsky's System of Ideas*, Oxford, Clarendon, 1992, Chapter 2).

5 Because pictorial representation is taken as the primary use, it is not just one kind of representation, but the paradigm. But compare J.E. Fetzer, 'What Makes Connectionism Different?', *Pragmatics and Cognition*, 2, 2, 1994, pp. 327–347. Wittgenstein in the *Tractatus Logico-Philosophicus* takes the pictorial, isomorphic concept of representation and extends it from pictorial phenomena to language. Arguably, it can then be further extended to distributed forms of

representation of the kind required by connectionism (L. Wittgenstein, *Tractatus Logico-Philosophicus*, London, Routledge, 1922).

6 It is important to distinguish between this process at the non-conscious level as in, for example, mother tongue learning, and at the level of everyday reasoning, where the operation of such rules may be much looser. See J.W. Garson, 'No Representations without Rules: The prospects for a compromise between Paradigms in Cognitive Science', *Mind and Language*, 9, 1, 1994, pp. 25–37. T. Horgan and J. Tienson, 'Representations Don't Need Rules: Reply to James Garson', *Mind and Language*, 9, 1, 1994, pp. 38–55, 56–87. The distinction is often not made clearly by cognitivist writers, which serves to deepen confusion. See, for example, N. Chomsky, op. cit.

7 Cf. Frank Smith, *Reading*, Cambridge, Cambridge University Press, 1985, pp. 88–89.

8 For a critique of confusions surrounding the concept of *rule*, see G.P. Baker and P.M.S. Hacker, *Language, Sense and Nonsense*, Oxford, Blackwell, 1984, Chapters 7 and 8, especially pp. 294–300, p. 259. See also Baker and Hacker, *Wittgenstein: Rules, Grammar and Necessity*, Oxford, Blackwell, 1985, pp. 45–47, for reference to, and explanation of, normative activities. Note that a commitment to the presence of normative activities does not imply that these are *necessarily* social rather than solitary activities. That point requires further argument (see Chapter 4). See also: T.S. Champlin, 'Solitary Rule-Following', *Philosophy*, 67, 1992, pp. 285–306, esp. p. 298; N. Malcolm, 'Wittgenstein on Language and Rules', *Philosophy*, 64, 1990, pp. 5–28.

9 J. Fodor, *The Language of Thought*, Cambridge, Mass., MIT Press, 1975.

10 See K. Sterelny, *The Representational Theory of Mind*, Oxford, Blackwell, 1990, Chapter 8, for a balanced discussion of these issues. It is also possible for cognitivists to maintain that connectionism is adequate to explain some if not all mental functions. For a contrasting view of the possibilities of connectionism, see Fetzer, op. cit. Some anti-cognitivists also see possibilities in a form of connectionism purged of representationalism. See, for example, J.R. Searle, *The Rediscovery of the Mind*, Cambridge Mass., MIT Press, 1992, pp. 246–247. However, representationalism of some kind is still adhered to by most connectionists; see, for example, C. Evers and G. Lakomski, 'Reflections on Barlosky: Methodological Reflections on Postmodernism', *Curriculum Inquiry*, 25, 4, 1995, pp. 457–465, pp. 463–464.

11 According to Fodor and others, a language of thought is needed in order to account for human abilities to form concepts. The principal empiricist accounts of concept formation, namely *abstractionism* (Locke) and *associationism* (Berkeley and Hume) and the problems raised by them are intended to be dealt with by the LOTH.

12 Sterelny, op. cit., pp. 43–44.

13 See D. Papineau, *For Science in the Social Sciences*, London, Macmillan, 1988.

14 Fodor, op. cit., pp. 95–96. In fact, Fodor appears to think that concept learning is the only kind of learning about which we can know anything and since we do not know anything about this, our ideas about learning must remain undeveloped.

15 It is also inaccurate for connectionists to say that representations are encoded in the brain, for they cannot answer the question as to *whom* the representation is made, which is a question that must be answered on the primary sense of 'representation'. On the impossibility of 'discharging the homunculus', see Searle, 1992, op. cit., pp. 212–214.

16 J. Searle, 'Minds, Brains and Programs', *Behavioural and Brain Sciences*, 3,

1980, pp. 417–457; Searle, *Minds, Brains and Science*, Cambridge, Mass., Harvard University Press, 1984; Searle, 1992, op. cit.

17 Searle, 1992, op. cit., p. 210.

18 Sterelny, op. cit., pp. 222–223.

19 Naturally this is an oversimplification; people communicate through expression and gesture as well, and a mechanism would not be able to do this. But if the Chinese Room is simply the syntactico-semantic mechanism underlying our use of language, then the analogy does work.

20 The connection is made explicit in, for example, Chomsky, 1988, op. cit., Chapter 5, esp. pp. 135, 143.

21 This is why the attempt to show the compatibility of connectionism with Wittgenstein's later philosophy of mind will not work. Connectionism cannot give a coherent account of representation because it cannot give a coherent account of rule-following. An attempt to show the compatibility of Wittgenstein's later work with connectionism can be found in Stephen Mills, 'Wittgenstein and Connectionism: A Significant Complementarity?', in C. Hookway and D. Peterson (eds) *Philosophy and Cognitive Science*, Royal Institute of Philosophy Supplement 34, Cambridge, Cambridge University Press 1993, pp. 137–158.

22 Which is not to say that a non-representational, brain-focused account of learning might not work, but that discussion is beyond the scope of this chapter.

23 Fodor, op. cit., p. 70.

24 For a tentative account of how this might be done, see R. Nolan, *Cognitive Practices: Human Language and Human Knowledge*, Oxford, Blackwell, 1994.

25 See, for example, B.Tizard and M. Hughes, *Young Children Learning*, London, Fontana, 1984, Chapter 5.

7 DEVELOPMENT

1 For a more cautious formulation of developmental constraints along these lines, see M. Donaldson, *Human Minds*, London, Penguin, 1992.

2 See K. Egan, *Individual Development and the Curriculum*, London, Hutchinson, 1986; A.N. Whitehead, *The Aims of Education*, New York, The Free Press, 1967.

3 Vygotsky is an important exception. For him, development and learning are interdependent and both depend on social interaction. Neither does he subscribe to a rigid stage theory of the development of general powers of the mind as do other developmentalists such as Piaget. See, for example, Chapter 6 in *Mind in Society*, Cambridge, Mass., Harvard University Press, 1978.

4 For a strong statement of this position in relation to language, see N. Chomsky, *Language and Problems of Knowledge*, Cambridge, Mass., MIT Press, 1988, pp. 134–135.

5 Vygotsky is, again, an important exception to this statement.

6 For a classic statement, see J.A. Green (ed.) *Pestalozzi's Educational Writings*, London, Edward Arnold, 1912, p. 195.

7 D. Hamlyn, *Experience and the Growth of Understanding*, London, Routledge, 1978, p. 41.

8 Ibid.

9 Cf. K. Sylva and I. Lunt, *Child Development*, Oxford, Blackwell, 1982, Chapter 3.

10 Following Kenny, I distinguish between capacity and ability by characterising a capacity as an ability to acquire an ability. For example, the capacity to learn a mother tongue may only be available during a certain period of biological

maturation. Cf. A. Kenny, *The Legacy of Wittgenstein*, Oxford, Blackwell, 1989, p. 139.

11 This point is ably made in R. Dearden, *The Philosophy of Primary Education*, London, Routledge & Kegan Paul, 1968, Chapter 3.

12 For a useful discussion of these issues which, nevertheless, does not place sufficient emphasis on the covert normativity of developmental theories, see K. Beckett, 'Growth Theory Reconsidered', *Journal of Philosophy of Education*, 19, 1, 1985, pp. 49–54.

13 J. Darling, *Child-Centred Education and Its Critics*, London, Chapman, 1994, Chapter 3.

14 Chomsky, 1988, op. cit., p. 136.

15 See, for example, J. Piaget and B. Inhelder, *the Psychology of the Child*, London, Routledge, 1969 (first published in French in 1966), for an overview of the theoretical position; J. Piaget, *Logic and Psychology*, Manchester, The University Press, 1953, for a more detailed account; and J. Piaget, *Biology and Knowledge*, Edinburgh, Edinburgh University Press, 1971 (first published in French, 1967) for an account of how the structures are reconstructed as development takes place.

16 See, for example, M. Donaldson, *Children's Minds*, London, Fontana, 1978; G. Brown and C. Desforges, *Piaget's Theory: A Psychological Critique*, London, Routledge 1979; B. Tizard and M. Hughes, *Young Children Learning*, London, Fontana, 1984. For a philosophical account that is generally sympathetic to the Piagetian enterprise, see D. Hamlyn, op. cit.

17 J. Piaget, *The Principles of Genetic Epistemology*, London, Routledge, 1972, pp. 85–93; Brown and Desforges, op. cit., p. 46.

18 Brown and Desforges, op. cit.; Donaldson, op. cit.; David Wood, *How Children Think and Learn*, Oxford, Blackwell, 1990, Chapter 3; Sylva and Lunt, op. cit., for useful reviews of the evidence.

19 This is a problem endemic in research into ability. It bedevilled the research into verbal deficit of Basil Bernstein and his associates and it vitiated much research into intelligence; see S.J. Gould, *The Mismeasure of Man*, London, Penguin, 1981, pp. 199–232.

20 See, however, H. Ginsberg, *The Myth of the Deprived Child*, New York, Doubleday, 1972, for evidence of the view that cross-class comparisons within a Western culture do provide comparative evidence for the unity of developmental stages. For a compelling account of the difficulties that members of non-literate cultures may have in understanding and solving problems belonging to the formal operational stage because of misperception of the nature of what is being asked of them, see D. Levi, 'Why Do Illiterates Do So Badly in Logic?', *Philosophical Investigations*, 19, 1, 1996, pp. 34–54.

21 This particular line of criticism has been developed by David Carr, cf. 'Knowledge and Curriculum: Four Dogmas of Child-Centred Education', *Journal of Philosophy of Education*, 22, 1, 1988. Redefinition of truth as viability does not really help the constructivist since it is clear that pre-operational structures are unviable because they are soon discarded. For an attempted defence of truth as viability, see E. von Glasersfeld, 'Cognition, Construction of Knowledge and Teaching', *Synthese*, 80, 1989, pp. 121–140.

22 Cf. P. Carruthers, *Human Knowledge and Human Nature*, Oxford, Oxford University Press, 1992, Chapter 10.

23 Sometimes this is simply not seen as a problem. See, for example, W. van Haaften, 'The Justification of Conceptual Development Claims', *Journal of Philosophy of Education*, 24, 1, pp. 51–70.

24 Piaget does all three of these unjustified things. The theory of intrinsic motivation is taken from Rousseau and was criticised in Chapter 3; the theory of underlying representational operations was criticised in the previous chapter and abstractionism is criticised in Chapter 9.

25 Sir Francis Bacon, *First Book of Aphorisms*, 1620, cited in M. Hollis, *The Philosophy of Social Science*, Cambridge, Cambridge University Press, 1994.

8 LEARNING LANGUAGE

1 See, for example, J. Piaget, *Le Langage et la pensée chez l'enfant*, Neuchatel-Paris, Delachaux et Niestle, 1923.

2 L.S. Vygotsky, *Thought and Language*, Cambridge, Mass., MIT Press, 1962, Chapter 2.

3 See J. Fodor, *The Language of Thought*, Cambridge, Mass., MIT Press, 1975, p. 70.

4 Noam Chomsky, *Language and Problems of Knowledge*, Cambridge, Mass., MIT Press, 1988, pp. 62–63.

5 Ibid., p. 45.

6 F. D'Agostino, *Chomsky's System of Ideas*, Oxford, Clarendon, 1992, Chapter 2.

7 D'Agostino's reservations about this are due largely to a desire for explanatory parsimony. But if something significant is lost by claiming that the neonate does not know the rules of language, namely the possibility of these being a *representational* system, then the claim will not be so easy to dismiss.

8 Chomsky, op. cit., p. 134.

9 Ibid., p. 27.

10 The available evidence does indeed suggest that children's acquisition of language proceeds through the use of structures of gradually increasing complexity. See, for example, P. Menyuk, *Language Development: Knowledge and Use*, London, Scott Foresman, 1988, Chapter 8.

11 Chomsky, op. cit., pp. 9–10.

12 See N. Chomsky, *Aspects of the Theory of Syntax*, Cambridge, Cambridge University Press, 1965, pp. 3–4; also Chomksy, 1988, op. cit., pp. 133–134.

13 For contrasting views of competence, see G.P. Baker and P.M.S. Hacker, *Language, Sense and Nonsense*, Oxford, Blackwell, 1984; P.H. Matthews, *Generative Grammar and Linguistic Competence*, London, Allen & Unwin, 1979; D. Cooper, *Knowledge of Language*, London, Prism Press, 1975.

14 Chomsky, 1988, op. cit., p. 179.

15 Ibid., p. 174.

16 In recent years, this claim has been modified, so that development takes place up to and beyond the onset of puberty. The claim has had to be modified in the face of overwhelming evidence. See K. Perera, *Children's Writing and Reading*, Oxford, Blackwell, 1984, Chapter 3 (pp. 88–158) and P. Menyuk, op. cit., pp. 33–34.

17 Cf. P.M.S. Hacker, *Wittgenstein's Place in Twentieth-Century Analytic Philosophy*, Oxford, Blackwell, 1996, pp. 190, 192.

18 See also E. Lenneberg, 'Natural History of Language' in F. Smith and G. Miller (eds) *Genesis of Language*, Cambridge, Mass., MIT Press, 1966.

19 See Perera, op. cit., Chapter 3, esp. pp. 156–158, for a summary of research in this area.

20 Perera, op. cit., p. 156.

21 Cf. Fodor, op. cit., pp. 95–96; Chomsky, 1988, op. cit., pp. 190–191.

22 See, for example, M.A.K. Halliday, *Learning How to Mean*, London, Arnold, 1978.

9 LEARNING AND CONCEPT FORMATION

1 These are not necessarily prior to language use, but underpin it, cf. R. Rhees, 'Language as Emerging from Instinctive Behaviour', *Philosophical Investigations*, 20, 1, 1997, pp. 1–14.

2 An early example was Geach's critique of abstractionism in *Mental Acts*, London, Routledge, 1957.

3 For the former, see J. Fodor, *The Language of Thought*, Cambridge, Mass., MIT Press, 1975; N. Chomsky, *Language and Problems of Knowledge*, Cambridge, Mass., MIT Press, 1988. For the latter, see P. Carruthers, *Human Knowledge and Human Nature*, Oxford, Oxford University Press, 1992.

4 See Carruthers, op. cit., p. 55, but note that Geach does not take this view.

5 I am not using 'particular' in the technical sense introduced in P.F. Strawson, *Individuals*, London, Hutchinson, 1961, but as a generic term to cover spatio-temporally persistent objects and also the sense data of traditional empiricisim. It is possible to be an abstractionist without adhering to some of the particular doctrines of empiricism. Indeed, abstractionism is an older doctrine than empiricism, but was appropriated by Locke.

6 See Chapter 2.

7 As Carruthers points out, nonconscious but conceptual noticing is subject to the same objection as was raised for conscious noticing, namely that it implies the possession of the conceptual ability that is to be explained. However, nonconscious abstraction need not be a conceptual process. Locke, for example, at times talks about the operations of the mind in abstracting, without thereby implying that this is itself a conceptual process (see J. Locke, *An Essay Concerning Human Understanding*, London, Dent, 1961, Book II, Chapter XI, p. 126). However, his proposal that children find it difficult to abstract suggests that he sees the process as more or less a conscious one.

8 For a different view, see Carruthers, op. cit., pp. 55–56.

9 Locke's comments on this point seem to be deeply ambiguous; it is not clear whether he means that ideas are formed by reflection or that reflection is the means by which I become aware of the ideas that I have formed. See Locke, op. cit., Book II, Chapter 1, p. 78, already quoted in Chapter 3.

10 Berkeley anticipates Hume by attacking abstractionism and showing how a particular idea of, for example, a triangle may stand for all triangles without being an abstract idea of a triangle (*Principles of Human Knowledge*, Introduction, esp. pp. 114–115, first published 1710, available in *Berkeley: Selections*, edited by Mary W. Calkins, New York, Scribner, 1929). See D. Hume, *A Treatise of Human Nature*, Oxford, Oxford University Press, 1978, pp. 18ff.

11 Berkeley, op. cit., paras 12–17; Hume, op. cit., pp. 18ff.

12 This customary association is a mental rather than a social one.

13 The associationist proposal is one of the main targets of the private language argument as it is developed in L. Wittgenstein, *Philosophical Investigations*, Oxford, Blackwell, 1953, paras 258–265.

14 Berkeley, op. cit. paras 18–19.

15 Chomsky, 1988, op. cit., pp. 190–191.

16 L. Wittgenstein, op. cit., paras 65–67. For this particular view of Wittgenstein's claim, see R.W. Beardsmore, 'The Theory of Family Resemblances', *Philosophical Investigations*, 15, 2, 1992, pp. 111–130.

17 Fodor, op. cit., pp. 95–96.
18 D. Lieberman, *Learning*, California, Wadsworth, 1990, pp. 429–430.
19 Cf. D. Papineau, *For Science in the Social Sciences*, London, Macmillan, Chapter 4, for an attempt to explain human action on the desire + belief = action model.
20 Carruthers, op. cit., pp. 95–97.
21 Vygotsky claimed that the linguistic ability was prior to and presupposed the mental one; see L.S. Vygotsky, *Thought and Language*, Cambridge, Mass., MIT Press, 1962, Chapter 2.
22 Carruthers, op. cit., pp. 104–107. It is not clear from the account whether or not paradigms are themselves concepts. One is inclined to think that they are not, otherwise they could not serve in an account of concept formation. However, the marks of the concept *inference to the best explanation* suggest that these prototypical properties *are* concepts.
23 Carruthers, op. cit., p. 106.
24 When I say that this is a non-discursive agreement, I do not mean that there are no conceivable circumstances in which a language user might be moved to express such a judgement.
25 Geach, op. cit., pp. 7–8. A recent major work on the nature of concepts does not mention Geach's account but says that possession of a concept *requires* the capacity to make judgements without identifying the concept with that capacity. See C. Peacocke, *A Study of Concepts*, Cambridge, Mass., MIT Press, 1992, p. 44.
26 For the sake of simplicity, I am excluding the use of certain kinds of second level concepts in the Fregean sense derived from names. A recent writer on the nature of concepts, although working within a Fregean paradigm, uses the term 'concept' to refer to the mode of presentation of all kinds of expressions, including proper names (Peacocke, op. cit.).
27 Geach, op. cit., p. 14.
28 Ibid., pp. 75–78.
29 For a recent discussion, see R. Nolan, *Cognitive Practices: Human Language and Human Knowledge*, Oxford, Blackwell, 1994.
30 B. Tizard and M. Hughes, *Young Children Learning*, London, Fontana, 1984, Chapter 5.
31 M. Sainsbury, *Meaning, Communication and Understanding in the Classroom*, Aldershot, Avebury, 1992, pp. 112–113.
32 Wittgenstein's discussion of family resemblance concepts can be found in *Philosophical Investigations*, op. cit., paras 65–76. It is important to note that Wittgenstein is not talking about concepts with blurred boundaries but a common core, but about concepts that do not necessarily have a central core of meaning.
33 For a critical discussion of the idea that there are intrinsic natural properties (extensions) of natural kinds, see P.M.S. Hacker, *Wittgenstein's Place in Twentieth-Century Analytic Philosophy*, Oxford, Blackwell, 1996, pp. 250–253.
34 Guy Robinson, 'Language and the Society of Others', *Philosophy*, 67, 1992, pp. 329–341.
35 Carruthers, op. cit., p. 107.

10 MEMORY AND LEARNING

1 Cf. Richard Wollheim, *The Thread of Life*, Cambridge, Cambridge University Press, 1984, Chapter 5; also M. Warnock, *Memory*, London, Faber & Faber, 1987.

2 Aristotle, *On Memory and Reminiscence*, in R. Mckeon (ed.) *The Basic Works of Aristotle*, New York, Random House, 1941; Augustine, *Confessions*, Book X, London, Dent, 1907. See D. Locke, *Memory*, London, Macmillan, 1971, for a good account.

3 John Locke, *An Essay on Human Understanding*, Volume I, London, Dent, 1961, Chapter X, p. 118.

4 David Hume, *A Treatise of Human Nature*, Book I, Section 3, Oxford, Oxford University Press, 1978.

5 See D. Locke, *op. cit.*, p. 24.

6 Cf. Frances Yates, *The Art of Memory*, London, Ark, 1984. Paradoxically, although conceptualisation of memory as a storehouse leads to all kinds of philosophical problems in the understanding of memory, *heuristically* it may be very helpful in the training of memory.

7 N. Malcolm, *Memory and Mind*, Ithaca, NY, Cornell, 1977, Chapter 8.

8 See Descartes, *Rules for the Direction of the Mind*, Rule XII, in *Philosophical Writings*, selected, translated and edited by E. Anscombe and P.T. Geach, London, Nelson, 1966.

9 Malcolm, op. cit., p. 203.

10 N.S. Sutherland, 'Outlines of a Theory of Visual Pattern Recognition in Animals and Man', Proceedings of the Royal Society, B.171 (1968), 301. Cited in Malcolm, op. cit., p. 206.

11 Malcolm, op. cit., p. 209.

12 Ibid., pp. 224–229.

13 Ibid., pp. 224–225.

14 Connectionism posits a form of learning that is called 'training', but it is quite unlike training as it is normally understood (see Chapter 5). Cf. Stephen Mills, 'Wittgenstein and Connectionism: A Significant Complementary?', in C. Hookway and D. Peterson (eds) *Philosophy and Cognitive Science*, Royal Institute of Philosophy Supplement 34, Cambridge, Cambridge University Press, 1993.

15 Cf. Rhona Stainthorp, *Practical Psychology for Teachers*, London, Falmer, 1989, Chapter 6.

16 Cf. Ibid., Chapter 6, for an example of the computational approach to memory. This is discussed and criticised in greater detail in Chapter 11. Stainthorp does allow a limited role for training in memory, however.

17 Cf. Yates, op. cit., for a full account of the ancient and Renaissance art of memory.

18 Author's own personal experience of working in British primary schools.

19 See, for example, Robin Barrow and Ronald Woods, *An Introduction to Philosophy of Education*, London, Methuen, 1975, Chapter 7.

20 Yates, op. cit., p. 144. To see memory as a storehouse may be useful heuristically, but it is quite another matter to make the image of a storehouse as the core of a philosophical account of the nature of memory.

11 ATTENDING, THINKING AND LEARNING

1 For an extended critical discussion of this, see O. Hanfling, ' "Thinking", a widely ramified concept', *Philosophical Investigations*, 16, 2, 1993, pp. 101–115.

2 It is, perhaps, in the idea of taking one's thoughts seriously that we come nearest to the idea that thinking could be a distinctive activity.

3 In this sense, thinking and attending are closely related: cf. R.K. Scheer, 'Thinking and Working', *Philosophical Investigations*, 14, 4, 1991, pp. 293–310.

4 René Descartes, *Meditations*, p. 68. Compare Hume: 'when I enter most intimately into what I call *myself*, I always stumble on some particular perception or other, of heat or cold, light or shade, love or hatred, pain or pleasure' (*A Treatise of Human Nature*, Oxford, Oxford University Press, 1978, p. 253). Later, he goes on to compare the mind with a theatre, 'where several perceptions successively make their appearance; pass, re-pass, glide away and mingle in an infinite variety of postures and situations' (ibid, p. 253).

5 As we saw in Chapter 2, however, this does not commit him to the *substantial* as opposed to the *modal* existence of ideas.

6 It is not essential at this stage because all that Descartes needs to do is to offer a *description* of what it is to focus on one's thoughts.

7 The difficulties described here are related to those connected with ideas as representations which are discussed in Chapter 2. However, even if my thinking about the sun were the exercise in judgement of a badly formed concept of the sun, then, in an important sense, my thought of the sun would be different from the sun. In other words the difficulties described are not peculiar to a representational account of concepts.

8 See, for example, R. Stainthorp, *Practical Psychology for Teachers*, London, Falmer, 1989, Chapter 5.

9 L. Wittgenstein, *Philosophical Investigations*, Oxford, Blackwell, 1953, para. 33.

10 Stainthorp, op. cit., Chapter 5.

11 To keep a sense of balance, it is also important to recognise the role that concentration and attention plays in the lives of young children. See in particular, B. Tizard and M. Hughes, *Young Children Learning*, London, Fontana, 1984, Chapter 5.

12 A. Gramsci, *Selections from the Prison Notebooks* (edited by Quinin Hoare and Geoffrey Nowell Smith), London, Lawrence & Wishart, 1971, p. 37.

13 See, for example, P. Mortimore *et al. School Matters: The Junior Years*, Wells, Open Books, 1988; R. Alexander, *Policy and Practice in the Primary School*, London, Routledge, 1992.

14 Cf. L. Wittgenstein, *Zettel*, Oxford, Blackwell, 1967: 'Love is not a feeling. Love is put to the test, pain not' (para. 504).

15 See I. Murdoch, *The Sovereignty of the Good*, London, Routledge, 1970; I. Murdoch, *Metaphysics as a Guide to Morals*, London, Penguin, 1992, for a development of the idea that attention is an aspect of love.

12 LATER LEARNING

1 'Teacher' in this sense refers not just to the professional educator but to all who may be involved in imparting knowledge.

2 The best-known exponent of this view is Paul Hirst, *Knowledge and the Curriculum*, London, Routledge, 1975. But a similar position can be found in J. McPeck, *Critical Thinking and Education*, Oxford, Martin Robertson, 1981. Stephen Toulmin's *The Uses of Argument*, Cambridge, Cambridge University Press, 1957, is one of the key texts to outline what a multi-subject account of logic and argument would look like.

3 'If there were a know-how of it all, there wouldn't be the problems, and so long as there are the problems there can't (save in respects that are trivial and subordinate) be a know-how'; R.F. Holland, *Against Empiricism*, Oxford, Blackwell, 1980, p. 23.

4 This point is particularly well developed in C.A. MacMillan, *Women, Reason and Nature*, Oxford, Blackwell, 1982; see Chapter 3 in particular.

5 For a defence of folk psychology, see M.E. Malone, 'On Assuming Other Folks Have Mental States', *Philosophical Investigations*, 17, 1, 1994, pp. 37–52.

6 See C. Hamm, *Philosophical Issues in Education: An Introduction*, Lewes, Falmer, 1989, for a good account in Chapter 5.

7 C. Winch, 'The Curriculum and the Study of Reason', *Westminster Studies in Education*, 1987.

8 Toulmin, op. cit., p. 120. It is wrong because there are many tautological statements where the conclusion is not stated in the premises (see next section). Contrast P.F. Strawson who, while no defender of the idea of context-independent inference, defines analyticity in truth functional terms and identifies it with tautology. See his *Introduction to Logical Theory*, London, Methuen, 1952, p. 74.

9 Toulmin, op. cit., p. 132.

10 See D. Cooper, 'Labov, Larry and Charles', *Oxford Review of Education*, 1984; C. Winch, 'Cooper, Labov, Larry and Charles', *Oxford Review of Education*, 1985.

11 Winch, 1985, op. cit.

12 Cf. L. Wittgenstein, *On Certainty*, Oxford, Blackwell, 1969, para. 98. See also paras 94–99.

13 Hirst's claim that different forms of knowledge embody different forms of inference can be partly accommodated by pointing out that warrants differ between forms. In the next chapter I shall show how different emphases on different kinds of reasoning in different subjects can still be accommodated to conventional accounts of inductive and deductive reasoning.

14 Depending on the nature of the backing statement, this may be either an inductive or a deductive argument.

15 R. Gaita, *Good and Evil*, London, Macmillan, 1991, for example, p. 236.

16 It might be thought that this is not necessary for practical subjects, but there are good reasons for thinking that it is. See S. Prais, 'Vocational Qualifications in Britain and Europe: Theory and Practice', *National Institute Economic Review*, 136, May 1991, pp. 86–89.

17 Quoted in S.J. Gould, *Wonderful Life: The Burgess Shale and the Nature of History*, New York, Norton, 1989, p. 281.

18 Ibid., p. 281.

13 LEARNING ABOUT RELIGION

1 D. Bastide (ed.), *Good Practice in Primary Religious Education 4–11*, London, Falmer, 1992, p. 11.

2 Schools Curriculum and Assessment Authority, *Model Syllabuses for Religious Education, Consultation Document Model 1*, London, HMSO, January 1994.

3 Ibid., p. 3.

4 On teachers' own uncertainties on this matter, see Bastide, op. cit., pp. 5–6.

5 For a recent neo-realist account of religious belief, where a minimal correspondence theory is argued for, see David Carr, 'Knowledge and Truth in Religious Education', *Journal of Philosophy of Education*, 28, 2, 1994, pp. 221–238, esp. p. 225.

6 For two examples, one ancient and one modern, see Plato, *Theaetetus*, Part 3 in F.M. Cornford, *Plato's Theory of Knowledge*, London, Routledge, 1935; Ernest Gettier, 'Is Justified True Belief Knowledge?', in A. Phillips Griffiths (ed.) *Knowledge and Belief*, Oxford, Oxford University Press, 1967.

7 Cf. Carr, op. cit. The *Tractatus* account of truth is not a correspondence theory

because it maintains that 'p is true' is the equivalent of 'p'. Any attempt to explain 'p is true' in terms of correspondence would, on the Tractarian account, be nonsense.

8 D. Carr, 'Towards a Distinctive Concept of Spiritual Education', *Oxford Review of Education*, 21, 1, 1995, pp. 83–98.

9 For a discussion by Phillips of this and related issues, see 'Wittgenstein, Religion and Anglo-American Philosophical Culture', in *Wittgenstein and Culture*, Wittgenstein Vienna Society, 1997, forthcoming, esp. Section 2.

10 It can be doubted whether the 'fideist' description accurately describes Phillips's current views. See a more nuanced view in, for example, D.Z. Phillips, *Wittgenstein on Religion*, London, Macmillan, 1993.

11 Cf. C. Hamm, op. cit., pp. 68–69.

12 D. Carr, 1995, op. cit. makes similar points in relation to spiritual education.

13 P.H. Hirst. 'Morals, Religion and the Maintained School', *British Journal of Educational Studies*, November 1965.

14 Paul Hirst, 'Education, Knowledge and Practices', in R. Barrow and P. White (eds) *Beyond Liberal Education*, London, Routledge, 1993, pp. 184–199.

15 D.Z. Phillips, 'Philosophy and Religious Education', *British Journal of Educational Studies*, XVIII, 1, February 1970, pp. 5–17.

16 'Searle on Language Games and Religion', esp. pp. 23–25 in Phillips, *Wittgenstein on Religion*, London, Macmillan, 1993, pp. 22–32. 'Primitive Reactions and the Reactions of Primitives' and 'From Coffee to Carmelites', in Phillips, 1993, op. cit., pp. 103–122, 131–152 respectively.

17 Carr, 1995, op. cit.

18 Natural historical accounts, such as that of David Hume, which seek to elucidate the cause and significance of religion in human life, come close to this position. See his *Natural History of Religion* (first published in present form 1777), Oxford, Oxford University Press, 1993.

14 MORAL LEARNING

1 For a discussion of the distinction, see, for example, J.P. White, *Education and the Good Life*, London, Kogan Page, 1990; R. Norman, ' "I Did it My Way": Some Reflections on Autonomy', *Journal of Philosophy of Education*, 28, 1, 1994, pp. 25–34.

2 For an argument against strong autonomy as a possible aim of public education systems, see C.Winch, 'Autonomy as an Educational Aim', in R. Marples (ed.) *Aims in Education*, London, Routledge, forthcoming.

3 For a qualified defence of strong autonomy, at least in modern societies, see White, op. cit.; Norman, op. cit. I shall show later in this chapter that adoption of strong autonomy as an aim of moral education renders moral education problematic.

4 P.F. Strawson, *Freedom and Resentment and Other Essays*, London, Methuen, 1974, p. 19. T. Kazepides, 'On the Prerequisites of Moral Education: a Wittgensteinian Perspective', *Journal of Philosophy of Education*, 25, 2, 79.

5 Aristotle, *Nichomachean Ethics*, Book 2. Translated by Sir David Ross, Oxford, Oxford University Press, 1925, pp. 28–29.

6 W.H. Auden, 'The Shield of Achilles', in *Collected Shorter Poems*, London, Faber, 1966, p. 294.

7 Thomas Hobbes, *Leviathan* (first published 1651), London, Penguin, 1968, p. 319.

8 This might be construed as a commitment to 'moral realism' but, if it is,

it does not commit one to any ontologically mysterious features of these situations.

9 The vicarious experience of moral situations is of the greatest importance in allowing judgement to develop. What the proper materials for such vicarious experience are is not so easy to determine.

10 Which is not to say that the consequences are the only considerations of importance, but if morality is bound up with the bringing about of harm or well-being, consideration of consequences of action is sometimes inevitable and right.

11 The golden rule, as a high-level moral principle, occurs in moral philosophies as diverse as those of Hobbes (*Leviathan*, p. 190) and Kant (*Groundwork of the Metaphysic of Morals* first published 1785; available in H.J. Paton, *The Moral Law*, London, Hutchinson, 1948). It should be noted, however, that it may yield different answers when applied by different individuals.

12 This should not be interpreted as suggesting that morality and the practice of the virtues is really some kind of *aesthetic* sensibility. The connection with human need, where it exists, ensures that that will not be so. Cf. R. Gaita, *Good and Evil*, London, Macmillan, 1991, pp. 85–86.

13 This is a point that receives emphasis in D. Carr, *Educating the Virtues*, London, Routledge, 1991, Chapter 12.

14 For example, Gaita, op. cit., p. 326.

15 Evan Simpson, *Good Lives and Moral Education*, New York, Peter Lang, 1989.

16 Ibid., Chapter 5.

17 L. Kohlberg, *The Philosophy of Moral Development*, Volumes I–III, San Francisco, Harper & Row, 1981.

18 Simpson, op. cit., Chapter 5.

19 Cf. Simpson, op. cit., pp. 150–161.

20 See, for example, L. Kohlberg, 'Stages of Moral Development as a Basis for Moral Education', in C. Beck, B.S. Crittenden and E.V. Sullivan (eds) *Moral Education: Interdisciplinary Approaches*, New York, Newman Press, 1971, p. 75.

21 See, for example, A. MacIntyre, *After Virtue*, London, Duckworth, 1981.

22 Gaita, op. cit., p. 86.

23 These remarks apply particularly to the Critical Philosophy. It is not clear that Kant always made such a rigid distinction between duty and inclination, either before or after the period of his Critical Philosophy. Cf. Keith Ward, *The Development of Kant's Views of Ethics*, Oxford, Blackwell, 1972.

24 C. Winch, *Quality and Education*, Oxford, Blackwell, 1996, esp. Chapters 3 and 7.

25 For a fuller discussion, see C. Winch, 'Authority in Education' in the *Encyclopedia of Applied Ethics*, edited by R. Chadwick, California, Academic Press, forthcoming; C. Winch, 'Autonomy as an Educational Aim' in R. Marples (ed.) *Aims in Education*, London, Routledge, forthcoming.

15 LEARNING TO MAKE AND TO APPRECIATE

1 I shall treat the artistic and the aesthetic as one, although aware of David Best's distinction between artistic and aesthetic experience. In practice, it is not possible to separate a concern for beauty with a concern for life issues. Although such a distinction may well be useful for certain purposes, it is not helpful as a general distinction to be employed in all circumstances. See D. Best, *The Rationality of Feeling*, Brighton, Falmer, 1992, p. 173.

2 One influential strand of thinking about this, which stems from the work of

John Dewey, is that children should learn about artistic production through *experimentation* with materials (see his *Democracy and Education*, New York, Macmillan, 1916). Subjectivist approaches would deny that one could make objective judgements about the quality of children's as opposed to adults' artistic production.

3 There is often a strong moral element to these activities, as can be seen in collected oral stories such as those of the Brothers Grimm.
4 For a useful historical discussion of this idea, see B. Tilghman, *Wittgenstein, Ethics and Aesthetics*, London, Macmillan, 1991, Chapter 2.
5 Best, op. cit. offers trenchant criticisms of both of these ideas and I shall not pursue them here.
6 See I. Murdoch, *Metaphysics as a Guide to Morals*, London, Penguin, 1992, for a lengthy pursuit of this and related themes.
7 Examples of this are to be found where regulative principles govern the creation and use of codes of action, for example, in morality and politics.
8 Cf. L. Wittgenstein, *Zettel*, Oxford, Blackwell, 1967, para. 320.
9 See G. Robinson, 'Language and the Society of Others', *Philosophy*, 67, 1992, pp. 329–341.
10 See M.J.A. Howe, *The Origins of Exceptional Abilities*, Oxford, Blackwell, 1990, for a demystificatory account of the lives of people of exceptional abilities.
11 Cf. I. Reid (ed.), *The Place of Genre in Learning*, Geelong, Typereader Press, Deakin University, 1987.
12 According to Plato, this mystery arises from the fact that the artist is divinely inspired. See *Ion*, in *Plato; The Collected Dialogues*, edited by E. Hamilton and H. Cairns, Princeton, New Jersey, Princeton University Press, 1963, 219–221.
13 Cited in Best, op. cit., p. 81.
14 See the discussion in Chapter 4. See also my own 'Vocational Education: A Liberal Interpretation', *Studies in Philosophy and Education*, 14,4, 1995, pp. 401–415.
15 According to Best, art involves human issues while aesthetics is concerned with appreciation detached from life issues. His tendency to separate the two is particularly unfortunate in the case of architectural education, where the aesthetic/artistic distinction is difficult to maintain as Best acknowledges (op. cit., pp. 178–179). Although there is not the space to do so here, it is possible to argue that it is precisely an emphasis on aesthetic considerations, devoid from a concern with the human, and hence moral space in which people relate to one another, which has rendered much modern architecture so unpopular.
16 Cf. C. Hamm, *Philosophical Issues in Education*, London, Falmer, 1989. For a criticism of Hirst's views, see J. Gingell, 'Art and Knowledge', *Educational Philosophy and Theory*, 17, 1985, pp. 10–21.
17 However, the lifelike and naturalistic character of some art forms, notably cinema, may mislead people into thinking that here is a more or less direct depiction of reality. Even the darkness and the flickering nature of the screen is redolent of Plato's cave and it would be interesting to see what he would have made of this particular art form.
18 A work of art is necessarily a pretence only in the sense that it is a representation rather than the real thing. It is contingently a pretence when it represents untruthfully. See H.O. Mounce, 'Art and Real Life', *Philosophy*, 55, April, pp. 183ff. Cited in Best, op. cit.

REFERENCES

Abbs, P., 'Training Spells the Death of Education', *The Guardian*, 5 January 1987.

Alexander, R., *Policy and Practice in the Primary School*, London, Routledge, 1992.

Aristotle, *Nichomachean Ethics*. Translated by Sir David Ross, Oxford, Oxford University Press, 1925.

Auden, W.H., 'The Shield of Achilles', in *Collected Shorter Poems*, London, Faber, 1966, p. 294.

Augustine, *Confessions*, London, Dent, 1907.

Baker, G.P., and P.M.S. Hacker, *Language, Sense and Nonsense*, Oxford, Blackwell, 1984.

————, *Wittgenstein: Rules, Grammar and Necessity; Volume Two of an Analytical Commentary on the 'Philosophical Investigations'*, Oxford, Blackwell, 1985.

Baker, G.P., and K.J. Morris, *Descartes' Dualism*, London, Routledge, 1996.

Barrow, Robin, and Ronald Woods, *An Introduction to Philosophy of Education*, London, Methuen, 1975.

Bastide, D. (ed.), *Good Practice in Primary Religious Education 4–11*, London, Falmer, 1992.

Beardsmore, R.W., 'The Theory of Family Resemblances', *Philosophical Investigations*, 15, 2, 1992, pp. 111–130.

Beckett, K., 'Growth Theory Reconsidered', *Journal of Philosophy of Education*, 19, 1, 1985, pp. 49–54.

Berkeley, B., *The Principles of Human Knowledge*, in Berkeley, *Selections*, edited by Mary W. Calkins, New York, Scribner, 1929.

Best, D., *The Rationality of Feeling. Understanding the Arts in Education*, Brighton, Falmer, 1993.

Brown, G., and C. Desforges, *Piaget's Theory: A Psychological Critique*, London, Routledge, 1979.

Bryant, P., and L. Bradley, *Children's Reading Problems*, Oxford, Blackwell, 1985.

Carr, David, 'Knowledge and Curriculum: Four Dogmas of Child-Centred Education', *Journal of Philosophy of Education*, 22, 1, 1988.

——, *Educating the Virtues*, London, Routledge, 1991.

——, 'Knowledge and Truth in Religious Education', *Journal of Philosophy of Education*, 28, 2, 1994, pp. 221–238.

——, 'Towards a Distinctive Concept of Spiritual Education', *Oxford Review of Education*, 21, 1, 1995, pp. 83–98.

Carruthers, Peter, *Human Knowledge and Human Nature*, Oxford, Oxford University Press, 1992.

Champlin, T.S., 'Solitary Rule-Following', *Philosophy*, 67, 1992, pp. 285–306, 298.

Chomsky, Noam, *Aspects of the Theory of Syntax*, Cambridge, Cambridge University Press, 1965.

——, *Language and Problems of Knowledge*, Cambridge, Mass., MIT Press, 1988.

Cooper, D., *Knowledge of Language*, London, Prism Press, 1975.

——, 'Labov, Larry and Charles', *Oxford Review of Education*, 1984.

Cottingham, John, *Descartes*, Oxford, Blackwell, 1986.

D'Agostino, Fred, *Chomsky's System of Ideas*, Oxford, Clarendon, 1986.

Darling, J., 'Understanding and Religion in Rousseau's *Émile*', *British Journal of Educational Studies*, 33, 1, 1985, pp. 20–34.

——, 'Rousseau as Progressive Instrumentalist', *Journal of Philosophy of Education*, 27, 1, 1993, pp. 27–38.

——, *Child-Centred Education and Its Critics*, London, Chapman, 1994.

Dearden, R., *The Philosophy of Primary Education*, London, Routledge & Kegan Paul, 1968, Chapter 3.

——, 'Education and Training', *Westminster Studies in Education*, 7, 1984, pp. 57–66.

Dent, N., 'The Basic Principle of Émile's Education', *Journal of Philosophy of Education*, 22, 2, 1988a, pp. 139–150.

——, *Rousseau*, Oxford, Blackwell, 1988b.

Descartes, René, *Oeuvres de Descartes*. Edited by Charles Adam and Paul Tannery, Paris, Cerf [1897] 1913.

——, *Philosophical Writings*. Selected, translated and edited by E. Anscombe and P.T. Geach, London, Nelson, 1966.

Dewey, John, *Democracy and Education*, New York, Macmillan, 1916.

Donaldson, M., *Children's Minds*, London, Fontana, 1978.

——, *Human Minds*, London, Penguin, 1992.

Egan, K., *Individual Development and the Curriculum*, London, Hutchinson, 1986.

Evers, C., and G. Lakomski, 'Reflections on Barlosky: Methodological Reflections on Postmodernism', *Curriculum Inquiry*, 25, 4, 1995, pp. 457–465.

Fetzer, J.E., 'What Makes Connectionism Different?', *Pragmatics and Cognition*, 2, 2, 1994, pp. 327–347.

Fodor, J., *The Language of Thought*, Cambridge, Mass., MIT Press, 1975.

Gaita, R., *Good and Evil*, London, Macmillan, 1991.

Galton, M., B. Simon and P. Croll, *Inside the Primary Classroom*, London, Routledge, 1980.

Garson, J.W., 'No Representations without Rules: the Prospects for a Compromise between Paradigms in Cognitive Science', *Mind and Language*, 9, 1, 1994, pp. 25–37.

Geach, P.T., *Mental Acts*, London, Routledge, 1957.

Gettier, Ernest, 'Is Justified True Belief Knowledge?', in A. Phillips Griffiths (ed.) *Knowledge and Belief*, Oxford, Oxford University Press, 1967.

Gingell, J., 'Art and Knowledge', *Educational Philosophy and Theory*, 17, 1985, pp. 10–21.

Ginsberg, H., *The Myth of the Deprived Child*, New York, Doubleday, 1972.

Glasersfeld, E. von, 'Cognition, Construction of Knowledge and Teaching', *Synthese*, 80, 1989, pp. 121–140.

Gould, S.J., *The Mismeasure of Man*, London, Penguin, 1981.

——, *Wonderful Life: The Burgess Shale and the Nature of History*, New York, Norton & Co., 1989.

Gramsci, A., *Selections from the Prison Notebooks*. Edited by Quinin Hoare and Geoffrey Nowell Smith, London, Lawrence & Wishart, 1971, p. 37.

Green, J.A. (ed.), *Pestalozzi's Educational Writings*, London, Edward Arnold, 1912.

Hacker, P.M.S., *Wittgenstein's Place in Twentieth-Century Analytic Philosophy*, Oxford, Blackwell, 1996.

Haften, W. van, 'The Justification of Conceptual Development Claims', *Journal of Philosophy of Education*, 24, 1, 1990, pp. 51–70.

Halliday, M.A.K., *Learning How to Mean*, London, Arnold, 1978.

Hamlyn, D., *Experience and the Growth of Understanding*, London, Routledge, 1978.

Hamm, C., *Philosophical Issues in Education: An Introduction*, Lewes, Falmer, 1989.

Hanfling, O., ' "Thinking", a Widely Ramified Concept', *Philosophical Investigations*, 16, 2, 1993, pp. 101–115.

Hirst, Paul, 'Morals, Religion and the Maintained School', *British Journal of Educational Studies*, November 1965.

——, *Knowledge and the Curriculum*, London, Routledge, 1974.

——, 'Education, Knowledge and Practices', in R. Barrow and P. White (eds) *Beyond Liberal Education*, London, Routledge, 1993, pp. 184–199.

Hobbes, Thomas, *Leviathan* [1651], London, Penguin, 1968, p. 319.

Holland, R.F., *Against Empiricism*, Oxford, Blackwell, 1980.

Hollis, M., *The Philosophy of Social Science*, Cambridge, Cambridge University Press, 1994.

Horgan, T., and J. Tienson, 'Representations Don't Need Rules: Reply to James Garson', *Mind and Language*, 9, 1, 1994, pp. 38–55, 56–87.

Howe, M.J.A., *The Origins of Exceptional Abilities*, Oxford, Blackwell, 1990.

Hume, David, *A Treatise of Human Nature* [1739–40], Oxford, Oxford University Press, 1978.

——, *Natural History of Religion* [1777], Oxford, Oxford University Press, 1993.

Jessup, G., 'Implications for Individuals: The Autonomous Learner', in G. Jessup (ed.) *Outcomes: NVQs and the Emerging Model of Education and Training*, Brighton, Falmer, 1991.

Kant, I., *Groundwork of the Metaphysic of Morals* [1785], cited in H.J. Paton, *The Moral Law*, London, Hutchinson, 1948.

——, *Critique of Practical Reason* [1788], translated by L.W. Beck, Indianapolis, Bobbs-Merrill, 1956.

Kazepides, T., 'On the Prerequisites of Moral Education: a Wittgensteinian Perspective', *Journal of Philosophy of Education*, 25, 2, 1991, pp. 259–272.

Kenny, A., *Descartes*, New York, Random House, 1969.

——, *The Legacy of Wittgenstein*, Oxford, Blackwell, 1989.

Kirk, R., 'Rationality without Language', *Mind*, V, 76, 1967, pp. 369–386.

Kohlberg, L., 'Stages of Moral Development as a Basis for Moral Education,' in C. Beck, B.S. Crittenden and E.V. Sullivan (eds) *Moral Education: Interdisciplinary Approaches*, New York, Newman Press, 1971.

——, *The Philosophy of Moral Development*, Volumes I–III, San Francisco, Harper & Row, 1981.

Lenneberg, E., 'Natural History of Language', in F. Smith and G. Miller (eds) *Genesis of Language*, Cambridge, Mass., MIT Press, 1966.

Levi, D., 'Why Do Illiterates Do So Badly in Logic?', *Philosophical Investigations*, 19, 1, 1995, pp. 34–54.

Lieberman, D., *Learning*, California, Wadsworth, 1990.

List, F., *The National System of Political Economy* [1841], New Jersey, Augustus Kelley, 1991, Chapter XVII.

Locke, D., *Memory*, London, Macmillan, 1971.

Locke, J., *An Essay Concerning Human Understanding* [1690], London, Dent, 1961.

MacIntyre, A., *After Virtue*, London, Duckworth, 1981.

Mckeon, R. (ed.), *The Basic Works of Aristotle*, New York, Random House, 1941.

Macmillan, C.A., *Women, Reason and Nature*, London, Macmillan, 1982.

McPeck, J., *Critical Thinking and Education*, Oxford, Martin Robertson, 1981.

Malcolm, N., *Memory and Mind*, Ithaca, NY, Cornell, 1977.

——, 'Thoughtless Brutes', in N. Malcolm, *Thought and Knowledge*, Ithaca and London, Cornell University Press, 1977.

——, 'Wittgenstein on Language and Rules', *Philosophy*, 64, 1990, pp. 5–28.

Malone, M.E., 'On Assuming Other Folks Have Mental States', *Philosophical Investigations*, 17, 1, 1994, pp. 37–52.

Matson, William I., and Adam Leite, 'Socrates' Critique of Cognitivism', *Philosophy*, 66, 256, 1991, pp. 145–168.

Matthews, P.H., *Generative Grammar and Linguistic Competence*, London, Allen & Unwin, 1979.

Menyuk, P., *Language Development: Knowledge and use*, London, Scott Foresman, 1988, Chapter 8.

Mills, Stephen, 'Wittgenstein and Connectionism: A Significant Complementarity?', in C. Hookway and D. Peterson (eds) *Philosophy and Cognitive Science*, Royal Institute of Philosophy Supplement 34, Cambridge, Cambridge University Press, 1993, pp. 137–158.

Mortimore, P., P. Sammons, L. Stoll, D. Lewis and R. Ecob, *School Matters*, Wells, Open Books, 1987.

Mounce, H.O., 'Art and Real Life', *Philosophy*, 55, April 1980, pp. 183ff.

Murdoch, I., *The Sovereignty of the Good*, London, Routledge, 1970.

——, *Metaphysics as a Guide to Morals*, London, Penguin, 1992.

Nolan, R., *Cognitive Practices: Human Language and Human Knowledge*, Oxford, Blackwell, 1994.

Norman, R., ' "I Did It My Way". Some Reflections on Autonomy', *Journal of Philosophy of Education*, 28, 1, 1994, pp. 25–34.

Papineau, D., *For Science in the Social Sciences*, London, Macmillan, 1988.

Peacocke, C., *A Study of Concepts*, Cambridge, Mass., MIT Press, 1992.

Perera, K., *Children's Writing and Reading*, Oxford, Blackwell, 1984.

Peters, R.S., 'Authority', in A. Quinton (ed.) *Political Philosophy*, Oxford, Oxford University Press, 1967.

——, *Essays on Educators*, London, Allen & Unwin, 1981.

Phillips, D.Z., 'Philosophy and Religious Education', *British Journal of Educational Studies*, XVIII, 1, February 1970, pp. 5–17.

——, *Wittgenstein on Religion*, London, Macmillan, 1993.

——, 'Wittgenstein, Religion and Anglo-American Philosophical Culture', in *Wittgenstein and Culture*, Wittgenstein Vienna Society, forthcoming.

Piaget, J., *Le Langage et la pensée chez l'enfant*, Neuchâtel-Paris, Delachaux et Niestle, 1923.

——, *Logic and Psychology*, Manchester, The University Press, 1953.

——, *Biology and Knowledge*, Edinburgh, Edinburgh University Press, 1971 (first published in French, 1967).

——, *The Principles of Genetic Epistemology*, London, Routledge, 1972.

Piaget, J., and B. Inhelder, *The Psychology of the Child*, London, Routledge, 1969 (first published in French in 1966).

Plato, *Theaetetus*, pt 3, in F.M. Cornford, *Plato's Theory of Knowledge*, London, Routledge, 1935.

——, *Ion*, in *Plato; The Collected Dialogues*, edited by E. Hamilton and H. Cairns, Princeton New Jersey, Princeton University Press, 1963.

——, *Meno*, in B. Jowett, *The Dialogues of Plato*, London, Sphere Books, 1970.

Prais, S., 'Mathematical Attainments: Comparisons of Japanese and English Schooling', in B. Moon, J. Isaac and J. Powney (eds) *Judging Standards and Effectiveness in Education*, London, Hodder & Stoughton, 1990.

——, 'Vocational Qualifications in Britain and Europe: Theory and Practice', *National Institute Economic Review*, 136, May 1991, pp. 86–89.

Reid, I. (ed.), *The Place of Genre in Learning*, Geelong, Typereader Press, Deakin University, 1987.

Rescorla, R.A., and A.R. Wagner, 'A Theory of Pavlovian Conditioning: Variations in the Effectiveness of Reinforcement and Non-reinforcement', in A.H. Black and W.F. Prokasy (eds) *Classical Conditioning II: Current Research and Theory*, New York, Appleton Century-Crofts, 1972.

Rhees, R., 'Language as Emerging from Instinctive Behaviour', *Philosophical Investigations*, 20, 1, 1997, pp. 1–14.

Robinson, Guy, 'Language and the Society of Others', *Philosophy*, 67, 1992, pp. 329–341.

Rogers, Carl, *The Carl Rogers Reader*, edited by H. Kirschenbaum and V. Land Henderson, London, Constable, 1990.

Rosenow, E., 'Rousseau's "Émile": an Anti-utopia', *British Journal of Educational Studies*, XXVIII, 3, 1980, pp. 212–224.

Rousseau, J.J., *Émile ou l'éducation* [1762]. English edition translated by Barbara Foxley, published London, Dent, 1911. (French edition, Paris, Garnier-Flammarion, 1966.)

——, *Discourse on Inequality*, London, Dent, 1913.

Ryle, G., *The Concept of Mind*, London, Hutchinson, 1949.

Sainsbury, M., *Meaning, Communication and Understanding in the Classroom*, Aldershot, Avebury, 1992.

Searle, J.R., 'Minds, Brains and Programs', *Behavioural and Brain Sciences*, 3, 1980, pp. 417–457.

——, *Minds, Brains and Science*, Cambridge, Mass., Harvard University Press, 1984.

——, *The Rediscovery of the Mind*, London, MIT Press, 1992.

Scheer, R.K., 'Thinking and Working', *Philosophical Investigations*, 14, 4, 1991, pp. 293–310.

Schools Curriculum and Assessment Authority, *Model Syllabuses for Religious Education, Consultation Document Model 1*, London, HMSO, January 1994.

Simpson, Evan, *Good Lives and Moral Education*, New York, Peter Lang, 1989.

Smith, Frank, *Reading*, Cambridge, Cambridge University Press, 1985.

Stainthorp, Rhona, *Practical Psychology for Teachers*, London, Falmer, 1989.

Sterelny, K., *The Representational Theory of Mind*, Oxford, Blackwell, 1990.

Strawson, P.F., *Introduction to Logical Theory*, London, Methuen, 1952.

——, *Individuals*, London, Hutchinson, 1961.

——, *Freedom and Resentment and Other Essays*, London, Methuen, 1974.

Stretton, H., and L. Orchard, *Public Goods, Public Enterprise and Public Choice*, London, Macmillan, 1993.

Sutherland, N.S., 'Outlines of a Theory of Visual Pattern Recognition in Animals and Man'. Proceedings of the Royal Society, B.171, 1968, 301.

Sylva, K., and I. Lunt, *Child Development*, Oxford, Blackwell, 1982.

Taylor, C., *The Explanation of Behaviour*, London, Routledge, 1964.

Tilghman, B., *Wittgenstein, Ethics and Aesthetics*, London, Macmillan, 1991.

Tizard, B., and M. Hughes, *Young Children Learning*, London, Fontana, 1984.

Tizard, B., P. Blatchford, J. Burke, C. Farquhar and I. Plewis, *Young Children at School in the Inner City*, Hove, Lawrence Erlbaum, 1988.

Toulmin, Stephen, *The Uses of Argument*, London, Cambridge University Press, 1957.

Verheggen, C., 'Wittgenstein and "Solitary" Languages', *Philosophical Investigations*, 18, 4, 1995, pp. 329–347.

Vico, G., *The New Science* [1725], Ithaca, New York, Cornell University Press, 1968.

Vygotsky, L.S., *Thought and Language*, Cambridge, Mass., MIT Press, 1962.

——, *Mind in Society*, Cambridge, Mass., Harvard University Press, 1978.

Ward, Keith, *The Development of Kant's Views of Ethics*, Oxford, Blackwell, 1972.

Warnock, M., *Memory*, London, Faber & Faber, 1987.

White, J.P., *Education and the Good Life*, London, Kogan Page, 1990.

Whitehead, A.N., *The Aims of Education*, New York, The Free Press, 1967.

Winch, C., 'Cooper, Labov, Larry and Charles', *Oxford Review of Education*, 1985.

——, 'The Curriculum and the Study of Reason', *Westminster Studies in Education*, 1987.

——, 'Education Needs Training', *Oxford Review of Education*, 21, 3, 1995, pp. 315–326.

——, 'Vocational Education: A Liberal Interpretation', *Studies in Philosophy and Education*, 1995.

——, *Quality and Education*, Oxford, Blackwell, 1996.

——, 'Authority (Education)', in the *Encyclopedia of Applied Ethics*, edited by R. Chadwick, California, Academic Press, forthcoming.

——, 'Autonomy as an Educational Aim', in R. Marples (ed.) *Aims in Education*, London, Routledge, forthcoming.

Winch, P., 'Authority', in A. Quinton (ed.) *Political Philosophy*, Oxford, Oxford University Press, 1967.

——, 'Understanding a Primitive Society', in *Ethics and Action*, London, Routledge, 1972.

——, *The Just Balance*, Cambridge, Cambridge University Press 1989.

Wittgenstein, L., *Tractatus Logico-Philosophicus*, London, Routledge, 1922.

——, *Philosophical Investigations*, Oxford, Blackwell 1953.

——, *Blue and Brown Books*, Oxford, Blackwell, 1958.

——, *Zettel*, Oxford, Blackwell, 1967.

——, *On Certainty*, Oxford, Blackwell, 1969.

——, *Philosophical Grammar*, Oxford, Blackwell, 1974.

——, *Remarks on Philosophical Psychology*, Volume 1, Oxford, Blackwell, 1980.

——, *Culture and Value*, translated by Peter Winch, Oxford, Blackwell, 1980.

Wollheim, Richard, *The Thread of Life*, Cambridge, Cambridge University Press, 1984.

Wood, David, *How Children Think and Learn*, Oxford, Blackwell, 1990.

Yates, Frances, *The Art of Memory*, London, Ark, 1984.

INDEX

212